I0085485

Captive Revolution

Captive Revolution

Palestinian Women's Anti-Colonial Struggle
Within the Israeli Prison System

Nahla Abdo

PLUTO PRESS

First published 2014 by Pluto Press
345 Archway Road, London N6 5AA

www.plutobooks.com

Copyright © Nahla Abdo 2014

The right of Nahla Abdo to be identified as the author of this work
has been asserted by her in accordance with the Copyright, Designs
and Patents Act 1988.

British Library Cataloguing in Publication Data
A catalogue record for this book is available from the British Library

ISBN	978 0 7453 3494 3	Hardback
ISBN	978 0 7453 3493 6	Paperback
ISBN	978 1 7837 1184 0	PDF eBook
ISBN	978 1 7837 1186 4	Kindle eBook
ISBN	978 1 7837 1185 7	EPUB eBook

Library of Congress Cataloging in Publication Data applied for

10   9   8   7   6   5   4   3   2   1

Typeset by Stanford DTP Services, Northampton, England
Text design by Melanie Patrick

Contents

Acknowledgements   vii

Introduction   1

1. Forgotten History, Lost Voices and Silent Souls: Women
   Political Detainees   14

2. Anti-Colonial Resistance in Context   42

3. Colonialism, Imperialism and the Culture of Resistance   84

4. Political Detainees and the Israeli Prison System   124

5. Prison as a Site of Resistance   167

Conclusion   208
Afterword   212
Notes   213
Bibliography   225
Index   241

This book is dedicated to all women, especially Palestinians, who struggled and continue to struggle against all forms of oppression, particularly against colonialism and imperialism.

Acknowledgements

This book would not have seen the light had it not been for the collective efforts, time and stories of the many Palestinian women political fighters and ex-detainees. The mutual trust expressed by all the women in the conversations, their belief in 'the cause' and hope for a better future which were at the centre of our conversations, both the one-on-one and the focus group, have contributed to the depth of the information in this book. Each of these women deserves a special thank you. Many thanks to Amne, Rawda, Khuloud, Itaf, Haleema 'F', Haleema 'A', Ahlam, Rawda, Munia, Aisha Ghada, Sonia, Ahlam, Ameena, Aida, Salwa, Doris and Iman. The contribution of other women who I also met outside of these two major events is also highly appreciated. I would also like to thank Mr. Issa Qaraqe who at the time was the chair of Nadil-Asir (The Detainees Club) and now is the Minister of Detainees. Many thanks to lawyer Walid Fahoum whose direct information on some of the women ex-detainees was very valuable. Thanks should also go to Ina'ash al-Usra organization for making available their documentation on political detainees. My thanks also go to the Social Science and Humanities Council in Canada for the institutional grant provided to carry out the field research.

To reiterate, this is truly a collective project to which various other people have contributed. Special thanks to my research assistant Maha Abdo-Sabbagh, whose knowledge and activism made my task a pleasant one. I am indebted to her for introducing me to these great women whose voices and words gave this book the value it deserves. Special thanks should also go to my editor Stephan Dobson for his extra patience with me and to Thérèse Saba for her copy-editing work. Many thanks to David Shulman from Pluto Press, whose enthusiasm and encouragement throughout the writing process kept me going. Lastly, my gratitude to all those who contributed to this book would not be completed without paying a special tribute to my partner, Sami Zubi who did everything possible to keep me going and interested, despite the many ups and downs I underwent during the long process of writing this book. While all these people helped shape the book, the responsibility for it is mine alone.

Introduction

This book aims at making audible the hidden voices, stories and histories of women political detainees while simultaneously raising international awareness of the plight of over 5,000 Palestinian political prisoners who currently suffer torture and inhumane treatment in Israeli prisons. The significance of the issue of women political prisoners is rather clear, as it occupies a central position in current international – and especially US – politics. There is little doubt that the insistence of the United States on pushing the current Israeli–Palestinian 'peace negotiations', in which the issue of political prisoners is placed at the centre of the talks, is a result of the failure of this imperialist power to bring about any stability in the Middle East. The stories and documentaries produced on the systematic torture, sexual mutilation, rape and atrocities committed against women (and men) in the US controlled prison of Abu Ghraib has drawn international public attention to the question of political detainees, especially in the case of women.

The absence of academic and especially feminist institutional interest in the lives and experiences of women's anti-colonial armed struggle casts a question mark around the so-called progressive leanings of such institutions. Concerning Palestinian women's political struggle in Israel/ Palestine, for example, an excess of feminist literature has been produced worldwide about women's involvement in the First Intifada (1987–92), and a plethora of Israeli Zionist and overwhelming orientalist writings were produced about Palestinian women freedom fighters and armed resisters after the Second Intifada (2000–03), yet hardly any literature analysing or accounting for the experiences of women's armed resistance historically, especially during the period of 1960–80 exists. All what existed then and continues until this day is an Orientalist depiction of Palestinian women as uneducated, anti-democratic and over-oppressed by their own culture and religion.

The significance of this study goes beyond a corrective mission; additionally, it voices what has been silenced or rendered invisible. This study is also concerned with demonstrating the difference between the status and role of Palestinian women (often lumped together as Muslims, Arabs and even terrorists in the Western imagination) and the latter's real lived experiences. This study also makes visible women's roles in anti-colonial and anti-imperialist struggles, especially among Third World peoples (both in the West in the Diaspora and in the Third World itself) which have hardly, if ever, attracted the attention of institutionalized feminism.

The question of positionality, identity or location occupies an important space in the making of feminist methodology, particularly when research involves epistemological production and especially the type of knowledge which is based on women's lived experiences. Dorothy Smith's 'institutional ethnography' (2005), which theorized an epistemology for understanding women's everyday experiences has contributed to feminist methodology. This was the starting point in conceiving the current project: uncovering the invisibility of Palestinian women freedom fighters, especially those militant fighters in the anti-colonial national liberation movement. The period in discussion here is the 1960s through the 1980s, a historical phase which included a high level of women's militant resistance throughout the globe. On a personal level, this research also was 'the season' for sharing my personal experiences as an ex-political detainee, the fate which most political activists – militant and not militant – face.

Sharing or reflecting on my detention experience during the discussions with women political detainees played an important role in eliciting the sharing of information and knowledge among all participants; it also facilitated the conversations by removing what otherwise would have been seen as power relations between the 'researcher' and the 'researched'. The sensitivity of some of the discussions, especially stories related to sexual torture, require equally sensitive approaches to release deep and valued personal information. This methodological point does not suggest that women without the experience of political detention cannot understand or write about other women political detainees. The work, for example, of Barbara Harlow (1992; 1994; 1996) is very important here. When the research involves personal discussions with women ex-militant detainees, as is the case in this project, sharing one's experiences (especially that of the researcher), I argue, can play an important role in facilitating lively discussions and the overcoming of certain taboos with a certain degree of ease. More importantly, the researcher's sharing of experiences of political activism with women in discussions presents a form of validation of political activism. In such research, the gap between the Academy and activism narrows. Further explanation of the methodology used in this research is presented later in this chapter.

For many decades the voices of most women involved in anti-colonial resistance movements, including political detainees, have largely been lost in the official histories and stories of nation building and national struggles. This project aims to restore some of the silenced and otherwise invisible voices and therefore histories of women militant fighters turned political detainees by reintegrating them into their proper 'public' space as participants, agents, and makers of their history.

Chapter 1 reaffirms the international character of women militant fighters and their experiences as fighters both outside prison in the society and inside prisons as political detainees. It does this by recounting the experiences of women from various parts of the world, including the United States, Northern Ireland, Algeria and elsewhere. While attempting to make visible the voices and experiences of such women, Chapter 1 also establishes the strong relationship between, on the one hand, colonialism and imperialism as forms of oppression and, on the other, women's resistance to these forms, arguing that the phenomenon of women political detainees is as old as the anti-colonial, anti-imperialist liberation struggles. At least since the 1960s, militant anti-colonial fighters including women have filled prisons and detention camps in many parts of the world. Women's active participation in resistance movements including the armed struggle has left and continues to leave its marks on our human history.

One common theme in all states, colonial, settler colonial, imperialist and so on, is the presence of people, including women, who challenge, defy and resist the state. While recognizing the historical specificity of each country and each struggle, Chapter 1 focuses on some of the shared and common experiences of women political detainees in various parts of the world, for example, Moroccan, Algerian, Lebanese women and women from Northern Ireland. Chapter 1 also demonstrates the shared character of all such states: the criminalization of political resistance and the use of sexuality and women's bodies as an instrument of torture. It argues that the state (and its prison authorities) uses women's bodies as a site of victimization and a tool of control; it also demonstrates how women use the same tool, that is, their own bodies, as a tool to challenge and resist their victimization by prison authorities. These topics are discussed in further detail later in the book.

Revolutions, anti-colonial struggles, and national liberation movements often evolve in a particular environment in which the articulation of the social, the economic, the political, and the ideological takes place in the context of the local, the regional, and the international. For example, the 'Palestinian Question', to use Edward Said's notion (1980), the so-called Israeli–Palestinian conflict, has been at the heart of the regional and international arena since at least 1948 and the creation of the state of Israel, and this 'conflict' has been fought at the social, economic, political, and ideological levels throughout all those years. The centrality of Israel for US (and European) imperialist interests, many argue, is detrimental not only for the maintenance and expansion of capitalism, but also for the overall hegemony of the United States over the Arab Middle East and its rich resources (see, for example, Chomsky 1999, 2011; Said 1980; Mooers 2006a).

It should come as no surprise, Chapter 2 argues, that such policies (e.g. those serving US imperialism) continue until this day to be imposed upon the Arab world, the most recent examples being the US intervention in the countries of the so-called 'Arab Spring' (i.e. Egypt, Tunisia and Libya), with attempts to hijacking the people's revolt and aiding Muslim Brotherhood to gain control.

Chapter 2 establishes a strong link between Israel–Palestine (and especially the Palestinian struggle) and the global forces of imperialism and colonialism and their racist Orientalist ideology. This ideology and its widespread circulation in the West including Israel have been central to how the Palestinian struggle is perceived. It is this ideology that constructs a new epistemology for perceiving the Middle Eastern people, the Muslim, the Arab and specially the Palestinian. This chapter challenges the hegemonic Orientalist perspective that depicts peoples' resistance as terror while justifies state terrorism as a means for spreading 'Western values of democracy'. In doing so, it re-examines the definition of 'violence' and differentiates between the violence of the state and the violence of the anti-colonial resistance.

The ideology of imperialism expressed partly in the Orientalist perspective of Arab including Palestinian women, Chapter 2 argues, is not the trait of the official institutions of the state alone. This perception is also hegemonic in the Academy and especially among what I refer to as Orientalist feminists and imperialist feminists. In her study of Western feminist writings about Algerian women, Marnia Lazreg (1988) highlighted the collusion between feminism and the colonial (and the imperialist) state in speaking about women of the colonies. Examples provided include the Orientalist hegemonic discourse on Palestinian women's resistance that describes them as terrorists, as uneducated, as fallen women, and so on. Orientalism, this chapter also argues, constitutes an important part in the criminalization and dehumanization of women militant fighters at the hand of the colonial state and its prison authorities. Chapter 2 also provides a critique of the Orientalist discourse, emphasizing its ahistorical approach and demonstrating its ideological stand against resistance and anti-colonial struggles. The chapter develops the anti-colonial, anti-imperialist feminist approach adopted throughout this book. It does so partly by drawing on the works of Fanon (1970), Jenkin (1987), Harlow (1986a, 1992, 1996) and Mooers (2006a), among others. This approach is also used in challenging imperialism and Orientalism including the notions of 'democracy', 'individual rights' and 'human rights', concepts used to camouflage atrocities committed by the state while it expands the imperial interests.

One important force in driving women in general and Palestinian women more specifically into joining the anti-colonial resistance struggle while knowing full well the risks of such involvement is the influence of the culture of resistance within which women find themselves. Resistance culture, Chapter 3 argues, provides a rich base from which female (and male) fighters draw upon in their anti-colonial struggle. Resistance culture is produced not only locally/nationally but also regionally and internationally. This was particularly so during the period of the book's focus (from the 1960s through the 1980s). Drawing on examples from various world revolutionary moments, this chapter established the importance of this culture in, for example, translating a political poem from its written abstract state into an empirical reality. Special emphasis in Chapter 3 is placed on the very rich national (Palestinian) culture of resistance, produced at that time in the forms of poetry and novels.

Palestine, Barbara Harlow argues (1992, 1994, 1996), was pioneering in producing an impressive body of resistance culture, especially *adab al-muqawama* (resistance literature) and *adab al-sujoun* (prison literature). These forms of cultural resistance, Chapter 3 demonstrates, formed a central building block in *fikr al-muqawama* (resistance thought) among Palestinian freedom fighters, including female ones. The heavy price paid by most cultural producers at the time (ranging from imprisonment and assassination) was acknowledged and honoured by women involved in the militant struggle.

Historically, one major dilemma in the history of the Academy has and continues to be the apparent gap between those who make history and those who write history. Activism and the Academy often collude, not only in the hard sciences but in the social sciences as well. This is true in our case study; thus, whereas Palestinian women were involved in the making of their/our history, the nation's history, until at least the last decade or so, has been written by men. This has undoubtedly led to the seeming invisibility of Palestinian women involved in the anti-colonial and national struggle. Women's invisible role in the making of their history, Chapter 3 argues, is not peculiarly Palestinian. In fact, it is also global: most resistance literature, historically, has been expressed in the male language, where the nation is depicted as gender neutral as if women do not matter.

Chapter 4 shifts from the general to the specific, detailing the individual experiences of political detainees. It highlights the voices and experiences of Palestinian women ex-political detainees. This chapter provides a strong rebuttal of the Orientalist feminist perception of Palestinian women involved in the armed struggle ... their images as uneducated, as fallen women, or as women 'who dishonoured their families' and thus joined the armed struggle to cleanse their families' names. Conversations with the women reveal the healthy relationship they all had with their families and for some the especially close relationships they had with their brothers and fathers before being involved in the armed struggle. In fact, in many cases it was such healthy family experiences which provided a smooth environment for their involvement in the resistance. This chapter demonstrates that it was the history of the family (especially relationships with parents) during the Nakba or other tragedies caused by Israel that pushed these women into the armed struggle. The chapter also reveals the importance of education for most of these women, a sizeable number of whom had already acquired university degrees before joining the struggle. In addition to responding to the question of why these women joined the armed resistance, Chapter 4 details the unreported violence exercised by the prison authority against these women from the moment of their arrest to the gruelling interrogation, which is mostly based on forms of torture to the humiliation and intimidation practised against them throughout their years of detention. The prison as a state institution, this chapter argues, has developed particularly gendered or sexual methods it uses to torture women, methods focusing on their bodies and psychological states.

Kumari Jayawardena's seminal work *Feminism and Nationalism in the Third World* (1986), which establishes a strong relationship between women's participation in national liberation movements and their feminist awareness, is only partially correct, as Chapter 5 demonstrates.

The difference established between gender consciousness and feminist consciousness argued by Julie Peteet (1991) seems more applicable to Palestinian women freedom fighters turned political detainees. Chapter 5 demonstrates that most women involved in the military resistance voiced their belief in gender equality: they interpreted the carrying of arms as an expression of gender equality, and they did not see themselves oppressed within their families. As Chapter 5 demonstrates, the rise of feminist consciousness among women political detainees has followed different paths and has not been a necessary result of their struggle in the national liberation movement. Considering that the western hegemonic feminist movement at the time was expressed in liberal and radical forms, it is no surprise that most first-generation women detainees did not see itself as part of this movement. These women have clearly prioritized the national cause over the feminist. As Chapter 5 shows, the second generation women detainees in our discussion were more comfortable expressing feminist beliefs and identifying with feminism.

Finally, Chapter 5 provides very rich material concerning methods of resistance that women invented while in prison. Thus, along with various forms of resistance such as work stoppages, hunger-strikes, and refusing to obey orders, women used their innovative and creative skills, turning the prison into an Academy where they learnt and taught others many subjects and facilitated the completion of high school by young detainees; they also initiated gender and political consciousness-raising sessions, discussing world topics and social-gender relations. This process, as many admit, has undoubtedly contributed to their personal, social, and political development. Finally, this chapter makes the point that women's struggle which began before their incarceration and continued throughout their detention time was not over. These women continued the struggle even after their release, but this time in order to continue living as productive members of their society (e.g. finding a job, achieving social recognition and finding the proper partner).

Reflections on Methodology and Research Methods

To begin with, the field data collected for this project involved one-on-one conversations with 17 female political ex-detainees and a one-day focus group with 14 women participants, the majority drawn from participants previously interviewed but also including others who had not. Data collection also included archival work (covering newspapers, magazines, and records kept at various women's organizations, particularly those of Ina'ash al-Usra, the organization which kept records on all women political prisoners, especially during the 1960s through the 1980s, and which celebrated the release of each prisoner). All private conversations as well as the day-long focus group discussions were tape recorded. Investigating and analysing workers' conditions, does not necessarily require one to be a member of the working class, nor does researching conditions of the 'natives' obligate one to be an aboriginal, as Fanon's extensive research on the Algerian revolution reveals (Fanon 1970). Doing research with female political detainees is not different: you do not have to have experienced detention and prison torture in order to study and analyse women's experiences in political detention. However, it is important to note that experiencing political detention and all of its ordeals and forms of resistance and sharing such experiences with the women during conversations – such as the case of the current author – has proven useful in that it made women much less reluctant to divulge their experiences with confidence.

Sharing my own political detention experience with the women has undoubtedly facilitated more open, smooth and participatory discussions. While I surely learned much more from the women's rich and long experiences than they did from my relatively short and pale experience, the moments shared reduced and even eliminated the sense of tension that often occurs in research on sensitive issues such as political detention and the ordeals related to it. Going into the field having a history and experiences similar to the women in conversations undoubtedly reduces if not eliminates the power relations between the researcher and the women who are the subject of this study. This was true during the face-to-face conversations conducted with the women and the more so during the focus group. Conversations in both forms of data collection lose their detached character, turning instead into an intimate discussion with friends.

Familiarity with the culture and language of the women one works with is an important constituent in research methods. Equally if not more important is a researcher's knowledge of the history, especially the political and cultural history, which is the crucible of women detainees' experience. Even with the presence of all these factors, a judgement has to be made on the exact terminology the researcher needs to use when arranging and publishing the results of the research. For example, one of the issues raised during my conversations with the women ex-political detainees was the precise terminology to be used in labelling them, that is, whether they were political prisoners or political detainees, and in addition whether the places in which they were incarcerated should be called prisons or detention camps. Politically, differentiating between the terms political detention and political prisons becomes important (and also in terms of how one sees and defines oneself). Susan Rosenberg's discussion of these two terms, described in the first chapter or in the following chapter, is pertinent here. The term political prisoner that Rosenberg uses to identify a person's struggle and resistance against her or his state is applicable to Palestinian citizens of the state of Israel. This term, she argues, 'complies with international legal definitions of political detainees' (Rosenberg 2006: 1). On the other hand, as will be discussed in the next chapter, people 'who are in pursuit of the recognition of their national liberation struggles for self-determination, are defined as political detainees' (Rosenberg 2006: 2). This definition resonates well within the context of women's struggle in the Occupied Palestinian Territories (OPT) against Israeli settler colonialism. In recognition of the fact that every woman interviewed considered herself a political detainee, the latter term will be used throughout this book as a manifestation of the identity of the overwhelming majority of Palestinian political prisoners, who until recently numbered over 10,000 people.

First and foremost, appreciating the sensitivity and delicacy of the topic of this research, I was exceptionally concerned with the security of the women involved. At the outset of the one-on-one interviews as well as during the focus group discussions, my intention to use pseudonyms in publication was made clear. To my great surprise, however, I learned that none of the women in the study were as concerned with the issue of security and anonymity as I was; they all said that I could use their real names and that they were not afraid of the Israelis. This response might be explained by the fact that, for most of these women, a relatively long time has passed since their release, and that the torture and humiliation they faced under Israeli occupation and especially as political prisoners was too pronounced to try to hide it from the public. In other words, nothing could happen to them worse than what they have experienced and continue to experience, hence the lack of concern in revealing their identities. In addition, a number of the Palestinian women political detainees have already voiced their experiences publicly, have given interviews to filmmakers, or have published their experiences, as is the case with Aisha Odeh who, by the time of my research between 2007 and 2009, had already published two books (Odeh 2004, 2007) narrating her experiences. This is also true of Ittaf Alian, who published her experience (Alian 2011), of Itaf who revealed part of her experience through an interview on Al-Jazeera (Al-Jazeera 2006), and Rasmiyya Odeh whose story was reported in the British *Sunday Times* Report on 19 June 1977, as well as in the account by Soraya Antonius (1980).

Another issue which will be discussed in more detail later in the book needs to be mentioned here: the issue of insider/outsider in research methodologies. The substance of the debate here includes the native researcher who lives the experience of her society but might not necessarily be familiar with the debates going on outside of her country, especially in the West. There is another aspect to this debate which is of particular relevance to this book, namely the issues relating to exilic researchers and those who live in the diaspora but who do their research on their own community. This category of researchers and to which the author belongs, as will be seen shortly, has the potential of further enriching the research and the data gathered. After all, the one significant question in research is not who can speak for or represent a group, rather how that group, especially a marginalized one, is being presented.

This issue concerns the position and politics of the researcher herself; it is about where she stands on the issues of discussion. Equally important, if not more so, the issue here is about the researcher's familiarity with the culture and history of the women she is conversing with or interviewing, which creates a situation of familiarity between the interviewer and those interviewed. This is particularly so if the researcher, as in our case, has also undergone a similar experience as the other women. Despite the ease with which I found myself while conducting interview conversations with the women political detainees, a number of culturally specific issues arose. For example, the use of certain terms in a public setting was a contentious issue. The use of a number of sexual terms in Arabic are tabooed and normatively women should refrain from using them in public. These include terms like *sharmouta* or *manuouka* (whore) or *qahba* (prostitute or whore). Such slurs were frequently used by the interrogators against every female political detainee interviewed. This issue created a dilemma for most of us during both the face-to-face conversation as well as during the focus group. Some of the women who used these terms defended their use, saying that this was necessary for telling their story accurately, while others refrained from using the terms, referring to them through circumlocutions such as 'You know! These bad names', 'I cannot say these words', and so on.

The dilemma for me was whether to leave the issue and not go into it in any detail, or to explore it through an exercise of feminist mutual learning. The openness of most young female political detainees to social and political discussions encouraged me to pursue the issue. Recounting my own experience in which I also encountered the same insults during my interrogation on a daily basis, I used and repeated such terms in both my one-on-one interviews as well as during the focus group. My rationale for using such terms, as explained to the women in both cases, was that it is important to record events exactly as they happened because of the social, cultural and political implications of the sexualized language used against women. Participants, both older and younger, were well aware of the reasons interrogators used socially and culturally tabooed words, especially against female political detainees. They were well aware that Israeli prison authorities, especially interrogators, use sexual slurs to de-humanize them, knowing full well how particularly harsh and inappropriate women find such terms. Similar terms, incidentally, are used by Arab men in public; for example, a man can pour scorn on another man by calling him *ibnel-sharmouta* (son of a whore) or *akhul-qahba* (the brother of a whore) – these are very demeaning and socially unacceptable slurs in public, yet in a male hegemonic culture, men use their prerogative and employ such terms in private and in public as well. It is worth noting that women who used these terms publicly also identified themselves as feminists. Still, the ease in which such conversations were conducted, my personal comfort in uttering and in hearing such terms, and my challenging of the silences imposed only upon women in the use of such terms, undoubtedly contributed to the lively discussions. The end result was that during the focus group, which included all women with whom I had already conducted private interviews, these terms were used publicly by many of the participants, both the older and the younger.

Another issue of language use encountered during our conversations was how to label the women in relation to their activity, as most if not all of them were detained for their participation or alleged participation in the armed struggle. This issue is crucial not only for understanding the historical context within which the women's armed resistance movement evolved, namely between the 1960s and 1980s, but also in today's context of imperialism or globalization, especially after the events of September 11 and the Second Palestinian Intifada, as we shall see in Chapter 1. *Munadela* (freedom fighter or revolutionary resister), for example, was the term used by almost all women to define themselves and to describe their political activism against Israeli colonialism and occupation. For most of these women, their struggle was part of the '*fidai'yyeen* movement' (freedom fighters movement), a movement as mentioned that was banned by the West (especially by the USA and Israel) and dubbed as a terrorist movement.

Throughout the various research and work that I have conducted among Palestinian women since the late 1980s, I have come to learn that while the emic (insider) research results in a better understanding of the language, culture and history as compared to an etic (outsider) orientation, the latter can contribute as well, in subtle and not too subtle ways: an etic perspective allows for the seeing of social organization that an emic perspective might not be able to see. In the late 1980s, I conducted several roundtable and focus-group discussions among Palestinian women leaders from the various factions of the PLO. As I would learn later, these discussions were the first to bring together women who otherwise would not have met face-to-face or talked to one another, on account of political differences. Female leaders who were invited explained the success of the meeting as a result of my status as an 'outsider' for, as far as all women involved in the focus groups were concerned, I was considered an outsider; I was seen as neutral, as not belonging to any political faction, and therefore as a person who would not adopt one position over another concerning the issues of friction within and between their respective parties.

During the research for this book, I found myself in familiar territory in that I know many women in the political movements, some of whom had already experienced political detention. Through these women, in what is known as a snowball method, I was able to meet with their friends who had similar experiences and thereby ended up with a relatively large pool of women political detainees with whom to conduct conversations. With the help of my local research assistant, we contacted around 25 women ex-political detainees; while most initially agreed to participate, only 17 of them showed up to the interviews that were conducted in Ramallah. Of these 17 women, 14 participated in the focus group. Still three more women were reached by phone and were briefly interviewed. Most of the face-to-face conversations lasted between four and seven hours each; they included a lunch and breaks for snacks which I provided in my home in Ramallah. Interviews were conducted before and after the focus group as well.

As in my previous experience with roundtable and focus-group discussions among Palestinian women leaders in the 1980s, the focus-group discussion component of this research brought together women from different parts of the West Bank, including the cities of Nablus, Jenin, Jerusalem, Beit Lahem, Beit Sahour, Al-Khalil (Hebron) and Ramallah. As with my previous research in the 1980s, bringing these women together was significant for the women themselves. Political ex-detainees from both the first and second generations of activists expressed deep satisfaction and pleasure, as the focus group was the first event which had brought them all together – and it was also the first time many of them were able to meet with each other after their release from detention. More significantly, the focus group brought together two generations of women political detainees; some of the women in each generation were detained together in the same prison or detention centre and in some cases in the same cell as well. For all of us, these coincidences turned the conversation into a most vibrant and dynamic one. On the one hand, and for first-generation female political detainees, this was an occasion to remember their shared past, memorialize their pain and recall their agency. On the other hand, it opened a space for second-generation female political detainees to voice their gratitude to and disagreements with the first-generation female detainees who, according to them, prioritized the political (national) over the social and were not sufficiently open to social-cultural discussions around issues concerning the female body and sexuality. A comprehensive discussion of these conversations is recorded in Chapters 4 and 5.

1

Forgotten History, Lost Voices and Silent Souls: Women Political Detainees

This chapter contextualizes and historicizes the phenomenon of female political detainees by drawing on experiences from various places around the globe, including Northern Ireland, the USA, the Middle East and North Africa. Emphasis in this chapter and throughout the book will be placed upon the gender-specific treatment of women political prisoners/detainees (later in this chapter, I will explain my choice for using the term 'detainee' or 'political prisoner' over that of 'prisoner'). It is argued that in political detention, women's bodies are transformed into sexualized and racialized objects stripped by the colonial state in general and the prison authorities more specifically of any and all human meaning, and thus these bodies are turned into a tool of oppression. Elsewhere (Abdo 2011b) I have used the terms settler-colonial and racist to define the Israeli state. Here I would like to add another definition, namely that of racialization. Following David Theo Goldberg's definition in *The Racial State* (2002), Israel is defined by its power to exclude and include in racially ordered terms, aiming to produce a homogenous population by keeping racialized others and by legislating against the 'degeneracy' of indigenous minorities (Goldberg 2002: 141–47). Israel, it is argued, employs all the components of racialization against its Palestinian Other: the surveillance system, considering Palestinians as a 'demographic threat', military occupation, a racist legal system which includes the Law of Return, the Absentees' Property Law, the Jewish National Fund Law and the law of agricultural settlement which bars the selling, leasing and owning of land by 'non-Jews', namely Palestinians (Abdo 2011b). Israel's national regime, as Lentin writes, is one of justifications which produces its own logic in relation to national security, immigration, pro-natalism and 'judaicization' policies to deal with the Arab 'demographic threat'. These justifications, she adds, are part of a process of racialization which assigns racial characteristics – not necessarily skin colour – to certain groups with the effect of constraining their full equality (Lentin 2008).[1] Directly related to women political detainees is Israel's policing of the Palestinian populations and the constructing of 'docile bodies'.

The settler colonial state and its prison institution's use of women's bodies as a site of oppression and victimization, however, does not turn women into docile subjects nor is it capable of silencing them. As will be clear throughout this book, and especially in Chapters 4 and 5, women's agency and resistance can be much stronger behind bars than it is in the free air. Women political detainees, it will be argued also turn their bodies and sexuality into a site of resistance.

I argue that all female political detainees, albeit to varying degrees, have similar experiences of humiliation, de-humanization, torture and other forms of oppression, while many if not most exercise moral and political agency and resist the prison authority and its agents. Similarities in struggle during the different stages of detention, however, do not translate into sameness: context, culture, detention circumstances and historical specificity separate and distinguish each case. Hence, the analysis presented here is not about one uniform voice of resistance; women's individual stories, voices and experiences as told by them are rather varied.

The actual voices of women political detainees all over the globe, including that of Palestinian women, has largely been lost or rendered invisible in the histories and stories of nation or state building and in the national struggles and the anti-colonial, anti-imperialist struggles in general; the academe and the research community have little to no interest in these struggles, nor are they accounted for in the growing body of resistance literature. Excluding women from recorded history in general and from the epistemology of nationalism and resistance movements more specifically exacerbates these silences and renders the women further invisible. The invisibility of female detainees' lives and experiences in the male-dominant writings of history is also shared by the almost total absence of recognition of their voices among most female or feminist writers. Still, if and when accounted for – as will be discussed in Chapter 2 – female political activists, especially those involved in militant struggles against colonialism and occupation, are portrayed negatively, are described as submissive, and are depicted as powerless subjects lacking agency or simply as 'terrorists'. In reality, *the subjectivity and agency of the women involved in the struggle deserves memorialization.* Their stories and voices also deserve to become sources for future knowledge in general and for a more comprehensive understanding of the Palestinian history of struggle and resistance in particular.

The phenomenon of women's political resistance and detention is as old as colonialism, imperialism and the capitalist state (and indeed is older). Yet it is possible to trace it back, especially in the context of national liberation movements both in the North and in the South, to the 1960s. Since then and up until this day females, albeit at a lower rate than their male counterparts, have been facing the predicament of political detention. Nonetheless, this type of struggle has not generated the concern, attention and academic visibility which other forms of violence have been given, such as domestic or other types of violence in the 'private' sphere. In fact, academic and particularly feminist work on female political detainees has either not been done or, when attended to, remains virtually invisible within academic and other circles, hence the added value of writing about women's struggle and resistance.

Detainees or Prisoners

There is little to no consensus in the literature on prisons and prisoners regarding the definition of 'political prisoners'. Some maintain that there is a difference between 'political prisoners' and 'political detainees'. To begin with, there is hardly any state which recognizes the category of 'political prisoners', let alone 'political detainees'. In fact, while the USA uses the term political detainees for *other* countries' practices, it would deny that it has any of its own; examples include the American treatment of Cuba or their position on ex-political prisoners.[2] The ex-political prisoner and US feminist Susan Rosenberg for one distinguishes between the two terms. Using the context of struggle and resistance within the USA, she argues that 'a political prisoner is someone whose beliefs or actions have put them into direct conflict with the US government, or someone who has been targeted by the government because of his/her beliefs and actions' (Rosenberg 2006: 1). This description, she argues, 'complies with international legal definitions'. On the other hand, 'individuals who make the claim of prisoners of war, such as the Puerto Rican and New Afrikan/ African-American liberation movements, who are in pursuit of the recognition of their national liberation struggles for self-determination, are defined by legal scholars as political detainees.' (Rosenberg 2006: 2)

These people, she continues, 'have been criminalized or wrongly defined as "terrorists" ... and have been repressed to the maximum' (Rosenberg 2006: 2).[3] In other words, unlike the term political prisoner, that of political detainee remains legally unrecognized both within the USA and internationally.

Of equal importance is that most women, especially Palestinian and Lebanese ones detained in Israeli prisons, prefer to describe themselves as political detainees – an indication of the illegal acts on the part of the Israeli settler colonial regime. Responding to an Israeli reporter who kept referring to her as a prisoner and to her place of detention as a prison, internationally known Lebanese fighter Suha Bishara had the following to say: 'I resisted his [use of the] term of prison. I am in a detention camp ... the word prison refers to the place where people are kept after a transparent legal process and trial; this was not the case for us.' (Bishara 2001: 179–80)

The African-American activist Angela Davis, a member of the communist party and a Marxist feminist anti-racist scholar, on the other hand, remains reluctant to distinguish between the two terms and argues that prisoners incarcerated for social or economic offences are also political prisoners. Speaking within the context of the USA, she argues that the fact that the majority of inmates in US prisons are African Americans testifies to their poverty and lower social and educational status resulting from the state's systematic policies of economic and racial discrimination against this population (Davis 1971). In other words, for Davis virtually all prisoners are political prisoners. While I accept Davis's principal logic regarding political prisoners, it is important to note that her talk is specifically about the USA. On the other hand, Rosenberg's failure to bring the state into the equation in her notion of 'political detainee' – a concept largely applicable to the study of the struggle of Palestinian women (and men) under Israeli occupation since 1967 – is problematic. In almost all cases of political detention, the struggle against colonialism and occupation is simultaneously a struggle against the state. After all, it is the state which embodies, personifies and practises colonialism, occupation and imperialism.

A sort of vagueness seems to engulf the concept of political prisoners at levels other than the state or government. For example, Amnesty International refrains from using the term 'political prisoners'; instead, it uses the term 'prisoner of conscience' to describe political prisoners who have used non-violent means to protest oppression. This definition, I argue, is somewhat elastic and rather vague, as it excludes freedom fighters and anti-colonial, anti-imperialist strugglers or resisters who might also use armed struggle against colonialism and occupation. This holds also true for the recent attempts by international human rights organizations that have tried to assist in the release of political prisoners on humanitarian grounds. Although the intention of such organizations is novel, their ideological or political stand remains limited to a small number of individuals, seen by them having been as wrongly incarcerated on religious or belief grounds. In other words, a mission which refrains from acknowledging the right to anti-colonial armed struggle and the need to defend political detainees.

Within certain historical conjunctures, the act of generalization and theorization of some concepts (e.g. ones such as political detainees or prisoners) can misrepresent or omit certain particularities considered by the detainees as being very crucial. In prisons and detention camps, the concept of being a political prisoner or a political detainee becomes part of the identity of the detainee; it is the one which they refuse to change or give up and for which they are willing to struggle in order to keep it as their chosen identity under their lived circumstances. Most political prisoners, especially among Northern Irish and Palestinian women (and men), have historically used and continue to use the notion of political detainee as an identity which distinguishes them from other inmates (deemed as criminals). This is so, for example, in the case of Northern Ireland women fighters who, beginning in 1974, staged major strikes against the introduction of the Prevention of Terrorism Acts.[4] All of these acts, which allowed internment without trial, single-judge courts, powers of detention and search, and the designation of criminal status to political prisoners, caused a major upheaval in prisons. In the late 1970s, both women and men political detainees staged major demonstrations and held protests known as the 'blanket protest' and the 'dirty protest' in which they refused to wear prison uniforms and insisted on their status as political detainees and not as 'criminals'.[5] The issue of criminalization of political detainees and its impact on political detainees will be explored further in this chapter.

There are other specific reasons for differentiating between the terms prisoners and political detainees. In general, prisoners who are considered by the state to be criminals or felons (murderers, offenders, thieves and so on) are incarcerated as criminals: in general they are captured by the civil police, detained for a period of time until a court hearing is held and then a judgement made, and then incarcerated. Political detainees or political prisoners, on the other hand, undergo a totally different course of incarceration: they are often captured by the military police, gendarmerie, the security or other special forces outside of the civil sphere, and they often spend long periods in detention and interrogation without trial, sometimes spending years in prison without the right to due legal recourse. Political detainees, especially during their lengthy periods of interrogation, face physical, psychological and sexual violence in an attempt by the prison to force them to confess or divulge information needed by the prison authority.

Political prisoners and detainees, I argue, constitute a historically specific phenomenon: women (and men) in this category are incarcerated for reasons different from those of 'regular prisoners' and are treated differently under specific military or security regulations. I consider political detainees to be those individuals who were (or are) activists, politically conscious of different modes of oppression, and who have struggled and continue to engage in a struggle, including the armed struggle against oppressive conditions. Political detainees also differ from other prisoners in that they continue their political struggle during detention and re-invent new modes of determination for exercising their rights to resist and to further the goal of justice and freedom. The term political detainees used here can include prisoners of conscience: persons locked up for speaking out against their government or state, for practising their religion, or on account of their culture, race or gender. This said, the focus of this book will be on women activists and resisters who actively challenge the state, be it colonial, occupying, settler or totalitarian.

The *aseera* or *moa'taqala* (Arabic for a female political detainee or political prisoner), whether she spends a short period of time in detention camps or a long one, and similar to the tens of thousands of male *asra* or *moa'taqaloon* (plural forms for male political detainees), identify themselves and are recognized by their people as political detainees: they all challenge and resist the illegality of Israel, the occupying state. It is no coincidence that in the Palestinian Authority (PA), the name of the ministry which cares for political prisoners is known in Arabic as *wizarat al-asra wal-muaa`taqaleen* (Ministry of Detainees and Political Prisoners). Palestinian literature on this issue uses both concepts: detainees and political prisoners (see, e.g. Baker and Matar 2011). In some cases the terms are used interchangeably, while in others, the former (i.e. the detainee) refers to those detained without a charge, while the political prisoner refers to those who were charged and moved to Israeli prisons. All political detainees in this case are incarcerated and/or sentenced by security or military courts. With a vivid political resistance culture rich in political artefacts (including prose, poetry, theatre, films, caricature and so forth), as will be demonstrated later in this book, the term 'detainee', and not prisoner, is used here as the dominant term of reference. In this book, both terms are used – sometimes interchangeably.

Why the Silencing of Female Political Detainees?

Historically the period between the 1960s and the late 1980s has been globally recognized as the era of resistance, political activism and revolutions, during which strong resistance movements emerged, whether in the form of national liberation movements or anti-colonial and anti-imperialist struggles. This era involved the use of all possible means of resistance by a large number of male and female participants, including militant forms and armed struggle. This was also the era when tens of thousands of women (and men) were actively involved in militant activities of resistance in regions such as Africa and the Middle East and in countries such as the USA, Morocco, Algeria, Ireland and various Latin American countries – and most notably among Palestinians. The global atmosphere during those years, it can be argued, was also conducive to such activism, as major international bodies and international movements, such as the United Nations and the Third World movement, sanctioned resistance to colonialism and occupation, recognizing it as a right of the colonized or occupied to resist. It was not until the late 1980s that the global mood took a drastic shift, labelling all forms of resistance and anti-state activism as terrorist activities and de-legitimizing and criminalizing all forms of resistance.

The reluctance to deal with the phenomenon of female political detainees was partially addressed by Mary Helen Washington in the context of the USA. According to Washington, 'the class, gender, and racial politics of prisons in this country conspire to make most of us feel not only separate from the world of prison but indifferent to it, untouched and unconnected' (quoted in Bhavnani and Davis 2000: 231). This contention, particularly regarding the notions of race and racism, I find quite compelling and relevant to the cases of most female political detainees, but more specifically with regard to the case of Israel as a settler-colonial state.

Most literature on Arab societies, including Palestinian, remains ambiguous and rather dismissive towards the force of the concept of racism used by the state of Israel as a constituent element in its policies of oppression of the Palestinians. Arab Palestinians are often seen as a national collectivity and a homogeneous national group. Existing feminist analysis of Arab societies might provide elaborate accounts of issues of gender and even class, but issues of race and racism are hard to find; missing the force of racism or racialization in such analyses – particularly when dealing with states or societies such as Sudan (North and South), Egypt (especially its treatment of the Copts) and North Africa (particularly in relation to the Berber), and Israel (its treatment of Palestinians) – renders feminist analyses weak and rather untenable. In the case of the Palestinians in general and the citizens of Israel more specifically, any analysis of political detainees that omits or does not account for the force of race or of racialization remains flawed and indefensible.

Racism and racialization are primary constituents of the settler-colonial state: they are embedded in its structure and institutions, and especially so in its prison institution. Race is irreducible to factors of culture, tradition or religion. Within the Arab context in general and that of Palestine more specifically, we find notions of cultural traditions, religion and family patriarchy to be heavily employed in academic and feminist discourses on women. Cultural or even *culturalist* notions such as these are widely used as the context for explaining the reasons for violence against women and their submission. These are the same notions used by the state, and its institutions, including its prisons, as means for legitimating the use of force, dehumanizing and further subjugating Palestinian political detainees.

Still, the use of women's bodies and sexuality by the colonial state, and especially by its prison institutions, represents a prime tactic, or rather strategy, of control used against women's political activism. Women's bodies and sexuality are rendered a prime site of humiliation, subjugation and victimization. This is done not only through direct acts of sexual torture, but also through sexual psychological torture as well. For example, the fabrication of stories about women's sexuality and the threatening of female detainees with publication of such stories among family members and their wider community are well-known tactics used by prison authorities to force women into submission.

Women's bodies and sexuality become the colonial state's prime means of controlling women and threatening their families. Still, such victimization is not received silently by women: women's bodies are also used by the women themselves as sites of resistance, defiance and struggle, as Chapters 4 and 5 will demonstrate.

Cultural – or rather culturalist – literature, while making a rather wide space for women as sexualized bodies, fails to account for either racism or women as racialized bodies. Women's bodies are not only sexualized but also racialized, and as such occupy a central place in the narratives of female political detainees such as in the case of Irish women, African Americans, or Hispanics, as will be seen shortly. The racial oppression of Arab women, particularly of Palestinian women living under Israeli rule, as well as the racialization and ethnicization of women political detainees in Israeli military prisons, remains an issue that is very under-discussed, if ever addressed at all. Through the voices and words of political women ex-detainees, this book aims to analyse and highlight this aspect of women's oppression. Racism, it is argued elsewhere (Abdo 2011b), is at the centre of the policies and practices of the settler-colonial state. Racism is embedded in the Israeli state's legal, judicial and administrative institutions as well as in the very social fabric of the society, and informs its politics and practice. It is not surprising therefore to find the bodies of political detainees being used as the site of the state's oppression. These bodies 'are governed, colonially and postcolonially, through their constitutive positioning as racially engendered and in the gendering of their racial configuration' (Abdo and Lentin 2002: 99).

Since the 1960s the anti-capitalist, anti-imperialist and civil rights movements in the USA have drawn a considerable number of women into the struggle, including into its militant forms. It is no surprise, therefore, that the majority of detainees have been Blacks or African Americans as well as Puerto Rican women. In 1970, Angela Davis had to go underground; she was captured by the FBI and charged with possession of weapons. By then, Davis was just one of several other American women who were on the FBI's ten most-wanted fugitives list. Susan Rosenberg was another political activist involved in the armed struggle in 1979 and the early 1980s. A member of '"New Afrikan/African-American" liberation movements', as she puts it, Rosenberg was a militant activist and was underground for six months before she was captured by the FBI and charged with several arms-related offences. Not unlike Davis, Rosenberg was also kept in the high-security unit of the prison, living in horrible conditions there

(Rosenberg 2006). During the same period, Puerto Rican women also took part in their national liberation from the USA. Alejandrina Torres is an example of a woman who was involved in the armed struggle and detained and tortured for her political activism (Jones 1997; Kogan 1990; Torres 1998).

Again during the same period, African women (from both the North and the South), Latin American and Arab women and women from Northern Ireland also joined the struggle for national liberation and against colonialism. It is in this context that one remembers the heroic anti-colonial freedom fighter, Jamila Bouhaired (also known as Djamila Bouhaired), the internationally renowned Algerian woman who was brutally tortured with electricity and sentenced to death by the French in 1957.[6] Whereas most female political detainees were detained for their active involvement, other women faced a similar fate because of the involvement of a member of their family. Moroccan Malika Oufkir, for example, whose writings have enriched feminist resistance literature, was also imprisoned along with all of her family (her mother and five siblings) for over 20 years. They were placed in an isolated desert prison and underwent tremendous hardships in what Oufkir terms the 'dungeon' (Oufkir and Fitoussi 2001). Later in this chapter the experience of Malika Oufkir will be detailed.

The internment and detention of Irish women for alleged or actual involvement in the armed struggle against British rule in the early 1970s is another example. The number of women detained during this decade within a period of less than six months reached about 300 women. Mairéad Farrell, Mairéad Nugent and Mary Doyle, among others, provide just a few examples. These women have spent many years in the Armagh Prison (the women's prison), only to be later transferred to the 'Maze Prison' (also known as Long Kesh).

The lot of thousands of Palestinian women political detainees involved in resisting Israeli colonialism since the 1950s is not very different. Palestinian women, as will be discussed later in this book, were adamant in resisting their criminalization and insisted on identifying themselves as *munadelat* (freedom fighters). They recognized their struggle as one of justice and freedom against Israeli colonialism and occupation, and consider it to be a just one. For most of these women, as their voices will tell us, their armed struggle was part of the *fidai`yyeen* (freedom fighters) movement. The term *fidai`* has been used by most Arab national anti-colonial resistance movements, from Algiers to Morocco, to Syria and

Palestine. This term was also used by Frantz Fanon in the 1950s and 1960s to describe the Algerian armed strugglers against French colonialism and in order to distinguish them from 'terrorists' (Fanon 1970: 43).[7] Yet, with the emergence of US imperialism as the sole power in the world and with its 'war against terror' campaign, the term *fidai`* (freedom fighter), especially in the West, began to take on a different meaning, indicating instead a criminal and terrorist, while the freedom fighter proper also became a terrorist, vilified and targeted. This usage has not been confined solely to state or official circles but was equally used by mainstream and radical white Western feminists, as will be discussed in Chapter 2.

Mechanisms of Silencing

Women detained for their activism in the armed struggle for freedom and liberation share similar experiences behind bars. They all suffer physical, psychological, verbal and sexual abuse. Notwithstanding their activism, agency and struggle for freedom, a fundamental lack of academic interest in the lives and experiences of these women remains. One of the general similarities among most political detainees is their reluctance to publicly share their detention experiences, instead, keeping their voices silent and their daily ordeals private. They articulate their reasons for their own reluctance in different ways. In her 'History is a Weapon: Political Prisoners, Prisons, and Black Liberation', Angela Davis (1972) explained her reluctance to tell her story of political detention, considering it an indulgence compared to the many Black men and women who spent many years in detention with no due legal recourse or public attention; this is a rationale shared by various other women, including Palestinians. The Algerian freedom fighter Jamila Bouhaired, until this day, has not told or published her experiences. It is worth noting that this fighter has had many cities and streets named after her throughout the Arab world, and in her honour two major films were produced, namely, *The Battle of Algiers* (1966) by the Italian film-maker Gillo Pontecorvo and *Jamila the Algerian* (1958). by the well-known Egyptian director Youssef Chahine. In 2007, 50 years after her release, the *Al-Sharq Al-Awsat* newspaper referred to her as the 'present–absent' hero who lives in exile in her own country (Shwar 2007).

Bouhaired's refusal to flaunt her individual suffering and experience over that of her female and male comrades who remained in prison after her release, in the context of a country that has sacrificed more than one and a half million people for its national liberation, is not uncharacter-istic of women political detainees, whose commitment to the struggle for freedom and justice has been and remains unwavering. In a recent interview with her, as her life was being celebrated in Lebanon she said: 'The national pride is more precious than the body. I did not do more than what I thought was my responsibility. I am still alive, unfortunately, it is the martyrs who ought to be celebrated,' (Al-Mayadeen 2013).[8] In my conversation with female Palestinian ex-political detainees, the issue of flaunting the individual over the collective repeatedly emerged as a reason for some women to continue to struggle and survive under difficult conditions and a reason for not divulging their own experiences. For most of these women, this study and the conversations on which it is largely based have provided a unique space for voicing their detention experiences among other ex-detainees and also publicly.

The love for justice, for freedom and for the homeland has been a driving force for struggle among most women political detainees before, during and after detention. The words of Northern Ireland's Mairéad Farrell, Mairéad Nugent and Mary Doyle on this issue are telling. In a letter they collectively wrote during their hunger strike at Armagh Prison, Farrell, Nugent and Doyle wrote: 'We are prepared to fast to the death, if necessary, but our love for justice and our country will live forever' (Daugherty 2002).

There are other reasons which can account for women's reluctance to speak up about their silent or silenced experiences, for example, the issues of one's own safety. This is true, for example, in the case of Irish women who were released before the signing of the 1998 'peace treaty' with Britain and whose future under occupation was unclear (Corcoran 2006). This is also the case for most Palestinian women political detainees, especially those released through 'exchange deals' between the Palestinian Liberation Organization (PLO), and later the Palestinian Authority (PA), with Israel. Most women were released in such exchanges. Especially between the 1970s and the late 1980s, they were barred from going back to their homes in the occupied territories of 1967, or from entering Israel proper, as was the case for Therese Halasa, a political detainee who was also a citizen of Israel; the women were all exiled and transferred to various Arab countries. A rupture in the lives of released political detainees was evident in both categories: those exiled as well as the others who were allowed to return to their homes in the Israeli occupied territories. Thus, whereas the exiled lived away from their natural environment, from their families and community, those who returned home after a decade or more of detention went back to occupation and colonialism, and not unlike the exiled, most of them found that their family homes had been demolished as a collective punishment measure. In the absence of a labour market capable of absorbing them, even many of those who were highly educated, as will be shown in Chapter 5, became financially dependent on their families and had to face or rather observe certain social and traditional codes restricting their movement – all conditions which further solidified their silences.

Finally, what I think is quite compelling in terms of female ex-political detainees' unwillingness or averseness to voice or document their experiences is the feeling of distress, frustration and anguish at one's own national or political leaders. This feeling, I believe, holds true in the case of Jamila Bouhaired, as well as in other cases. For many Arab women and in most Arab countries, release from prison was not translated into freedom or liberation; rather, most women found themselves in a larger prison ruled by autocratic, dictatorial and repressive regimes ... the colonizer came to be from within. This is what many Algerian nationals faced – despite the fact that, as mentioned earlier, more than one million lives had been sacrificed for the country's liberation. Ahlam Mostaghanmi's *Dhakirat al-Jassad* (Memory in the Flesh), which since its first publication in 1993 has been reprinted over 35 times and which was turned into a theatre production during Ramadan of 2010, eloquently described the Algerian peoples' frustration and disillusionment in the post-liberation national leadership.[9] This is also what most Palestinian female ex-detainees have suffered: dissatisfaction with the continued Israeli occupation and colonialism, and disappointment with the PA, which for the almost two decades after the so-called peace agreement has failed to deliver any substantive changes.

In other words, the very national or collective feeling and consciousness which played a central role in women's commitment and determination to resist and sacrifice their freedom has in fact disappointed them, becoming a major source of their frustration. Statements such as 'Why bother?', 'Who cares?', 'No one is interested', or 'No one listens' were repeatedly pronounced by Palestinian ex-political detainees during our conversations.

Different Prisons, Similar Experiences

As noted earlier, women political detainees share many common characteristics. The first and foremost is the struggle for freedom, justice and against all forms of oppression, a struggle which they undertake before, during and after detention. In detention camps or prisons women endure similar experiences of torture, humiliation, solitary confinement and isolation, with beatings, the application of electrical shocks, torture through the alternate pouring of hot and cold water, and blindfolding. In the case of confinement, often in unsanitary cells, there is too often no running water and toilet facilities that consist of buckets placed in each cell and emptied every few days (and in some cases the urine would flood the cell). For example, in the case of Irish female political detainees in Armagh, the urine-saturated cells became a primary reason for the staging of the 'dirty protest', as will be discussed here.

Psychological torture is also a characteristic feature of detention camps for female political detainees. Most political detainees experience similar methods of psychological torture. These include the torture of their male counterparts or other family members, especially their mothers, in front of their eyes, sleep deprivation, solitary confinement, rooms infested with pests such as cockroaches, worms and ants, exposure to very loud music or to sounds of screaming with the victim hooded using a heavy, dirty sack sometimes soaked in urine or polluted with faeces, and so on. Although such experiences are also shared by male political detainees, psychological torture remains gender specific: it has a specific impact on women. The forced nudity of women political detainees, including parading them naked in front of their male comrades, is specifically tormenting and dehumanizing for female detainees. Psychological torture is particularly distressing for pregnant women who spend months in detention with little to no medical attention. It is also specifically poignant for those who give birth while in detention, or for menstruating women who are deprived of sanitary napkins. The highly publicized cases of Irish freedom activist Róisín McAliskey[10] and Palestinian political detainees Mirvat Amin and Manal Ghanem are just a few cases in point.[11] In various cases, including ones involving women of Palestine and Northern Ireland, strip-searching was one particular form of sexual abuse experienced by women detainees. Although strip-searches, especially in airports and at other border crossings, have currently become a daily routine within self-proclaimed democracies such as the USA and Israel, such tactics were not highly visible during the 1970s and the 1980s. In the case of the Northern Irish women resisters, the strip-search was used to further sexually, physically and psychologically harass the political detainees. The threat of rape, attempted rape and actual rape, which are more prevalent among female political detainees than among males, remains most agonizing for women political detainees, as will be discussed further.

This said, it is worth noting that sexual torture is not targeted at women alone; it has been and continues to be experienced by male political detainees. Sexual abuse of men and young boys, including rape, has been heavily documented in the cases of the Abu Ghraib and Guantanamo detention camps under the auspices of the USA. Without going into too much detail about the torture in Abu Ghraib detention camp perpetrated by US soldiers and security contractors, I would only like to mention one particular report, a US military psychology assessment report on detainees' abuse at Abu Ghraib. According to this document, 'soldiers were immersed in Islamic culture, a culture with a different worship and belief system that they were encountering for the first time'. It goes on to explain how the 'association by soldiers of Muslims with terrorism could exaggerate difference and lead to fear and to a devaluation of people'. The differences between the US soldiers and the Iraqi prisoners reached such a level whereby, according to a military dog handler, even the dogs 'came not to like Iraqi detainees. They [the dogs] did not like the Iraqi culture, smell, sound, skin tone, hair-color or anything about them' (quoted in Nusair 2008: 181).

Horrifying sexual assaults on men and children are not unheard of in the case of Palestinians held in Israeli detention camps.[12] In one highly documented case, that of Mustafa Dirani, a lawsuit was – and remains at the time of writing – filed against the prison authorities and the Israeli state for his sexual assault. Dirani spent seven years in the recently discovered 'secret prison facility' known as 'Facility 1391'. Mustafa Dirani, the security chief of the Lebanese militia group Amal, was – and remains – the most high-profile former detainee of Facility 1391; he was kidnapped from his home in Lebanon by Israeli agents in 1994, together with other people visiting him at the time. After his release through an exchange of prisoners between Hizbullah and Israel, Dirani filed a lawsuit accusing his interrogator of two counts of sexual assault; in one incident, his interrogator, known as 'Major George', tortured him and inserted a wooden baton into his rectum, while in the other, 'Major George' ordered a soldier to rape him (Cook 2003).[13]

With this said, the fact remains that in general, gender remains a primary constituent of the ideology behind the treatment of political prisoners, and Palestinian political prisoners in Israel and a force that distinguishes the treatment of male and female detainees. In this context, racialized and sexualized state policies become highly visible. In detention camps, women's bodies are used as the primary site for torture and persecution. From sexual abuse, sexual assault, attempted rape and rape on the one hand, to deprivation of necessary services, including sanitary ones, to torture and humiliation during pregnancy on the other hand, all are female-specific means used by the prison authorities for torturing women. Several Palestinian women political detainees have experienced the threat of rape and attempted rape, and some actually were raped. In my conversations with women ex-political detainees, one described her fierce resistance to rape; two others mentioned attempted rape against them, while the rest admitted to experiencing the threat of rape, sexual harassment and intimidation at the hands of prison authorities.

The Criminalization of Political Detainees

Earlier in this chapter the issue of the criminalization of political detainees was raised as a rationale given for women's silenced voices. In the following, a comprehensive account of the role of the criminalization of political detainees and prisoners will be provided. To begin with, this issue is common among all freedom fighters and activists resisting oppressive regimes. In today's imperialism, national liberation struggles and resistance to colonialism and occupation is seen as violence and often delegitimized. Women (and men) activists fighting for national liberation or for freedom from colonialism, imperialism and other forms of oppression are incarcerated or 'imprisoned' as criminals: they are not detained as political activists. Criminalization of political detainees is an a priori judgement – or rather punishment – levied on the activists even prior to any investigation. The designation of criminal status to political prisoners or political detainees does not intend to only denigrate and dehumanize them. Labelling political detainees as 'criminals' and 'terrorists' aims, first, at justifying the state's as well as its agents' rationale for imprisoning them. It also charts the way, the means and the methods used in torturing them and forcing them to submit or confess to their 'criminal behaviour'. Criminalizing political detainees, moreover, intends the transformation of these people into the other, inferior and less worthy of due process and legal procedures.

The Othering of political detainees expresses a relationship of power that is class, gender and race informed. For example, sending the message that Irish women resisters and detainees are criminals and terrorists is a means for the British authorities to justify its colonial rule and policies over Northern Ireland. The struggle of Northern Irish women political detainees against their criminalization has led to years of protests and strikes by both women and men detainees. The 'dirty protest', led by female political detainees in Armagh Prison, staged as resistance against their criminalization by the state in 1980, speaks volumes about the agency and resistance of Northern Irish female political detainees to their criminalization. Mary Corcoran's *Out of Order* (2006), her account of women's resistance in Armagh prison, is the first detailed documented account of protests by women prisoners in Armagh Prison and in the Mourne House Unit of Maghaberry Prison during the time well known as 'the troubles'. She traces a history of the present by charting the evolution of the punishment of female political prisoners in Northern Ireland over a 26-year period. To do this, she structures her account according to the three key stages of prison administration and penal regimes she identified as operating in Armagh Prison during that period: reactive containment (1969–76), criminalization (1976–81) and normalization (1982–98). During the criminalization period, Corcoran discusses women's resistance to the removal of their political status by staging what the prisoners called 'dirty protest'. The protest actions included women's refusal to bathe and smearing their cells with faeces and menstrual blood. In addition, women detainees participated in a nearly year-long hunger strike, both to resist and to demonstrate their agency as political prisoners and to show their solidarity with and support of their male counterparts in H-Block. After winning some concessions, women political detainees began to normalize their forms of resistance through employment of formal procedures including legal litigation against the administration, campaigning against strip-searches, and by demanding improvements in their prison conditions (Corcoran 2006: 207).

Palestinian women's political detainees' resistance to their criminaliza-tion, intimidation and dehumanization by the Israeli prison authorities, which has involved hunger strikes, the refusal to perform chores, and various other modes of creative resistance, will be discussed especially in Chapters 4 and 5. But what is rather historically specific about this case is that the presentation of Palestinian women as being submissive, lacking agency and blaming them for resisting colonialism has come from many sources, including unexpected ones such as Western feminists. Although hundreds and probably thousands of Palestinian women were part of the anti-colonial resistance movement, estimated by Soraya Antonius at 2,000 women between 1967–79 (Antonius 1980: 29), there was virtually no interest, especially among feminists in this phenomenon. Palestinian women in general were viewed from an Orientalist perspective, described either as terrorists or seen as Arab/Muslim victims of their own culture, religion, family and patriarchy (Said 1979; Abu-Lughod 2002). During our period of discussion (1960–80) most Western media and not necessarily the academy, were fascinated by the resistant act of well-known Palestinian fighter, Leila Khaled who hijacked a plane to free Palestinian prisoners from Israeli prison. Khaled was presented by most Western media as a terrorist and criminal with no concern for the reasons for her actions. The process of victimization and vilification of Palestinian women, especially those involved in the armed struggle, took a special turn after the development of the feminist movement and its institutionalization through women and gender studies departments, a movement which emerged in the early 1990s. Hence the emergence of a plethora of Western (and Israeli) feminist literature – especially after September 11 and since the second 'Al-Aqsa' Intifada (which began in 2000 and ended roughly around 2006) joining the slanderous campaign against Palestinian women fighters, describing them as terrorists, as submissive, and as lacking agency (Victor 2003; Tzoreff 2006; Schweitzer 2006; Reuter 2006; Patkin 2004).

Political Detainees and Administrative Detention

While in general, prisons arbitrarily exercise their authority and adopt administrative detention or detention without a due legal process against political detainees, the Israeli state has turned this practice into an extreme and regularized procedure, used against thousands of Palestinian political detainees. Detention orders are often authorized by administrative orders, including ones originating from the police and the military, and not by judicial decree (B'Tselem 2011). Detention of Palestinian political prisoners, including women as mentioned earlier has been going on since the 1960s. In her 'Prisoners for Palestine: A List of Women Political Prisoners' (1980) Soraya Antonius recorded over 200 women political detainees, and adds that the list does not include the hundreds of women and girls rounded up in the Gaza Strip and kept in detention camps in Saina in 1972 (Antonius 1980: 29). During the first two or three decades of the Israeli 1967 occupation, information on Palestinian political detainees was scant, partly because Israeli officials did not release the names or locations of all detainees (Antonius 1980: 30), and partly because Palestinian official documentation of political detainees began after the Oslo Accords – which represented the Declaration of Principles on Interim Self-Government, and was an attempt in 1993 to set up a framework that would lead to the resolution of the ongoing Israeli–Palestinian conflict. In 1998, the first Palestinian Ministry of Detainees was established.[14] As the Palestinian struggle for liberation continued, the phenomenon of women fighters and their detention also developed further. Commenting on more recent waves of detention, the human rights organization B'Tselem (the Israeli Information Center for Human Rights in the Occupied Territories) states the following:

> Over the years, Israel has administratively detained thousands of Palestinians for prolonged periods of time ... ranging from several months to several years, without prosecuting them, without informing them of the charges against them, and without allowing them or their attorneys to study the evidence, making a mockery of the protections specified in Israeli and international law to protect the right to liberty and due process, the right of defendants to state their case, and the presumption of innocence. The highest number of administrative detainees was documented during the first intifada. On 5 November 1989, Israel was holding 1,794 Palestinians in administrative detention.
>
> B'Tselem (2013)

What distinguishes the Israeli case from, say, the US state regime is that the overwhelming majority of Palestinian political detainees are being detained by either the Shin Bet (Israel Security Agency, or ISA), the military police, or by the Israel Defense Forces (IDF). According to data compiled by B'Tselem, up until 2007 adults aged 18 years and over as well as children under the age of 18 were largely incarcerated by or 'kept under the custody' of the IDF. In 2005, there were 1,233 Palestinian children detainees between the ages of 16–18 and 63 were under the age of 16. In 2007, 196 political detainees were between the ages of 16–18 years. All these children were in IDF detention camps (B'Tselem 2005). Palestinian children are also placed in administrative detention. In 2009, the number of children political detainees reached 311. Between 31 January and 31 October 2010, 132 child political detainees and 16 children were placed under administrative detention. Most children detainees were under the age of 16, while 16 others were placed under administrative detention (B'Tselem 2011).

Despite the loudly announced exchange of prisoners in January 2010 (with the exchange of Palestinians for the Israeli soldier, Shalit) suggestive of a large decrease in the numbers incarcerated, in fact the release of about 1,000 detainees during the exchange did not reduce the overall number of detainees; the number of Palestinian detainees in Israeli prisons was estimated at 4,700, of which there were 185 children and 320 administrative detainees. Between January 2012 and 23 March 2012, there were about 900 detentions throughout the 1967 occupied territories. These included tens of children, women, members of the Palestinian Legislative Council (PLC) and a number of those who were released, were then arrested again (Ferwana 2013). As I write this and as most Palestinians are celebrating Eid Al-Fitr, Ferwana reported the presence of about 4,550 Palestinian political detainees in the occupation prisons. These include 220 children, 6 female detainees, 17 members of the Palestinian Parliament and 250 administrative detainees. (Ferwana 2013)[15]

By confining political detainees in detention camps for prolonged periods of time, preventing them from seeing lawyers and family members and denying them access to legal recourse, administrative detention is designed to coerce detainees into submission. During this period, detainees undergo an arduous course of torture and humiliation. Still, for many, neither during the period of initial detention nor after the laying of charges do women political detainees accept their detention silently or acquiesce to their oppressors. Agency and resistance to the state and its prison institution continues.

Agency and Resistance in Israeli Detention Camps and Prisons

Resistance, struggle, and fighting against oppression do not stop at the doors of prisons or detention camps. The commitment to freedom, the love for the homeland, and the determination to struggle against oppression – elements which make up the agency of women fighters and drive them to resist – continue to be the driving forces for their survival in prisons or detention camps. Essential to all political resisters, both male and female, is the affirmation of their identity, namely, their insistence on being defined as political prisoners or detainees and not as terrorists. Against the silences, which characterize much of the Western academic and feminist perceptions of women political detainees, most political detainees are never silent recipients of oppression, regardless of the place or space they find themselves in. Literary writings, including novels, women's diaries, poetry and other forms of cultural artefacts, point to a variety of means used both collectively and individually by women political detainees in resisting their oppression while in detention camps and prisons.

Methods of resistance used by most female political detainees include hunger strikes, refusing to leave their cells, disobeying the orders of prison guards, persisting in making demands and the already discussed dirty protests. Resistance, in other words, can be active and direct or else passive. The social and political consciousness-raising provided by the older and younger generations of political detainees for new arrivals is also common among many political detainees globally. Resistance education in prisons, expressed in formalized education sessions, seminars, workshops and literacy awareness classes is also practised by female political detainees. A detailed discussion of this issue will be presented in Chapter 5. Moreover, steadfastness and perseverance in the face of harsh and brutal interrogation methods are also taught in the detention camp. Women, especially the senior political detainees who have gone through the terror and violence of interrogation, use their experience in order to morally and mentally comfort and aid more junior detainees going through similar experiences. While general means and forms of resistance are commonly and collectively shared by female political detainees, the individual experience of torture and resistance remains culturally and historically specific.

The following narratives of Moroccan and Lebanese women provide an example of the individual and collective struggles female political detainees engage in while in detention camps. The first narrative is Moroccan and is based on Malika Oufkir's 2001 *Stolen Lives: Twenty Years in a Desert Jail*. Malika Oufkir was never politically active, nor was she involved in any form of resistance prior to her incarceration; nonetheless, her relentless perseverance and struggle during her and her family's detention for about 20 years makes her case a worthwhile one to acknowledge. Oufkir and her whole family (her mother and five siblings) were detained for almost two decades for a political act her father had committed – trying to assassinate Mohammad V, the King of Morocco, as part of a military *coup d'état*. In other words, her detention was part of a collective punishment. Of particular interest here is that, despite the lack of any previous political consciousness or participation in any political activities, Malika Oufkir was able to wage a heroic struggle against the appalling conditions of the Moroccan jail in the desert. Malika Oufkir's struggle, while seemingly 'individual', has in fact been both individual and collective at the same time. The strength, courage and hope she gained in prison to pursue the struggle for the survival and anticipated freedom of her family is inspirational. The injustice that befell her and her family as a result of an act which they never participated in, or even knew about, and which landed them in prison ignited Malika Oufkir's agency and her will to resist. Malika Oufkir rediscovered (or perhaps revived) her agency partly by being the nanny and nurse for her sick three-year-old brother and partly through the resilience she demonstrated in the presence of her three sisters. Still, her major inspiration came from her younger brother, a teenager at the time, who himself acquired new and varying skills for enhancing communication and continuity within this family that had been divided by placing them in different cells.

Traces of social and not political agency in Malika Oufkir's pre-prison life – for example, in not accepting her mother's social or customary norms – cannot sufficiently account for her resilience in prison. In fact, the transformation in her life was literally from the palace to the prison. Mohammad Oufkir, Malika's father, was a high-ranking general under King Muhammad V and the closest aid to his son, King Hassan. She was adopted by the king at the age of five and lived lavishly in the palace until 1972, spending most of her teenage years being showered with gifts and imported clothes and being treated like a princess. The move to the desert jail with the resulting separation of the family ignited the need for Malika Oufkir to persist and resist prison life. It also made it possible for her and her family, in part through her determination, to endure the harsh treatment of prison. In prison, Malika Oufkir performed the roles of teacher, mentor and health provider and became the primary mental–emotional resource for her siblings while simultaneously ensuring their physical survival. She exercised her agency in order to change the dire situation into which she and her family were thrown. She was the leader, the thinker and the driving force behind her younger brother who as noted above, also began to develop new talents and practise them as means for a potential escape from the prison.

Over the years, Malika Oufkir's brother began collecting any metal objects that he could hide and, after making openings between the cells, dismantled an old radio for use in communicating with other members of the family. With the help, encouragement and hard work of all the family, after 15 years of isolation and horrifying prison conditions, and using their bare hands or kitchen utensils which they had hidden from the guards, they were able to dig a tunnel wide enough for the family to escape into the desert. (Oufkir and Fitoussi 2001)[16]

Malika Oufkir's case is a prime example of how oppression, as a thesis, creates its own antithesis of opposition, resistance and struggle. The 1970s marked the darkest years in Morocco's recent history: a monarchical and autocratic regime, the suppression of freedoms and the abuse of human rights. Whereas Malika Oufkir was immune from such oppressive conditions, until the *coup d'état* and her imprisonment, Fatna El-Beih and many other Moroccan women were not.

The following narrative relates the life and struggle of Fatna El-Beih, another Moroccan woman, and is based on her 2000 book *Hadeeth Al-A'tmah* (Talk of Darkness). Fatna El-Beih's life is one of struggle and resistance against the dictatorship of King Mohammad V, first declared as Sultan of Morocco from 1927–53 and King from 1957–61, and his son Hassan II who ruled Morocco from 1961 until his death in 1999. Fatna El-Beih began her struggle as a teenage school student, organizing protests and marching against the regime, and continued struggling as a political detainee against the Moroccan prison authorities. During the 1970s, under the monarchical reign of Hassan II, thousands of people were kidnapped, many disappeared, many were executed and many more were tortured in the jails of the Moroccan desert. Fatna El-Beih was one of those who was kidnapped and tortured for five years; she was kidnapped from a friend's house while both were studying for their exams. After showering her with a range of indecent names, including *qahba* (whore), *sharmouta* (prostitute) and so on, they placed her in solitary confinement and gave her a number and a new name – Rasheed, *a male name*: 'this was the beginning of stripping me of my identity: kidnapping and arbitrary detention, then erasing my female identity and treating me as a male', Fatna El-Beih says (2000: 15).[17]

In some respects, for example in reference to the meaning of 'time' in prison, Fatna El-Beih, like Malika Oufkir did not distinguish between day and night. Women political detainees experience 'time' in various ways. For some, time was about waiting, often expressed in statements such as 'What is next?' and 'What about tomorrow?' However, for activists and fighters like El-Beih, other issues were more pressing, especially during the first months of detention while living through the moment of horrific interrogation. Of significance to these women is the issue of when they would be called for interrogation – and when their next session of torture would begin, and what their response would be at that time. Although the Oufkir family went through many hardships, especially psychologically, they were spared physical and sexual torture, in contrast to the politically conscious and activist detainees. The latter, as will be demonstrated further in this book, go through unthinkable torture during interrogation, especially during the days or even the weeks of detention and interrogation. Reflecting on her detention and the prison authorities, especially on her interrogators, Fatna El-Beih says: 'No difference here between times or sexes ... no difference for them ... they aimed at destroying the self, and the sole through the body, whether the body is male or female.' (El-Beih 2000: 17)

Political detainees, moreover, experience *time* differently than other prisoners, especially in terms of the actions or activities they undertake. On the ways time is used during her detention, Fatna El-Beih has the following to say:

> We had a shortage of time. We had a full programme: study, making artefacts ... discussions, sports, writings, etc. We studied literature and philosophy, we studied economics, sociology, psychology; we used the quiet nights to organize cultural events and discussions and spent the whole night doing this. We chose to represent a whole generation and it was incumbent upon us to be in the position of leadership.
>
> Fatna El-Beih (2000: 35–36)

While all female political detainees experience torture in some similar ways, the methods of torture vary from one context to another. For example, Fatna El-Beih recounts her experience of the torture method called *tayyara* (airplane), saying: 'You feel yourself in a plane, but instead of taking off, you always crash. This is crucifixion *Moroccan style*' (El-Beih 2000: 18, emphasis in the original). Another method used by interrogators is called *falaqa* (thick baton), and it was used to beat the detainee constantly until she or he loses consciousness: 'They did this to me for seven months' Fatna El-Beih said (2000: 18).

New Skills and Alternative Senses

Because of the nature of political detention, in which detainees are labelled terrorists and deemed to be a threat to the 'security' of the state, prison authorities take strong measures to ensure that detainees do not see or recognize their interrogators. This is done partly through blindfolding the detainees whenever they are taken for interrogation, to court, transferred to other detention camps or dragged into the interrogation room. It is also accomplished by placing detainees for weeks, months and even years in solitary confinement, in cells built specifically for this reason: a tiny cell with usually one small barred window, often too high for the detainee to reach or see through. For many if not most detainees, sight, which in a significant sense, is often blocked. But the loss of sight, as Fatna El-Beih's case exemplifies, is often compensated for by a sharp sense of smell and hearing. Thus attests Fatna El-Beih: 'As I was blindfolded all the time, I learned to recognize them [the prison guards] through their smell and the sound of their shoes ... [And] through the marks of their fingers they left on my body I learned to differentiate between the interrogators' (El-Beih 2000: 19). In reference to the collective struggle she was involved in while in the detention camp, Fatna El-Beih recalls:

> We got used to hear without seeing, and to communicate without proper means of communication and to discern everything around us; to be patient even when patience dissipated ... We dry our flowing tears, and make sure our belief in the cause never waivers or is shaken ... This is what has strengthened us, solidified our determination and kept us aloof; our determination did not collapse.
>
> El-Beih (2000: 33)

Developing a strong sense of hearing to compensate for loss of sight during lengthy periods of isolation was one major skill acquired by Lebanese fighter Suha Bishara, our third example. In her book *Muqawama* (Resistance) (2001), which recounts her and her cell mates' time in an Israeli detention camp, Suha Bishara stated:

> We became accustomed to hearing the different sounds in the detention camp, to the degree that we became all ears and so experts in listening and recognizing the source of sounds. We were able to distinguish between the female guards through the sounds of their steps and the sounds they made when they opened the doors. Our hearing faculties became very sharp and always alert. We would clearly recognize movement within the detention camp ... We could guess who had been dragged to interrogation and who accompanied them, who returned and who was transferred.
>
> Bishara (2001: 186)

Using the senses of hearing and smelling to compensate for the loss of seeing, in other words, becomes a skill which incarcerated political prisoners develop. It also presents another stark example of the level of agency women exercise under stressful conditions.

It is true that while the general literature on resistance and political detention is slowly growing, most of this literature continues to focus on male detainees; it is either written by men or narrated by them and expresses their own experience. Few and far between is the literature which is written by women or men that narrates women's experiences or accords them importance. Thus, except for the works of Barbara Harlow (1992), Frantz Fanon (1970) and Mary Corcoran (2006), the overwhelming majority of written material on women prisoners or detainees comes in the form of cultural production, such as poetry, novels, diaries and biographies, written by women (see e.g. Odeh 2004, 2007; Langer 1975; Bishara 2001, 2010; Oufkir 2001; Agah, Parsi and Mehr 2007). Such writings, while valuable and while contributing to our understanding of women's experiences of political detention, unfortunately remain removed from the wider public and are often regarded as being just a personal experience, which lacks wider theoretical or historical relevance.[18] Another factor which restricts the circulation of such literature is often the local language within which such literature is written. For example, Aisha Odeh's three books, which recount her biography, are all in Arabic and none have yet been translated. Although Arabic readership could be large, the knowledge of the existence of such writings remains geographically and strategically restricted and does not reach a European or North American readership. One of the difficulties faced by female political detainees trying to obtain their deserved place as authentic voices is their reluctance to narrate their stories or voice their concerns – a point emphasised by Harlow, who argues that the talk (or narratives) of otherwise silenced women reveals volumes about the human condition (Harlow 1992). In recognition of the significance of women's voices, this study will include autobiographies and personal narratives of women detainees as an integral part of its data.

National Anti-Colonial Resistance in the Era of New Imperialism

The discussion above reveals the commonalities and differences in the individual experiences of women resisters to colonialism in various countries worldwide. The context for these discussions – the second half of the twentieth century – was one of a declining Western colonialism, a decline that seemed to be completed with the 'peace treaty' between Britain and Northern Ireland in 1998 and the end of South African Apartheid in 1994.[19] These events were central to the public statements which the late Edward Said made on various occasions. In the early 1990s, Said made strong statements condemning the Israeli colonization of Palestine and asserted that Israel was the only remaining bastion of colonialism in the world. The general global political atmosphere changed in the late twentieth century and leading into the beginning of the twenty-first century. Among such changes was the development by progressive academics, with Edward Said as a pioneer, of concepts like 'post-colonialism' to describe countries recently freed from colonial control. Left, progressive and radical critical feminists began to use this concept in studying, understanding and analysing Third World countries.

Unfortunately, however, and as will be demonstrated in Chapter 2, changes in the political environment during the 1990s did not last long. The end of the twentieth century witnessed some major political and economic changes worldwide. These included the incorporation of the former Eastern bloc into the capitalist leviathan, the expansion of the scope of the International Monetary Fund (IMF), and the NATO invasion of Yugoslavia. Insofar as the Middle East is concerned, the twenty-first century ushered in a new global era characterized by a heightened form of imperialism combined with a highly sophisticated military technology used in the direct military intervention and occupation of Iraq and Afghanistan. This era, known as 'the new imperialism', has undoubtedly shaken the very bases of the then-existing epistemological methods or frameworks, rendering them rather problematic if not irrelevant.

The debate on the difference between present-day imperialism, coined by Colin Mooers (2006) as the 'new imperialism' and the 'old imperialism', does not concern us here. What is important to note though is that there seems to be an ideological shift away from the colonial imperialism of the nineteenth and the twentieth centuries which involved the physical presence of the colonial forces to the new form of colonial imperialism achieved largely through wars of destruction, with the imperialist forces leaving the country in shambles (e.g. Iraq, Afghanistan and Libya): a shift from a 'civilization mission' to a 'democratization mission'.

In the hegemonic ideology of current imperialism which overemphasizes notions of 'democracy', 'individual rights and freedoms' as pretexts for its expansionist interests have, with the aid of new technologies, especially communication technology, travelled fast throughout the world. This official ideology was also adopted by the Western academy (including the Israeli academy) towards Palestinian women, and it became rather a mantra in Western feminist literature on Palestinian women resistance fighters. The spread of this ideology has largely contributed to the plethora of vilifying literature against Palestinian women anti-colonial fighters.

In conclusion, the notion of the seemingly 'voiceless' talk of women political detainees, as this book will demonstrate, is only true for those who ignore them, silence their voices and exclude them from history. In reality, these women were and remain a rich source of history, experience and knowledge. All that is needed to counter such notions is the inclusion of such experiences and voices back into the history of resistance, representing it in its complete and comprehensive form, which is the aim of this book. In other words, this book is an attempt to rewrite the Palestinian history of resistance and political detention, partly in order to reinstate the missing voices, stories and histories of women political detainees and partly because of the inaction of the Palestinian Authority and the international community concerning the issue of thousands of political detainees who are still incarcerated in Israeli prisons. In such incarcerations, the unspeakable atrocities committed against female (and male) political detainees by all colonial imperialist states will also be revealed. Such practices, it is argued, should never be ignored, hidden or kept on the backburner, especially insofar as they involve the physical, psychological, mental and sexual torture of political detainees including women.[20]

2

Anti-Colonial Resistance in Context

Resistance is not peculiarly 'Third World', nor is it specific to the colonies. As discussed in Chapter 1, political resistance to imperialism and colonialism in industrialized capitalist countries (especially the USA) has happened and continues to occur. In past decades, especially during the 1960s, 1970s and 1980s, we witnessed major uprisings in Western capitalist countries, some of which included armed struggle, such as the Republican resistance movement in England and Ireland and the Hispanic and African-American anti-imperialist struggles in the USA. Throughout the 1990s and on into the early twenty-first century, we have also witnessed the emergence of massive anti-imperialist protests and political actions in which different means of resistance and struggle have been employed. In 1999, for example, a demonstration in the USA managed to shut down the World Trade Organization (WTO) and occupy downtown Seattle (Juris 2008a). This was followed by a five-day general strike against capitalist exploitation of the farm workers in Immokalee, Florida and the chain of protests both 'peaceful' and 'violent' spread to many other European countries, including Mexico, Germany and Greece (Juris 2008b).

Although popular revolts and uprisings against imperial capitalist exploitation, especially those against large intra-state organizations such as the WTO, the World Bank or the International Monetary Fund (IMF), have declined – or rather been silenced – after the September events of 2001, they have not entirely vanished. The silencing, which was the by-product of the overwhelming control of the 'new imperialism', to use Mooers' term (2006a), has instead found its expression in various other forms of resistance, for example, the Occupy Movement in North American cities (2011) that demanded a more equitable distribution of wealth, better wages and free education – basically a demand for change if not an outright dismantling of the capitalist system. Still, the major anti-imperialist struggles and revolutions during the 1960s through to the 1980s were actually waged outside of the USA and Europe, in countries that the latter powers had already colonized, occupied and controlled, for example, in Vietnam (1961–75), Algeria (1954–62), Cuba (1953–59) and Nicaragua (1978–89). These revolutions, along with freedom fighter and revolutionary leadership figures (such as Ho Chi Minh, General Giap, Che Guevara and Fidel Castro) have had a great impact on the Palestinian resistance movement, especially in the form of armed struggle between the late 1960s and the late 1980s. As will be seen in the following chapters, Palestinian women freedom fighters-turned-political detainees and prisoners looked upon such revolutions and revolutionary leaders with approval and took their leaders as role models and educators.

> We are at a point in our work when we can no longer ignore empires and the imperial context in our studies.
>
> Said (1994a: 5)

Two decades later, today, Said's quote remains as pertinent as it was true several decades earlier when imperialism took different forms (colonialism and settler colonialism). A proper understanding of the Palestinian anti-colonial and anti-imperialist struggle requires a comprehension of the imperialist and colonial contexts within which the Palestinian struggle has unfolded and continues to unfold. This chapter argues that the so-called new imperialism which is largely linked to world changes since September 11, 2001, and particularly since the American imperialist onslaught on Iraq, is in many aspects, just a continuation of 'old' imperialism. This continuity, insofar as Israel/Palestine is concerned, is based on capitalistic expansionist bases, including resources and a geo-strategic interest and the 'securatization' of Israel, yet performed/enacted at the levels of discourse and ideology. More specifically, insofar as the Palestinian women's struggle was/is concerned, the imperialist context within which they were/are viewed has been largely one of an ideological nature and of discursive proportions: perception, representation and imagining by Western (including Israeli) official, popular, and mainstream media and academia – a context that was and has remained characteristically Orientalist and racist in essence.

Palestinian women's struggle from the late 1960s up until the late 1980s emerged as part of the anti-colonial anti-imperialist struggle which the people have been waging since the turn of the twentieth century. Unlike most Third World countries that were able to rid themselves of colonialism, especially by the British and French, British colonialism left Palestine in 1948 only to be replaced with another settler colonial regime – Israel. In 1967 and with the support of the West, especially the USA, settler colonial Israel expanded its territorial control over the rest of Palestine as well as parts of other Arab territories (Syria, Egypt and Jordan). Israel's settler colonialism and consequent territorial expansionism, resulting in further refugeeism and oppression of Palestinians, instead of being objected to by the West has in fact been condoned. Repeated vetoes by the USA and its Western allies of all UN attempts at doing some justice to Palestinians have resulted in maintaining Israel's colonial rule over the whole of Palestine since 1948. The international failure at resolving the Palestinian question has turned Palestinians into refugees, stripping them of their national identity.

The influence of the Zionist lobby especially in the USA and the Zionist perpetual myth of Palestine as 'a land without people for a people without land' loomed high in the agendas of most official circles and media and among the public at large in the West. In his rather long documentary *Peace, Propaganda and the Promised Land*, John Dworkin (2012) explores the public and popular perception of Israel and the Palestinians by the USA and explains the complicity of US journalists in carrying out Israel's public relations. He also explains how the imperialist ideology using language, words, framing and context uttered by various sectors of the US society, including the so-called Middle East Experts, scholarship, media critics and others succeeded in neutralizing Israeli settler colonialism, turning it from an offensive force to one for the defence of Israel (Dworkin 2012).

For at least three decades after the establishment of Israel, the Palestinians hardly existed on the international stage. At best they were seen as refugees – voluntarily leaving their homes and lands – living off the charities of the United Nations Relief and Work Agency for Palestine Refugees in the Near East (UNRWA), and at worst they were lumped with Arabs and Muslims represented as villains, terrorists, vile and backwards. In his 'US Media Bias: Covering Israel/Palestine', Remi Kanazi asks the question: 'Why are … media outlets such as The New York Times and CNN not reporting the Palestinian side of the story?'. His answer is that Israel has 'solidified itself as the strategic ally of the US in the Middle East after its victory in the Six Day War (1967 Arab/Israeli War). Israel was taken under the wing of the US – which saw its potential as a strategic, military, and political force.' (Kanazi 2006) It is worth noting that

Edward Said's trilogy: *Orientalism* (1979), *The Question of Palestine* (1980) and *Covering Islam* (1981), are basically devoted to the explanation and analysis of the representation of Arabs/Muslims/Palestinians, categories often conflated together to produce a monolithic image of the Other as backwards, terrorists and despicable – a subject which has been well developed and is quite exhaustive. However, similar to most scholarly work on Palestine until the late 1980s, Said's scholarly work was gender blind – a scholarly scene to be altered in the late 1980s with the emergence of Arab, Muslim and other progressive gender and feminist analysis and critique of Orientalism.

A balanced, or more precisely, ethical perspective on Palestinians at the time, while rare, was largely expressed by Arab authors or left-wing Western scholars. In an early piece on the detriment of the Palestinians caused by Israeli colonialism, Janet Abu-Lughod writes:

> Except for the extermination of the Tasmanians, modern history recognizes no cases in which the virtually complete supplanting of the indigenous population of a country [the Palestinians] by an alien stock has been achieved in as little as two generations ... Our natural tendency to assume that what exists today has always been, may afford us psychic peace but only at the terrible cost of denying reality. And once historic reality has been denied, our capacity to understand and react meaningfully to the present is similarly destroyed.
>
> Abu-Lughod (1971: 153)

Denial of the Palestinian reality and existence as a people and a nation and the deafening silence on the atrocities of the Zionist colonial project has been the name of the official international take on the Palestinians, at least until the 1980s. The denial of one rather long history on the land and the affirmation of the newly constructed one, on the other have also seeped into academic feminism at the time. Second wave feminism and radical feminism, which were prominent in the USA and the Western world until the late 1980s, were pre-occupied with issues such as patriarchy and sexuality, and were primarily inward or locally oriented. Western feminism at the time, was hardly concerned with the plight of Palestinians and their victimization, while Israel, its security and legitimate existence dominated public opinion and radical feminism. In her 'Israel: Whose Country Is It Anyway?', Andrea Dworkin (1990), explains how as a Jew growing up in the USA she was totally immersed in the Zionist ideology and movement in the USA. She begins by saying: 'It [Israel] is mine' and goes on to explain her Zionist upbringing, her involvement in supporting Israel: 'attending Hebrew schools', 'collecting donations to the Zionist movement', and 'planting trees' in a country that 'was built from scratch', a 'country without a people for people without a country' ... a total immersion in the Zionist imperialist propaganda which recognized no Palestinians but a country (Israel) that was surrounded by many Arab enemies (Dworkin 1990: 2–3). Although after her 1988 participation in the first official feminist conference in Israel and her change of mind as she attended, along with Robin Morgan, the alternative (non-governmental) feminist conference, meeting there one Palestinian feminist that she began to recognize the lack of rights of Palestinians in Israel and criticized the 1967 occupation. Yet, unlike Morgan whose *The Demon Lover: On the Sexuality of Terrorism* (1989) was based on interviews with Palestinian women under occupation, Dworkin never spoke with or visited Palestinian women under occupation or dared to visit any Palestinian city in Israel/Palestine.

It is no surprise that Dworkin's 1990 short piece on Palestinian women remains largely superficial, simplistic and seemed like an attempt to fend off the label of Orientalism or racism. Meeting one Palestinian woman, who, incidentally, was a token feminist for the Israeli Ashkenazi feminist movement, a movement that showed only contempt, disdain and racism towards not only Palestinians but also Mizrahi women who at the time made up more than 60 per cent of the total Israeli population (Abdo 2011b), made her an 'expert on Palestinian women'. Racism and Orientalism, as will be seen later in this chapter, have in fact characterized Dworkin's well publicized work on Palestinian freedom fighters during the Second Intifada.

As for Robin Morgan who spoke with and interviewed Palestinian women under occupation and wrote extensively about how these women were like 'us/western women' human beings who along with the oppression of patriarchy also suffered the oppression of occupation, she decided to cast Palestinian women's political struggle, including the armed struggle of the 1960s and 1970s as 'terrorism'. Referring to Morgan's analysis of the 'sexuality of terrorism', Sarah Irving has pointed to the distressing irony in the former's analysis in a book titled *Sisterhood is Global* (1984) where one of the main thesis of Morgan was that 'women who participate in terrorist acts generally do so as the pawns of men or as some kind of surrogate male themselves'. (Irving 2012: 100) Irving goes on to discuss Morgan's criticism of Leila Khaled and the Palestinian delegation to the 1980 Copenhagen's

International Women's Conference, a criticism, Irving states which was based on distortions, inaccuracies and demeaning to Arab/Palestinian culture (Irving 2012: 100). Not unlike Andrea Dworkin, for Robin Morgan and for the dominant radical feminism in the West, Palestinian women's struggle is approved of mainly if it was waged against their own social, sexual and patriarchal oppression, if it was against their men, families and culture. This type of feminism, this Orientalist and rather racist feminist perspective of Palestinian women has been and as will be seen later in this chapter, continued to dominate Israeli and liberal Western feminist perspectives of Palestinian women and their struggle.

While Western imperialism, along with its collaborators from the media and academia was framing, imagining and representing Palestinians in very negative terms, serving in the process its and Israel's interests, Palestinians, including women were engaged in the struggle against colonialism and imperialism. Palestinian women's struggle including the armed struggle was waged primarily internally, on Palestinian occupied land, as the case of almost all the women in our conversations. Still, for a short period of time (1968–1970) Palestinian women's struggle also involved hijacking of planes in international skies. It is true that the name of Leila Khaled has appeared internationally as the first and probably only woman hijacker, receiving tremendous international attention, seen both as an idol and/or terrorist, Ameena in our conversations as will be seen in Chapters 4 and 5 was in fact the first Palestinian woman hijacker, but was totally ignored nationally and internationally. The reasons for hijacking for Ameena to be discussed later in the book were no different from those widely reported to have been uttered by Leila Khaled: 'letting people in the West hear that the Palestinian people exists, not as refugees but as a people who was expelled from their homeland by force' (Hajjar 1973). Hijacking, in other words, was a tactic used to deliver the message about the plight of the Palestinians.

In her *Leila Khaled: Icon of Palestinian Liberation*, Sarah Irving says: 'Hijacking carried out by Palestinian groups in the late 1960s and early 1970s certainly meant that few people in the USA and Europe could continue to claim to have no idea who the Palestinians were.' Yet, Irving doubted the actual impact of this message on the West, adding: '[F]or many, it [hijacking] simply turned Palestinians from a group of people they have never heard of into a group of people they associated irrevocably with the word "terrorist"' (Irving 2012: 38).

All of the women in our conversations resented the term 'terrorism', calling themselves, as argued in Chapter 1, *munadelat* (freedom fighters). These women understood fully the difference between the terrorism of Israel and the imperialist block (state terrorism) and the violence of the armed struggle which was seen as a legitimate fight against the former. In an interview with *The Guardian*, when asked about 'violence' and 'terrorism' involved in her actions, Leila Khaled clearly responded:

> Whenever I hear this word [terrorism] I ask another question ... Who planted terrorism in our area? Some came and took our land, forced us to leave, forced us to live in camps. I think this is terrorism. Using means to resist this terrorism and stop its effects – this is called struggle.
>
> Viner (2001: 2)

Although the focus of this project is women's involvement in the armed struggle, it goes without saying that this was only one of the many other forms of struggles Palestinian women have been engaged in. Palestinian women have been heavily involved in political activism at international levels, women's delegations from the General Union of Palestinian Women (GUPW) were in fact present at every international UN conference (Mexico 1975, Copenhagen 1980, Nairobi 1985, Beijing 1995) and at the World Congress of Women in Moscow in 1990.[1] These forms of activism have in fact galvanized considerable support for and solidarity with the Palestinian struggle, especially by non-governmental groups, including feminist activists, union activists and human rights advocates, Black women, women of colour and Third World women who understood the meaning of colonialism and imperialism and fought against such forces in their own ways. One example of the achievements of women's international involvement was evident at the first UN International Conference on Women (Mexico 1975). This conference and 'in the revolutionary spirit of the time passed a motion condemning Zionism as Racism' (Irving 2012: 97), three years before the UN General Assembly (1978), passed the motion which declared Zionism as racism.

Similar Aims, Different Forms

In 2003, in a public lecture Edward Said announced that 'Israel was the last bastion of colonialism' (Suliman 2011). Said did not live long enough to witness the US (and its allies) military occupation of Afghanistan (2001–present) and Iraq (2003–2011), wars seen as part of the 'new imperialism'. 'New' imperialism however, does not substantially differ from 'old' imperialism. Both forms express aggressive capitalist expansion, both are in search of resources and labour and commodity markets – they are similar in aims and goals albeit different in the use of ideology: words, language and framing. In other words, 'new' imperialism is a continuation of the 'old' imperialism; it can also include the 'old' colonial forms, but differs in the modes of expression and manifestations in its practice. New imperialism has largely developed in a historically specific time during major international changes including the collapse of the Soviet Union and the socialist bloc, resulting in the emergence of the unipolar system. New imperialism, in other words is the product of the cumulative historical processes of capitalist development. This form, while it can use direct military invasion (physical colonialism), does not have to do so in furthering its expansionist aims.

By utilizing the most recent technological developments, including 'smart' weapons and 'precise' targets, new imperialism can spread its hegemony over vast areas of the globe.[2] One of the primary objectives of the new imperialism is to allow big capital a free reign throughout the globe, a process largely facilitated by an ideology which uses new words and language. The large intra-state institutions, such as the World Bank and the IMF, to a large extent adopt the ideology of 'development and democratization' through economic austerity measures such as cuts to social, health and educational services as well as actions leading to the shrinking of the public sphere and the expansion of the private market. Such measures have resulted in the amassing of greater political control in the hands of a few countries – particularly the USA – over the rest of the world, and within the USA, wealth has been massively and increasingly concentrated in the hands of yet much fewer people, leaving the masses of ordinary people largely destitute (Mooers 2006a; Wood 2006).

As Mooers and others have rightly observed, the globalization of the new imperialism is expressed in the scale and magnitude of its economic exploitation and through the complexity within which it articulates with the political and military ideology and practice; this is distinctively unique to the new imperialism. The new imperialism expresses the control of the vast majority of the world by a handful of organizations controlled by the USA.

As for the allegedly peaceful nature of today's imperialism, it should be noted that the new imperialism is anything but peaceful or free. To achieve its economic goals, it uses sophisticated military force in opening up new markets or coercing old ones to submit, as the case of Iraq has shown and the current imperialist intervention in the 'Arab Spring' indicates.

Imperialism old and new has always been accompanied by a racialized ideology, demonizing and dehumanizing the invaded peoples and colonized victims. The old imperialism had often presented itself as a civilizing mission, one that was meant to uplift the 'primitive', 'uncivilized' and 'uncultured' peoples of the colonies (Said 1994a; Kimmerling 2003; Abdo 2011b). But the new imperialism is much more nuanced and sophisticated: it has created a new epistemology for framing world peace, conflict and resistance and for dealing with what it perceives to be 'democratic' regimes acceptable and amenable to imperialist interests. It has also managed to re-frame what it deems as a 'threat' to world security – or, to put it bluntly, to its economic and geo-political interests. Some concepts have been given a new meaning, such as the notions of 'peace', 'violence', 'terrorism' and 'democracy'. Others, including notions such as 'just wars', 'duty to protect' and the 'right to intervene' (used by the NATO intervention in Bosnia (1995) and Kosovo (1999) and the 'free army' in the case of the 'Free Syrian Army', for example, were either invented or simply re-emerged. Disseminated through mass media and intellectuals and policy-making circles, this racialized epistemology, these ideological contexts, often precede the imperialist onslaught and are used to justify it.

The historic association of Palestinian freedom fighters with terrorism which has widely spread among not only Western officials but also the academy calls for a re-examination and reinterpretation of the new imperialist terminology especially those concerning terms such as 'violence', 'terrorism', 'democracy' and 'freedom', and the need to restore them to their logical place within the context of the Middle East in general and Palestine more specifically.

The New Imperialism, Israel and the Arab World

It comes as no surprise that a popularized discourse on the lack of 'individual freedoms' such as 'democracy', 'human rights' and 'women's rights' in both Afghanistan and Iraq preceded the devastating imperialist wars on these two countries. Such alleged absences have been and still are used by the new imperialism (primarily by the USA) to justify its military invasions and the expansion of its imperialist interests. For the USA and its allies, the imposition of 'human values and democracy' on such countries by means of war has been justified through the 'just war' concept. The term 'just war', recycled under the Reagan administration and currently upheld by the Obama administration, has been interwoven into the imperialist ideology. This concept has been and continues to be abstracted from its material reality of economic devastation, the destruction of civilization and the killing of hundreds of thousands of people in the Middle East. This and other reinvented terms used to justify the US imperialist onslaught on the Middle East are deployed as a means for a politics of aversion, or, to use Richard Falk's term, a 'politics of deflection': these terms deflect attention from the actual reasons for imperialist aggression by focusing on the ideological sphere (Falk 2009a).[3]

The new imperialist ideology of democracy has been popularized outside of the US government and administration, penetrating various other groups including the military, the academy and various think-tanks and also a wide sector of feminist and liberal intellectuals, mainly in the USA but also in Europe and Israel. To illustrate this point, we shall dwell on the case of liberal and radical Western feminists, especially but not exclusively American feminists, who 'suddenly' discovered Afghani and Iraqi women during the imperialist wars against these two countries and began to talk about the need to 'emancipate' or 'save' them. In the same vein, this chapter will argue that Western feminists have also 'suddenly' found interest in Palestinian women freedom fighters at the turn of the twenty-first century. But before moving into the feminist debate over Arab and Palestinian women, it is important at this historical moment of the so-called Arab Spring to shed some light onto the actual meaning and implications of 'democracy' both in terms of its actual value for the USA and what it implies for the Arab region.

It is worth noting that there is no contradiction between capitalism and formal democracy. Capitalism, as Wood writes, 'can coexist with the ideology of freedom and equality in a way that no other system of domination can.' (Wood 2006: 18) Capitalism can easily co-exist with neo-liberal democracy because of the ostensible separation between the sphere of politics, which guarantees formal equality, and the sphere of economics, which tolerates stark inequalities and wherein capital has disguised class contradictions and domination.

The imperialist project of opening up all borders to allow big capital a free reign throughout the globe – a characteristic feature of the new imperialism – is largely accompanied by and accomplished in part through ideological means. US imperialism is never concerned with the lives of ordinary people, but rather with the big corporations and conglomerates; it is the democracy and the freedom of capital that is being sought here. This democracy is permissible as long as the control of business is off-limits to popular deliberation or change, that is, 'in so long as it isn't democracy' (Chomsky 1999: 10). Capitalist democracy practised under the new imperialism, Chomsky adds, is the immediate and foremost enemy of genuine participatory democracy (1999: 11).

History is replete with cases wherein US imperialism has been genuinely opposed to real democracy, favouring instead reliable dictators who served its interests. This is true for US foreign policy in general (for example, Marcos of the Philippines, Suharto of Indonesia, the Shah of Iran, and so on). When a given dictator became unreliable and could not deliver as expected by their masters – basically when a given dictator came under domestic pressure – the USA would begin to re-think its position vis-à-vis the dictator. The case of the so-called Arab Spring is an example par excellence here. The strategic and economic importance of the Arab or Muslim Middle East for the Western (and especially US and Israeli) imperialist interests has turned this region into the centre of world attention for the past several years.[4] The renewed imperialist search for easy access to sources of oil and natural gas – in abundance in the Arab gulf countries and in Libya and in terms of natural gas which is said to be in great quantities in the shores of Syria – along with its concern about the rise of national anti-colonial resistance movements seeking independence has made it imperative for the USA to focus attention on the Middle East.

In the Middle East region the USA is not the only player; the other important player is its closest ally and right hand, Israel. The latter, which presents itself as the only democracy in the Middle East (while in reality it is far from being such), has a powerful role in facilitating the movement of the new imperialism in the area.[5] The hegemony of the imperialist and Zionist expansionist ideologies in the Middle East has turned both Israel and the USA into unique polities with exceptional status and above international laws. Thus, whereas the USA uses its veto power to block undesirable UN Security Council (UNSC) decisions, especially those related to the plight of the Palestinians under Israeli occupation and colonialism, Israel ignores UNSC decisions that have been passed against its interests simply by ignoring them.[6] It is not genuine democracy, in other words, which the USA and Israel are concerned with; after all, 'the US and its allies', as Chomsky notes, 'will do anything to prevent democracy in the Arab world' (Chomsky 2011).

Whereas the USA uses terms such as 'democracy' and 'individual freedoms' to advance its imperialist interests, Israel flags the notions of 'stability' and 'security' in order to justify its aggressive and military intervention in the region. It is under the guise of such terms, for example, that Israel has waged wars against all of its neighbouring Arab countries: the Suez war 1956; the wars of 1967 and 1973; the invasion of Lebanon in 1982 and again in 2006; the Gaza war in 2008–09 and the placing of the Occupied Territories under a long siege. Currently, in an attempt to quell all forms of national anti-colonial resistance in the Middle East, Israel, the USA and the West, along with some Arab dictatorships, monarchies and emirates such as Saudi Arabia and Qatar, wage a fierce ideological, economic and political war against Syria; they simultaneously sponsor, train and arm the so-called freedom fighters with the intention of destroying the country as a national sovereign state and as a power in anti-Israeli and anti-imperialist resistance in the region. It is important to note here that the conflict in Syria started with the emergence of a genuine opposition movement from within demanding regime changes; this movement however had soon turned into an armed movement with rebels from various parts of the world. The imperialist interest in destroying Syria as a power in the region shares the same aim of the war against Iraq, except that the current destruction of Syria is waged indirectly by the US military through the use of terrorist groups, along with the Syrian attacks in retaliation to such terrorism. The irony here is that among the so-called freedom fighters in Syria are members of Al-Qaeda, mercenaries from various countries including Afghanistan, Chechnya and Pakistan, and members of various Islamic fundamentalist organizations, including 'Jabhat Al-Nasra' and the Islamic State of Iraq and Syria (ISIS), labelled terrorist organizations by the USA itself (Abboud 2014, Press TV 2014) – a seeming contradiction in US foreign policy, but one deemed irrelevant to the thinking of US interests; even such 'terrorists' can be tolerated as long as they achieve 'our' interests. The fact that the ideology of imperialism is contradictory, paradoxical and ironic is no surprise. The ideology of imperialism, according to Wood, 'flies with the capitalist wind, sets foot wherever the latter lands and changes its ideological garb whenever it deems necessary.' (Wood 2006: 17) After all, Wood adds, what we are calling the new imperialism is not interested in strengthening democratic citizenship but, on the contrary, it strives to: 'preserve elite rule in the face of an unavoidable mass politics and popular sovereignty. The object was to depoliticize the citizenry and turn democracy into rule by propertied classes over a passive citizen body, and also to confine democracy to a limited, formal political sphere.' (Wood 2006: 17)

It is well known that Hosni Mubarak and Zein el-Din Ben Ali, the former presidents of Egypt and Tunisia respectively, were loyal guardians of US (and Israeli) imperialist interests in the region. It is also a fact that violations of human rights and democratic rights during their regimes were rampant, yet the USA chose to ignore these violations. The case of Saudi Arabia's gross violations of human rights, and especially women's rights, is similar; these violations are well known within the US administration and yet are grossly ignored on account of the vital role Saudi Arabia plays in serving imperialist interests.[7]

In other words, as long as the regime – any regime for that matter – serves imperialist interests, no questions will be asked by the imperialist power about democracy or human rights. However, when regimes are rejected by the masses, such leaders become a burden to the USA and the old friend and ally then begins to invest heavily in their replacement, even if the choice, as was in the case with the 'Arab Spring', is to support Muslim groups: Al-Ikhwan (the Muslim Brotherhood) in Egypt; Hizbul-Nahda (the Islamic party) in Tunisia; and the Islamists in Libya: Political Islams aimed at ruling Egypt, Tunisia and Libya according to their interpretation of the Shari'a. It is worth noting that among the 'Islams' that the USA has recently allied itself with and is heavily supporting is Wahhabism, a type of Sunni Islam found particularly in Saudi Arabia, well known for its gender exclusion and women's oppression. These forms of Islam are used by the USA and the West as a weapon against Shi'a Islam (in Lebanon and Iran) and against the A'lawites (in Iraq and Syria). In contrast to Wahhabism, which is deemed 'friendly' by the USA, the Shi'a and A'lawites – who historically have been and remain nationalist, anti-imperialist and resist Israel's colonialism – are deemed 'terrorists' and 'the enemy' by the USA and its allies.

The uneasy marriage between the new imperialism and Islam is characteristic of Western (especially US) foreign policy towards Arab and Muslim countries. Although the demonization of Islam and Muslims, including Islamophobia, has long existed in the West (Said 1979) – save Saudi Wahhabism – the new imperialism seems more willing to accommodate certain Islams and more specifically the Al-Ikhwan (Muslim Brotherhood) as long as they serve its (and Israel's) interests. Hassanein Heikal, Egypt's renowned historian and journalist, has nicely described this uneasy marriage between new imperialism and the Muslim Brothers when he suggested that 'what the Arab world is witnessing today is not an "Arab Spring", but rather a new Sykes-Picot Agreement intended to divide the Arab world and secure shares in Arab resources and strategic positions for the benefit of the West' (Heikal 2011).[8]

Advancing the imperialist interest through the use of military power, such as in the cases of Iraq, Libya and Syria today, is not a new strategy in US foreign policy. The kind of Middle East needed by imperialism does not require real democracy, human rights, or women's rights, nor does it concern itself with the lives of the people. The imperialist strategy in the Middle East is to divide and fracture Arab unity and turn the area into a free market, into a space free for the movement of capital. And for such a strategy to work, we need a special kind of a Middle East: one free of nationalist resistance and of anti-colonial sentiments and also one which is amenable to US and Israeli interests. The kind of a 'new' Middle East desired by new imperialism was emphatically expressed by then Secretary of State Condoleezza Rice during her visit to Lebanon in 2006. In the midst of the Israeli war on Lebanon and the devastation of Beirut, Rice described the devastation and ruin of the country and the people as the 'birth pangs of a new Middle East'; a new Middle East imagined as 'democratic, Hezbollah-free and amenable to US interests' (cited in Cohen 2010). It is in this vein that one can understand the legitimization and justification of Israel's devastating war on the Gaza Strip in 2008–09. This war as well was portrayed as a 'just' war, one against terrorists and villains.

While Israel's repeated invasions and destruction of the Gaza Strip (2008–09; 2012) were portrayed by Israeli and Western media as 'a war against terror', popular voices all over the world as well as international human rights organizations condemned Israel and described its acts as 'crimes against humanity'. The claim that Israel committed crimes against humanity in its war against Gaza in 2009 came as a result of investigative reports conducted by the UN Special Rapporteur on Human Rights in the Occupied Palestinian Territories, Richard Falk (2009) and Richard Goldstone's Report (2009) respectively. In retaliation to these reports, Israel expelled Falk, dismissed the Goldstone's report, and even put pressure on Goldstone to change his report. Since 1948 until today Israel has continued its settler-colonial policies in the region, its relentless aggression and occupation of Arab and Palestinian lands and its placing of millions of Palestinians in a large open-air concentration camp in the Occupied Territories, acts which did not seem to have affected the thinking of various Western feminists, both liberal and radical, for whom the logic of colonialism has been reversed: Israel (the settler-colonial regime) presented as the victim while the Palestinians, the colonized victims, remained vilified, viewed as terrorists. This imperialist position, as the following sections demonstrate, was also reflected in much of the Western feminist literature on Palestinian women resistance.

Orientalist Feminism and Palestinian Women's Resistance

The movement from old imperialism, that is, from imperialism in its colonial and settler-colonial form, to the new imperialism which is American in character has a corresponding parallel movement in the ideology and epistemology of Western feminism with regard to Arab and Muslim women; this movement within feminism, I argue, is one from Orientalist feminism to 'imperialist feminism'.

Western feminist debate on Arab and/or Muslim women in general and Palestinian women more specifically has largely emerged in the late 1980s following Said's work on *Orientalism* (1979). As we saw earlier, prior to the 1980s there was little concern with Palestinian women and their struggles. The emerging debate, which was largely discursive in nature, was not concerned with women's lived reality, let alone with their anti-colonial struggle. During Orientalist feminist debate, Arab and Muslim feminists have launched a strong critique of Western liberal and radical feminists who have constructed Arab and Muslim women as having no agency and as being helpless individuals oppressed by their men, their culture and their religion.

Thus, despite Edward Said's warnings against Orientalist epistemology which, among other things, homogenizes all Arabs, turning them into an undifferentiated whole while simultaneously conflating the terms Arab and Muslim, a large number of Western feminists have continued along the path of the Orientalism; they have continued to vilify Arab and Muslim women while simultaneously remaining silent about the colonial and imperialist contexts under which these women found themselves. In her 'Feminism and Difference: The Perils of Writing as a Woman on Women in Algeria', Marnia Lazreg (1988) criticized French Orientalist feminists' perceptions of Algerian women under colonialism; the latter were described as uncivilized and in need of education. Elsewhere I have provided a detailed discussion of the Feminist Orientalist debate, arguing that '[b]y challenging the monolith, Middle Eastern/Arab/Muslim which has been characteristic of traditional Amero-Euro writings on the region, these feminists have defied the Orientalizing-Othering approaches constructed as modes of knowing Arab/Middle Eastern women' (Abdo 1993: 29; see also Abdo 1996, 2002). A scathing criticism of some Western Orientalist writings on Arab/Muslim women has also come from Sherene Razack (2008), who writes against the exclusion of Arabs/Muslims from Western (especially US and Canadian) law and politics. Most telling in the majority of feminist Orientalist literature has been the essentialization of Arab and Muslim women and their description as lacking agency, as being silent victims of their religious, patriarchal and cultural oppression, as lacking control over self and body. These feminist debates and related discourses, which peaked in the late 1980s through the 1990s and much of the responses by Arab or Muslim feminists, were largely discussed in the realm of culture: they all focused on women's bodies and sexuality through related themes such as the 'veil', 'harem', 'polygamy' and other culturally-based gendered symbols. The responses to such debates by Arab and/or Muslim feminists has brought into the discussion other forces and factors, including the economy, class and in the case of Palestinians, issues of race and colonialism (Abdo 2002; Lazreg 1988; Hammami and Rieker 1988; Hammami 1995). Feminist Orientalist writings lacked a political dimension, were mainly ahistorical and largely misconstrued the actual lived conditions of Muslim and Arab women. Yet, whether in Morocco, Lebanon, Palestine or Algeria, Arab women have long been active agents of change and revolution, not passive victims of culture or religion.

It was not until the turn of the twenty-first century that a new feminist debate on Muslim and Arab women emerged, one in which the latter were described as helpless and in need of both pity and rescue/saving. This debate escalated after September 11, and took a special turn after the start of the Second Palestinian Intifada (2001) and reached its peak during the US war on Iraq and Afghanistan. It is during the latter events that Western feminists began to justify the US imperialist wars as a need 'to save the women from the patriarchy and oppression of their regimes' (Abu-Lughod 2002, 2006). During these imperialist wars, American feminist individuals and institutions began to show special interest in and organize around 'helping' Iraqi and Afghani women to achieve 'democracy'. With notions such as 'pity' and the need to 'save' and help the 'helpless', Western feminists began to call for world support for the cause of 'liberating' these women. The critique of these perceptions came from various Arab and other feminists, including Lila Abu-Lughod (2002, 2006). Abu-Lughod has in fact exposed the fallacy of liberal feminist epistemology, linking the corresponding feminist ideology to the wider imperialist ideology of the USA. The existence of a strong alliance between imperialism (the state) and the academy including feminists has been widely discussed by Arab and/or Muslim feminists (Razack 2008; Zine 2004; Abdo 2011b), an alliance which remained true to this date as the following will argue.

Although specific references to Palestinian women were hardly made in much of the feminist Orientalist literature between the 1960s until the late 1980s, they were included in the general debate on Arab/Muslim women, as part of the monolith, Muslim. More serious feminist writings on Palestinian women in struggle were produced basically during the First Intifada, a revolt seen as 'peaceful'. Considering the fact that Palestinian women have been active in their national and anti-colonial struggle for the last century or so, and considering the participation of hundreds of women in the armed struggle during the 1960s–1980s, the seeming silences of Western feminists around Palestinian women leaves the impression that the former had little to no interest in Palestinian women's lives or struggle. It should be noted here that this silence had also engulfed the national/local scene: very little media coverage on the plight of these women, especially during their imprisonment was published and hardly any serious academic or feminist discussion ensued at the time.

After the events of September 11 and the Second Palestinian Intifada of 2000 with the emergence of a new Western academic and feminist debate on Palestinian struggle and resistance, the rather historical lack of attention was replaced with a sort of a strong concern. This new concern in the form of debate, while it continued the Orientalist line of feminist argument which for example, depicted Leila Khaled as a 'terrorist' (Morgan 1989), was full of rage against and vilification, dehumanization and sexualization of Palestinian women resistance fighters. In other words, although in various ways the twenty-first century Western feminist debate on Arab (Palestinian) women is similar to that of the twentieth century, in that both are focused on Arab women's religion, culture, bodies and sexuality, the recent debate, which is also culturally framed, is political in spite of itself: a politics of positioning within Israeli colonial and US imperialist policies.

'Culture of Suicide' or Resistance Culture? Imperialist Feminism and Palestinian Women's Resistance

> Western feminisms appropriate and 'colonize' the fundamental complexities and conflicts which characterize the lives of women of different classes, religions, cultures, races and castes in these countries.
>
> Mohanty (2002: 260)

I use the term 'imperialist feminism' to refer to the epistemological frame of reference used by Western feminists for viewing Arab/Muslim women in general and Palestinian women more specifically. Imperialist feminism encompasses not only the characteristics of Orientalist feminism, but also goes much beyond such characteristics: it uses the Orientalist/racist approach, described above as culturalist in order to establish a wedge between 'us' and 'them'. Parallel to 'new' imperialism which is a continuation of 'old' imperialism, 'imperialist feminism' is the continuation of Orientalist feminism, with a different choice of words and language. Similar to Morgan's description of freedom fighter Leila Khaled, discussed above, imperialist feminism has been preoccupied with women's militant struggle, especially after the Second Intifada, referring to them as terrorists using 'suicide bombing' for personal, psychological, religious and cultural reasons (Bloom 2005, 2009; Victor 2003; Dworkin 2002; Chesler 2003; Tzoreff 2006).

It is important to note that the very term 'suicide bombing' is a Western construct and is no description of the mode of struggle used during the Second Intifada. 'Blood for honour', as Bloom (2005) wrote, became a central theme in almost all of this literature. According to such arguments, Palestinian women kill themselves or commit 'suicide bombing' in order to cleanse their or their family's 'defamed' honour.

Andrea Dworkin, whose earlier work was discussed above, has championed Western imperialist feminism, declaring that 'shame and dishonour' is the reason for women becoming 'suicide bombers'. 'These women idealists,' she writes 'crave committing a pure act of terrorism which will wipe away the stigma of being female ... After all those women were sexually abused by their men and threatened to be killed by them' (Dworkin 2002: 22). 'Terrorist bombing,' she continues, 'is a life-saving procedure used by women as a trade-off between the lowly status of the raped woman for the higher status of a martyr ... Suicide bombing can elevate self-esteem, restore personal honour, and raise social standing'

(Dworkin 2002: 21). Phrases like 'blood for honour' have become the epistemological frame of reference of and the mantra for the imperialist feminists: Palestinian women, it is argued, are willing to trade their deaths for 'restoring lost family honour'.

In her 'Female suicide bombers: a global trend' (2007) Mia Bloom asks 'Why do women become suicide bombers?' and provides the following response: 'Motives vary: to avenge a personal loss, to redeem the family name, to escape a life of sheltered monotony and achieve fame, or to equalize the patriarchal societies in which they live ... In many instances the women are seeking revenge' (Bloom 2007: 95). Still, the argument about 'restoring family honour' or cleansing the name of the family from the shame women supposedly caused remains central in most such writings: this claim runs throughout Barbara Victor's book *Army of Roses: Inside the World of Palestinian Women Suicide Bombers* (2003) and is evident in the works of Dworkin (2002) and Bloom (2005, 2007). This is how Bloom puts it:

> It is telling that the women who participate in suicide bombings are usually among the most socially vulnerable: widows and rape victims. In fact, in several instances, the women were raped or sexually abused not by representatives of the state but by the insurgents themselves. As such they are stigmatized, and thus easily recruited and exploited.
>
> Bloom (2007: 102)

Advancing a similar argument, Terri Toles Patkin asserts that 'suicide bombing' centres on defending the 'purity' of women within traditional roles. In her 'Explosive Baggage: Female Palestinian Suicide Bombers and the Rhetoric of Emotion', Patkin argues:

> Resentment and self-righteousness are often considered to be the underlying motivators for engaging in terrorism. Perceiving themselves as victims, the terrorists hone a very sensitive awareness of slights and humiliations inflicted upon themselves or their particular group, and picture themselves as part of the elite, heroically struggling to right the injustices of an unfair world.
>
> Patkin (2004: 80)

For Patkin, 'terrorists' share several characteristics; these include: 'over-simplification of issues, frustration about an inability to change society, a sense of self-righteousness, a Utopian belief in the world, a feeling of social isolation, a need to assert [one's] own existence, and a cold-blooded willingness to kill' (Patkin 2004: 80). Yet, as will be argued later in this chapter, an 'oversimplification of issues' is embedded in the mind of Patkin and similar authors who fail to see the wider context of Israeli colonialism and oppression, ignoring Palestinian history altogether.

Along with the religious and cultural factors suggested as the bases for women's motives for partaking in the armed struggle, this literature personalizes and psychologizes Palestinian women, removing in the process their collective or national identity. Female 'suicide bombers', it is claimed, are products of Palestinian traditional and patriarchal society, a society which does not tolerate divorce, where women are expected to bear children, where male–female relations are forbidden before marriage, and where some women are seen as not being candidates for marriage – factors which allegedly result in family dishonour and shame (Bloom 2005, 2009; Victor 2003; Beyler 2002; Dworkin 2002). Moreover, the literature on the so-called suicide bombers places emphasis on females' lack of education (Dworkin 2002; Victor 2003; Beyler 2002). According to Beyler, 'There will be problems in places where children represent a majority of the population, and not educated to look for long-term solutions instead of dreaming of becoming suicide bombers'. She adds, 'women suicide bombers took the opportunity to affirm themselves as human beings after having failed to or been denied the ability to affirm themselves as women' (Beyler 2009: 14). This genre of literature also makes claims about the 'traditionality' of the societies in which such women live. In his *Female Suicide Bombers: Dying for Equality?* Yoram Schweitzer (2006) maintains that 'Female suicide bombers appear almost exclusively in societies that are heavily traditionalist and conservative, where women lack equal rights and their status in society is much lower than that of their male counterparts' (Schweitzer 2006: 10). This construction of Palestinian society is also found in the work of Mira Tzoreff, for whom terms like 'suicide bomber', 'terrorist', and '*shahidah*' (martyr)[9] are interchangeable (Tzoreff 2006). In a reference to Wafaa Idris, a Palestinian woman involved in the armed struggle during the Second Intifada, Tzoreff writes:

Idris was twenty-five years old, divorced by her husband (who was also her cousin) after some eight or nine years during which she failed to bring an offspring into the world. Her status as a divorced and barren woman, and her return as a dependant to her parents' home where she became an economic burden, put her in what is a dead-end situation in a traditional, patriarchal society. She was non-normative in Palestinian society and her chances of building a new life for herself were close to zero. Wafaa Idris's only way of redeeming herself from the inferior status ordained by her surroundings was by choosing to become a shahida for the sake of her nation.

Tzoreff (2006: 19–20)

Even women who were educated and economically independent did not escape such dehumanizing descriptions. Writing on another woman militant fighter, Hanadi Garedat, Tzoreff states:

At the age of twenty-seven and still unmarried, Garedat was in an untenable position in a society that sanctifies marriage. Her non-normative status exposed her to its supervisory apparatus, which refused to recognize her as an educated and economically independent woman, and continued to scrutinize her every move, especially her sexual behaviour. Becoming a shahida rescued her from the lifelong spinsterhood dictated by her advanced age.

Tzoreff (2006: 21)

Whether married or not, being a parent or not, educated or not, the above arguments are used in a manner that constructs a sweeping generalization applied to all Palestinian women involved in the armed resistance against Israeli occupation and colonialism.

Dorit Naaman (2007) provided a strong critique of such literature, writing especially about the case of Ayat Akhras. Naaman writes:

Not only was she [Ayat Akhras] not male, she was not overtly religious, not estranged from her family, not openly associated with any radical groups. She can hardly be described as a woman without a future. She was young, she was a good student, and she was engaged to be married.

Naaman (2007: 936)

Naaman, whose research focuses on media representations of the so-called suicide bombers, has shown the hollowness of most of the literature on this issue, presenting alternative examples of various women whose personal profiles defy the very basis of most of this literature. She concludes her discussion with an affirmation that:

The discourse on terrorism is generally devoid of historical perspectives ('terrorists are pure evil' is one popular trope) and lacks any positionality because, it is assumed, terrorists simply live outside of morality and social norms. But such ahistorical and essentialist attitudes came to haunt this discourse when a former terrorist, Nelson Mandela, became a Nobel Peace Prize winner, or, more recently, when Osama bin Laden, a former American ally, 'turned' terrorist. The discourse on terrorism also does not account for state terrorism, whereby state institutions such as the army or police inflict violence on civilian populations, as was the case in Nicaragua and Chechnya (and by the US via the Contras). This last point is particularly missing from the discourse on the Palestinian–Israeli conflict. All attacks on Israelis, whether inside the 1967 border or outside, whether targeting soldiers or civilians, are dubbed terrorist attacks. But dropping a one-ton bomb from an Israeli airplane on a five-story Palestinian house, in which a militant may be present, knowing full well that dozens of civilians will be killed, is hardly ever described in Western media as terrorism.

Naaman (2007: 939)

In contrast to much of the feminist epistemology around 'suicide bombing' and in reference to the question of class and education in relation to Palestinian women's involvement in the armed struggle, Susan Galleymore has written that 'Many Palestinians who carry out these deeds, including women, are well educated and come from middle-class families; some have families themselves' (Galleymore 2009: 86). She adds:

Research findings indicate that the percentage of female suicide bombers who acted out of nationalist motives was more than twice as high as those who acted out of religious motives. In addition, some of them had academic education and/or were married with children.

(Galleymore 2009: 260)

There is one other, perhaps a more serious claim made by the reality-twisting and dehumanizing literature on Palestinian female resistance, namely, the claim that 'a driving force for suicide bombers to kill is Palestinians' hatred of Israel or of the Jews' (Bloom 2009: 4), or the claims that Palestinians are 'heavily influenced by anti-Israeli propaganda, hatred and fanaticism' as well as by 'anti-Semitism' (2009: 15). Thus Phyllis

Chesler, for example, writes in her 'A Jerusalem Conference to Combat Global Anti-Semitism: The Greatest Battle of the 21st Century':

> For years, the world stood by and did nothing as the Palestinians perfected their diabolical arts of airplane hijacking and suicide terrorism against the tiny Jewish state. On the contrary, the world cheered the terrorists on. Palestinian terrorists were seen as victims or as freedom fighters, Israelis were viewed as the 'genocidal' aggressors … Western progressives, including feminists, became more concerned with the occupation of a country that never existed (Palestine) than they were with the occupation of women's bodies, world-wide. The Arab and Muslim media, joined by their mainstream western counterparts have accused the Jews and the Zionists—falsely—of deliberately shooting down a young Palestinian boy, committing a massacre in Jenin, poisoning Palestinian water … The targeting and isolating of Israel continues.
>
> Chesler (2009: 15–16)

A full exposure of this dehumanizing literature alone could fill a whole manuscript.[10] In this section, we shall dwell on a couple of important issues while devoting the rest of the chapter to a fuller critique of this literature. It is true that the above imperialist feminist literature on Palestinian women emerged much after the period of the women's armed struggle (1960s–1980s), but the ideology and language used was not very different from that experienced by the women in our conversations. This language was in fact used by the Israeli interrogators (women and men) against the women in our conversations. All of the women in our conversations showed awareness of such accusations (e.g. dehumanization and denigration of their culture and religion and the focus on their bodies and sexuality) and have in fact responded to all such claims as will be seen in Chapters 4 and 5.

A feminist anti-racist, anti-colonialist critique should begin with the conceptual and methodological approaches used in the above-mentioned dehumanizing and unethical literature. First and foremost, that imperialist feminist literature is devoid of any measure of objectivity. Most information gathered by and referred to by the authors quoted above is based on reports of the Israeli mainstream media, the Israel Defense forces (IDF) and Israel's prison authorities, and specifically from 'research' conducted by Anat Berko, a US and Israel Defense Forces (IDF) counter-terrorism expert.[11] Using documents written by Israeli prison officials, uncritically, makes the question of where the above authors stand from the Palestinians' perspective quite clear: taking the Israeli official position has been characteristic of most Western literature on Palestinian militant fighters.

Siding with the Israeli establishment, praising Israel as the only democracy in the Middle East while simultaneously considering Palestinians as terrorists, villains and criminals has been the mantra of the imperialist ideology throughout. Since the establishment of the state of Israel, and especially in the last three decades or so, the West has regarded Israel as its most important ally and the prime protector of its imperialist interests in the Middle East. Mainstream media more specifically would not allow, let alone tolerate, any stance critical of Israel. Edward Said aptly captured this state of affairs in 1994 when he stated that:

> Now everyone knows that to try to say something in the mainstream Western media that is critical of U.S. policy or Israel is extremely difficult; conversely, to say things that are hostile to the Arabs as a people and culture, or Islam as a religion, is laughably easy.
>
> Said (1994b: 118)

On the same issue, he added:

> Of course, on the other hand, there is a virtual certainty of getting an audience if as an Arab intellectual you passionately, even slavishly support U.S. policy, you attack its critics, and if they happen to be Arabs, you invent evidence to show their villainy; if they are American you confect stories and situations that prove their duplicity; you spin out stories concerning Arabs and Muslims that have the effect of defaming their tradition, defacing their history, accentuating their weaknesses, of which of course there are plenty. Above all, you attack the officially approved enemies—Saddam Hussein, ... Arab nationalism, the Palestinian movement, and Arab views of Israel.
>
> Said (1994b: 118)

In such a political atmosphere, it is no surprise that voices critical of imperialism, of colonialism or of the USA and Israel would be silenced, while vilification and dehumanization of the victims of imperialism and colonialism finds an audience. It is here that the ideology of the new imperialism succeeds in penetrating most sectors of Western (including

Israeli) societies, including the media and academia. Canada, it might be noted here, has in fact become a staunch ally of Israel, especially since the coming to power of the Harper government. Not too long ago, on 8 January 2014, while addressing a Toronto gala held by the Jewish National Fund, Harper, in front of about 4,000 attendees described Israel as 'a light of freedom and democracy in what is otherwise a region of darkness [sic].' (Engler 2014)

Moreover, most, if not all such literature is flagrantly ahistorical in its approach and totally blind to and ignorant of the historical and contemporary oppression of Palestinians under Israeli colonialism whether in Israel proper or in the 1967 occupied territories.[12] This literature fails to ask the important question about the source of the violence and terror.

For Palestinians in general, living an honourable life means living as human beings, as a people with history and cultural roots. For almost all of the women militant fighters in our conversations and most of those after the Second Intifada, fighting for their political and national identity and freedom is an 'honourable' task.

Before continuing to rebut the above-mentioned dehumanizing claims made against Palestinian women in the armed resistance, the following will address the charges which this literature makes concerning 'anti-Semitism'. Chesler, Dworkin and Bloom mentioned above have implicitly and explicitly contended that Palestinians 'hate' Jews and are anti-Semitic. As various Palestinian and other authors have demonstrated (Ashrawi 2001; Odeh 2012; Abdo and Lentin 2002), such claims have been made by all of the Zionist and Israeli leaders, beginning with former Israeli prime minister Golda Meir (1969–74), who is quoted as having said that: 'Peace will come to the Middle East when the Arabs love their children more than they hate us' (quoted in Carlson 2003: 10; Levy 2004: 187). Addressing the 2001 World Conference against Racism in Durban, Hanan Ashrawi, the PLO spokeswoman during the Oslo Accords, had the following to say:

From the non-existent Palestinians or the claim that 'there is no such thing as Palestinians; they never existed' made by Golda Meir in 1969, we have undergone a metamorphosis wilfully inflicted upon us by Israeli-imposed diction and policies that have variously depicted us as two-legged vermin, cockroaches, beasts walking on two legs, a people that have to be exterminated unless they are resigned to live as slaves, grasshoppers to be crushed, crocodiles, and vipers.

Ashrawi (2001)

Other critical authors, including historians and geographers such as Said (1979), Masalha (2012), Pappe (2004, 2008) and Khalidi (1992), to mention just a few, have responded to the charge that 'Palestinians hate Jews' by documenting the history of destruction, atrocities and devastation brought about by the establishment of the state of Israel. An equally strong and perhaps more compelling response to such allegations has come from the Palestinian ex-political prisoners during my conversations with several of them who have also been accused of 'hating Jews'. Thus for example, in her *Thamanan Lil-Shams* (For the Sake of the Sun) Aisha Odeh criticized what she referred to as 'The Hatred Charge' levied against Palestinians by the Israelis. She recounted the experience of herself and two other detainees who were also her friends during one episode of interrogation in Al-Led prison for women (also known as Nve-Tertza):

One morning we were informed by the female prison guard that we were to meet the prison woman in charge. A white woman with European looks sat behind her desk. She kept us standing while staring at us. She looked at the papers in front of her and repeated that we need to listen to the guard's orders. We responded: We are political detainees and we have rights protected by the Fourth Geneva Convention, which stipulates the need for protecting our human rights. It also requires that we be provided with books, newspapers, papers and pens, and we should receive family visitations.

Upon hearing this she looked at us and said: 'You are not political prisoners. You are children killers, you were blinded by hatred and animosity towards the Jews which were aired to you by "Ahmad Said"[13] and other Arab radio stations encouraging you to kill Jewish children. Tell me, why do you hate the Jews? Why? Why?'

Odeh (2012: 37)

'Her accusation', Aisha continued:

fell on us like a heavy rock ... we were shocked. It felt like a stab to the heart of our struggle. Immediately pictures and memory of their hostility towards our people exploded in front of us. We responded: You have no right to judge our struggle because you belong to a state which was established on terror, forgery, robbery and massacres ... you appear to have forgotten or pretend to forget the many massacres you committed against our people; we shall remind you of a few: Deir Yassin, Qibya, Kufor Kassem and so on.

Upon hearing this she got very mad and ordered that we be returned to our cell. We could not believe what we heard. We never figured out the reasons for her allegations. Was she so ignorant? Or did she think we were stupid? Or what? How could she strip us from our noble cause, and our right to struggle for our freedom … As if we [had not been] expelled from our own homeland by them.

Odeh (2012: 38)

In this narrative, Aisha Odeh and her friends remind the world in general, and Israelis and their supporters more specifically, of part of their history as Palestinians. They bring that history back to life in their memory and present it to their oppressor clearly and straightforwardly. Aisha Odeh does not stop here. Her genuine feelings of anger and disbelief as a result of the accusation of race hatred led her to recall the history of her friend Rasmiyya Odeh, who was also with her during the interrogation. Here is what Aisha relayed about Rasmiyya:

Rasmiyya was more emotional and hurt by the accusation of the female prison guard. For the first time since she joined the group in Al-Moscobiyya detention camp in Jerusalem, she spoke with such anger and fury. Her words were so strong; they could melt iron … as if she was living the Nakba [the catastrophe of 1948] at that moment. Did she really need anybody to teach her what happened to her and her family? Silence engulfed us as we listened.

Rasmiyya, when a child, asked her mother: 'Why, mother, do we not have a house like our neighbours?'

Her mother answered that their house is more beautiful than all of their neighbours. Where is it? Let's go to our house.

Her mother told her about their house in Lifta [a village destroyed in 1948], and the story of running away and becoming refugees, and how they could not go back to it. Rasmiyya asks: Why did you leave it mother? 'We were concerned with your safety; we protected you from danger', the mother answered. The child keeps insisting: When will we go back to our home? 'When your father comes back.' Where is my father? 'He went to the United States'. Why did he go to the US? 'In order to work, make money so we could go back to our home'. We do not want money, I want my father, and I want to go back home.

The mother cried hard, and Rasmiyya failed to understand the reasons for this, but she became very sad and could not sleep out of fear that something bad might happen to her mother. She spent her nights thinking of what she could do to prevent her mother from crying. The little child would roam the streets of lower Ramallah looking for the United States in order to bring her father back and make her mother happy, and kept thinking of the day they could go back to their home in Lifta.

Odeh (2012)[14]

Rasmiyya's story as related by Odeh made mention of her family's experience living in the refugee camp, after leaving their village (Lifta). Rasmiyya spoke of the hunger they experienced as the UNRWA (United Nations Relief and Works Agency) used to supply them with insufficient food to live on for a month. As a child, Rasmiyya had go to garbage dumps and look for food (Odeh 2012: 38). Aisha Odeh recalls,

At this point Rasmiyya started crying non-stop ... then she burst out like a volcano:

They want us to not hate them? They want to deny us our emotions and memory the same way as they denied us our homes, land and our dignity? Do you think I needed Ahmad Said [Arab media commentator at the time] to tell us that we were expelled from Lifta, and that we lived the bitterness of exile, its oppression, hunger and humiliation? And that what prevented us from hysteria and loss is our hope to return to our home and our village? Or that he [Ahmad Said] played with our heads and made us think we were exiled from our villages and homes and we believed in him? Do we need him to tell us that they even hunted us in our refugee camps? Or is it that the occupation does not exist, it is just a fabrication, and we just imagine it?

Odeh (2012: 38–39)

Both Aisha and Rasmiyya were among the first generation of Palestinian fighters to join the armed struggle in the late 1960s, and both were detained for their political activism and given harsh sentences: Rasmiyya was handed three life-sentences plus ten years, while Aisha was sentenced to two life-terms plus ten years. These stories are not about a dead past and cannot be erased from Palestinian memory. For this memory, which is focused on the Nakba, is about their contemporary history, about how Palestinians became disposable and refugees; it is also about their hope for the future, for return and a freedom – one that nobody can deny them, not even the Israeli state with its constant efforts at erasing Palestinians and their memories.

Palestinian Resistance: a Historical Context

As argued earlier, the Western image or imagined perception of the Arab including Palestinian woman as docile, submissive, lacking agency and incapable of change is exactly that: an imaginary construct with no basis in reality. Palestinian women, like their Arab sisters and other women, and especially those who have lived through and experienced colonialism, have always resisted oppression and fought for their independence and humanity. Resistance to colonialism and imperialism, as already mentioned is as old as the forces of imperialism are. Palestinian women involved in the armed struggle, their determination to resist and their resolve to sacrifice themselves for the sake of their people, their stolen land, their ruined towns and villages, and their suppressed and distorted history is not a new phenomenon and is definitely not a product of the Second Intifada, when a plethora of distorted and derogatory literature on the female armed struggle emerged. Palestinian women have long recognized their right to resist colonialism as a human right, one enshrined in international law. Even if at the risk of repetition, it is worth remembering that Palestinian resistance during the two decades (1960–1980) was part of the international anti-colonial and national liberation movement internationally. It was particularly influenced, as will be seen in Chapter 3, by various revolutions including the Vietnamese and the Algerian anti-colonial, anti-imperialist struggles.

Palestinian resistance did not develop outside of this world history; it was very much part of this international phenomenon. The end of the British colonial rule in Palestine did not translate into an end to colonialism, but rather to a continued colonial control by the Zionist state – hence also the rise of Palestinian anti-colonial resistance. Palestinian revolts and revolutions have in fact marked Palestinian history since the early twentieth century: from the 1929 revolt against the British open-door policy towards the Zionist settler-colonial project, to the 1936–39 revolution against British and Zionist colonialism, and on to the taking up of arms after the establishment of the PLO during the decades of the 1960s through the 1980s (Masalha 2012; Sayigh 1979; Abdo 2011a). In all these movements, women played an active and important role: during the British and Zionist colonial rule they staged their own demonstrations, sit-ins, submitted petitions and conducted various other forms of resistance. They also partook in the armed guerrilla resistance in the 1936–39 revolution.[15] With the emergence of the Palestinian Liberation Organization (PLO), an umbrella organization, women came to be organized within the different political parties that made up the organization; they became an integral part of what was known – at least up until the Oslo Accords – as the Palestinian revolution.[16] During this period, women conducted military operations against the occupier and fought like their male comrades in the anti-colonial struggle. This was true for all sectors of the Palestinians: in the Occupied Territories of Gaza and the West Bank, in Israel/Palestine as well in the refugee camps in the Diaspora. As Chapter 3 will demonstrate, Palestinian women's struggle in general and their armed struggle during the 1960s–1980s and later has been largely supported by the strong culture of resistance which flourished during the time. Hence, any discussion of Palestinian women political prisoners which ignores or fails to understand this context will not be able to explain, let alone capture, the lived reality of these women.

Palestinian Women: Between Victimization and Agency

> I have been unable to live an uncommitted or suspended life ... I have not hesitated to declare my affiliation with an extremely unpopular cause.
> Edward Said in Barsamian (2003: ix)

In the aftermath of September 11, 2001, it became almost a crime to try and defend the resistance against occupation, colonialism and imperialism. The ideology of the new imperialism – which twisted, falsified and distorted notions, concepts and the meanings of resistance, turning, for example, the notion of resistance into terrorism and dictatorship into democracy, and which frames allies of the USA as 'good' while critics of the USA as 'bad' – was able to penetrate the consciousness of many people, including the victims of colonialism and occupation themselves. The social landscape at the time became dominated by the so-called 'war on terror'. During this period, as Sherene Razack pointed out,

> [t]hree allegorical figures have come to dominate the social landscape of the 'war on terror' and its ideological underpinnings of a clash of civilizations: the dangerous Muslim man, the imperilled Muslim woman, and the civilized European, the latter a figure who is seldom explicitly named but who nevertheless anchors the first two figures.
>
> Razack (2008: 18)

This racist context and 'threatening' atmosphere which sent waves of chills and fear, especially among Arab and Muslim countries, was largely met with silence and loss of interest, especially among women academics and feminists, in the Palestinian struggle in general and women's involvement in the armed struggle more specifically. It in fact has further intensified the Western hegemonic discourse of vilification and victimization. After all, Razack argues that some Western feminists 'participate in empire through the politics of rescue, unhesitatingly installing the idea that it is through gender that we can tell the difference between those who are modern and those who are not' (Razack 2008: 17), hence, the silencing of a progressive discourse on women's struggle and anti-colonial resistance.

Instead of considering women's resistance – including that of many women referred to as 'suicide-bombers', most of whom, as Galleymore (2009) said: 'acted out of nationalist motives rather than of religious ones' – as a rightful struggle against occupation and colonialism, Palestinian women were victimized and criminalized and denied their history and memory rooted in the Nakba. Women involved in struggle and resistance would look in vain to recognize themselves in this discourse: these women who define themselves as *munadelat* recognize all those who were killed during the armed struggle as *fidai`yyat*.

The distinction between terrorism and violence on the one hand and native resistance, including the use of armed struggle and the sacrifice of one's life, on the other was articulated almost half a century ago by Fanon. In reference to the Algerian anti-colonial resistance, Fanon was cognizant of the difference between the violence of the colonizer and that of the colonized in the struggle against colonialism. Although his terms of reference were largely masculine, he expressed this difference as follows:

> The native's violence was not life denying, but life affirming ... for he knows that he is not an animal; and it is precisely when he realizes his humanity that he begins to sharpen the weapons with which he

will secure its victory .... What distinguished native violence from the violence of the settler, its saving grace, was that it was the violence of yesterday's victims who have turned around and decided to cast aside their victimhood and become masters of their own lives ... He, of whom they have never stopped saying that the only language he understands is that of force, decides to give utterance by force. Indeed, the argument the native chooses has been furnished by the settler, and by an ironic turning of the tables it is the native who now affirms that the colonialist understands nothing but force.

Fanon (1970: 15–16)

Fanon expresses here the feelings of most women in our conversations: those who refuse to accept silence and oppression and refuse to accept colonialism and occupation, and who are determined to fight for their freedom.

The terms *shaheeds* and *shaheedas* heavily distorted by imperialist feminists are held high in Palestinian political culture and especially the culture of resistance. These women (and men) are considered to be true and courageous freedom fighters. For example, in his *Under Siege*, renowned Palestinian poet Mahmoud Darwish writes:

If you are not rain, my love, be tree, sated with fertility, be tree
If you are not a tree, my love, be stone saturated with humidity, be stone
If you are not stone, my love, be moon, in the dream of the beloved woman, be moon.
So spoke a woman to her son at his funeral.

Darwish (1995: 35)

Writing about a female child *shaheeda*, Tawfiq Zayyad, another renowned Palestinian poet, says:

This child has five bullets in her forehead
and a sun
and shahadah [the act of self-sacrifice]
She fell like a golden tulip
She fell chanting for victory ...

Zayyad (1994: 10–11).

Fanon has rightly made the point when stating: 'If the settler colonial work is to make even dreams of liberty impossible for the native, the native's work is to imagine all possible methods for destroying the settler' (Fanon 1970: 16). After all, the *fidai*`/*fidai*`*yyah* are not terrorists. They are *shaheed/shaheeda*, that are highly revered in Palestinian culture and are almost never referred to in negative ways. They sacrifice themselves for the larger cause: freedom and liberation of their people, of their nation.

Within the Palestinian context, in which both Muslims and Christians have been involved in the resistance, it is no coincidence that the terms for martyr and freedom fighter are used interchangeably. This is so historically, partly because of the initial secular nature of the Palestinian National Liberation Movement since its emergence in 1964. The *shaheed/ shaheeda* or that of the *fidai*`/*fidai*`*yyah* are not terrorists. As discussed in Chapter 1, all women in our conversations saw themselves as *munadelat* (freedom fighters or *fidai*`*yyat*). Fanon's distinction between the *fidai*` and the 'terrorist' is very clear. He declares that the *fidai*` lives the life of a revolutionary. He/she are one who 'does not shrink before the possibility of losing his [her] life or the independence of his [her] country, but at no moment does he [she] choose death.' (Fanon 1970: 43)

When Aisha, Rasmiyya, Itaf and many others decided to take the path of *fidaa* (the act of martyrdom), they all knew that they were risking death, but their belief in the potential freedom this sacrifice might bring to their people and country made them take that path. Interviews with the women recorded in Chapter 4 attest to this reality.

Any attempt at describing or accounting for Palestinian women (and men) in resistance, I argue, must be cognizant of the historical and cultural contexts within which these women lived, perceived themselves and articulated their experiences. Western attempts at imposing a foreign discourse on Palestinians cannot explain their resistance. Quite to the contrary, such elitist, patronizing (and matronizing) approaches only serve the state and the imperialist ideology. What ought to be blamed here, as argued earlier, are not the victims of colonialism, but rather occupation, colonialism and imperialism themselves.

The importance of history and context for Palestinians' militant resistance, including some women who participated in the so-called suicide bombings, was best articulated by Dr Eyad Sarraj, a psychologist and chair of the Gaza Community Mental Health Program. In his 'Why We Have Become Suicide Bombers' (2005), Sarraj provides a simple yet resounding response to the literature which has dehumanized Palestinian fighters.[17] He begins his response by historicizing the Palestinian tragedy and contextualizing its people's struggle and resistance. The author narrates the devastating effects of the Nakba, documenting the countless peaceful 'negotiations', 'agreements', 'dialogues', 'treaties' and 'deals' the Palestinians have entered into and accepted, all of which have failed to produce any resolution to the Palestinian problem. Sarraj poignantly observed:

> We simply became the slaves of our enemy. We are building their homes on our villages, and we clean their streets. Do you know what this does to you when you have to be the slave of your enemy in order to survive? No, you will never understand how painful it is unless your country is occupied by another force. Only then will you learn how to watch in silence pretending not to see the torture of your friends and the humiliation of your father do you know what it means for a child to see his father spat at and beaten before his eyes by an Israeli soldier? Nobody knows what happened to our children. We don't know ourselves except we observe that they lose respect for their fathers. So they, our children, the children of the stone as they became known, tried the Intifada – the Uprising. Seven long years our children were throwing stones and being killed daily. Nearly all our young men [and many of our young women] were arrested and the majority [were] tortured. All had to confess. The result was every one suspected that all people were spies. So, we were exhausted, tormented and brutalized. What else could we do to return to our home? We had almost forgotten that and all what we wanted was to be left alone.
>
> Sarraj (2005)

Sarraj's writings, especially his contention that Palestinians were exhausted, tormented and brutalized and that they were left with no means to return to their homes encapsulates their experience. His contention that Palestinians were left with nothing to defend themselves, without their families and homes, has been echoed by most of the women during our conversations. If desperation was at all a factor behind women's involvement in the armed struggle, it was because of the terror of the colonizer, because of the violence of occupation and the daily humiliation the occupied have been enduring. This desperation is economic, political, social and ideological and is caused largely by the colonizing state; it is definitely not personal, psychological or family related, as many analyses try to lead us to believe. Herein lies the true meaning of honour, or more correctly, dignity; Palestinian militants struggle to preserve and protect their dignity and their honour as a people. They participate in the struggle in order to regain their stolen homeland, identity, culture and humanity, reaching their ultimate dignity as independent and sovereign people.

In other words, Palestinian women active in the armed struggle consider themselves to be an integral part of their national resistance culture, one that sanctifies freedom fighting and is not hesitant to sacrifice the individual for the freedom of the collective, for the higher cause. This was exactly what Aisha and Rasmiyya and the rest of the women in our conversations also believed in, as will be seen in Chapter 4. In the context of freedom fighting, terms like honour, dignity and shame leave the realm of the individual and psychological and become part of the collective memory and will of a people who have historically been committed to the struggle for protecting and regaining their homeland. It is only in this context that the true meaning of honour for women becomes clear: the honour of freeing the homeland, and not the 'honour' or 'shame' associated with women's body and sexuality.

To conclude, Palestinian women involved in the anti-colonial struggle, whether historically since the 1960s or in more recent history after the Second Intifada, have been exercising their right to defend their homeland, their freedom and national honour. This involvement defies Orientalist and imperialist perceptions of Arab and Palestinian women by expressing a great deal of agency. After all, nowhere in the literature that dehumanizes women resisters are there any indications, let alone evidence, that these women were forced to become militants. In most cases, during the Second Intifada, or historically as our conversations will demonstrate in the following chapters, women partake in the armed struggle voluntarily and without coercion.

It is true that the national and international scene at the turn of the twenty-first century is different than that during the 1960s–1980s: Palestinian women's historical struggle, not unlike the general spirit of the Palestinian National Movement until the early 1990s was overwhelmingly secular, women with Muslim and Christian backgrounds were involved in the movement, while in the Second Intifada Hamas has already gained political control especially in the Gaza Strip, resulting in the emergence of a national atmosphere that was expressed more in religious terms. Another difference between the two forms of armed struggle was the tactics or forms of resistance used. Despite such differences, in general I would argue that women's armed resistance in the Second Intifada continued the path of armed resistance which existed three or four decades earlier. This struggle throughout Palestinian history has primarily been a struggle against colonialism, occupation and their daily oppression.

One cannot ignore the fact that the Palestinian culture of resistance, of which women's struggle was a part, has served as a source of power and resilience for them – a source in which women take pride and which they use to defy their victimization by Western (and Israeli) feminists. This culture, as will be discussed below, derives its resilience and defiance from the history of the Nakba and that event's central place in the memory and consciousness of Palestinians. This is the history that almost all the vilifying literature, including the earlier works of Morgan and Dworkin has ignored, and this is the history which Palestinians insist on remembering and reminding the whole world of.

The Nakba: Memory as the Guardian of History

Who is to tell Rasmiyya to forget about her family house in Lifta? Who is to tell her to forget about the absence of her father or to forget about how she roamed the streets of Ramallah looking for America in order to bring her father back? This is Rasmiyya's history memorized by her as an ordinary child who became a refugee. This is one memory among millions of others which make up the Palestinian collective memory of the Nakba: the history of their dispersal, of life in exile or in the Diaspora, of their annihilation as a collective identity and of the destruction of their homes, villages and towns. This is the history on which the Israeli state was established in 1948.

Since its establishment, the Israeli government has been attempting and continues to attempt to erase the memory of the Nakba at least from the Jewish consciousness and from Western public discourse and official media as well. This has been largely done through the destruction of Palestinian villages and towns, replacing them with Jewish settlements or through planting trees and turning these villages into resorts for example, Canada Park which is built on the ruins of the three villages of Yalu, Imwas and Beit-Nuba (Cook 2014). Such policies and practices could also be a reason for the historical amnesia that has predominated in Western literature on Palestinian resistance and women more specifically. Palestinian narratives are excluded from the discussion of Israel/Palestine by much of Western academia as well as by mainstream film, art, music and news media institutions (Al-Hardan 2008: 249; Khalidi 1997: 18; Pappe 2008: 152, 160; Mojab and Abdo 2004: 23–24; Abdo 2008: 174). Such an omission has undoubtedly impacted on public knowledge concerning Palestinian struggles against Israeli settler colonialism, limiting, in turn, greater public discourse on the question of Palestine. Until the 1980s, the Zionist rendition of the events of 1948, which lays all the blame for the war and its consequences on the Arab side, has gone largely unchallenged outside of the Arab world. In a lecture delivered by Israeli-British historian Avi Shlaim at the Palestinian Initiative for the Promotion of Global Dialogue and Democracy (MIFTAH), the author argues, 'this is a nationalist version of history and, as such, it is simplistic, selective, and self-serving. It is, essentially, the propaganda of the victors. It presented the victors as victims, and it blamed the real victims – the Palestinians – for their own misfortunes' (Shlaim 2004).

The emergence in the 1980s of the Israeli new historians, also known as the revisionist historians, has challenged the one-sided Western narrative of the establishment of Israel. The works of the new historians include Benny Morris' *The Birth of the Palestinian Refugee Problem, 1947–49* (1988), Simha Flapan's *The Birth of Israel: Myths and Realities* (1987), Avi Shlaim's *Collusion Across the Jordan: King Abdullah, the Zionist Movement and the Partition of Palestine* (1988), and Ilan Pappe's *Britain and the Arab–Israeli Conflict, 1948–51* (1988). In his *Palestine Nakba: Decolonising History, Narrating the Subaltern, Reclaiming Memory*, Nur Masalha (2012) provides a comprehensive analysis of the debate on the Nakba, arguing that it represented a complex process of 'politicide', 'memoricide', 'toponymicide' and cultural genocide. 'Politicide' refers to the Israeli atrocities against Palestinians conducted 'through their gradual but systematic attempts to cause their annihilation'; it is also the process of 'denying the Palestinians any independent political existence in Palestine' (Masalha 2012: 1, 4). The term 'toponymicide' is used by Masalha to refer to the erasure of ancient Palestinian place names and their replacement by newly coined Zionist Hebrew ones (2012: 10). 'Nakba memoricide' is used by Masalha to denote the systematic 'erasure of the expelled Palestinians and their mini holocaust from Israeli collective memory and the excision of their history and deeply-rooted heritage in the land, and their destroyed villages and towns from Israeli official and popular memory' (Masalha 2012: 10). Finally, as in the case of other authors before him (Pappe 1988; Abbas 2003), Masalha uses the concept of 'cultural genocide' to re-emphasize the erasure of Palestinian physical culture, buildings, streets, homes and the destruction of about 500 villages and towns and other Palestinian historic sites.

Although Israel has primarily targeted the Jewish consciousness through its erasure of the Nakba from its public and media discourse, it has and continues to put tremendous pressure on its Palestinian citizens to forget their catastrophic history. 'The passing of the Nakba Law on 23 March 2011, which aims at preventing Palestinians from holding their annual day of commemoration of the Nakba, the banning of the term Nakba from textbooks used by its Palestinian citizens' and Shimon Peres's lecture to Palestinian school students 'to forget about the past', (Abdo 2011b: 152), are just some examples.

For Palestinians, remembering the Nakba is not a choice or just a figment of their memories which can be selected or deselected at will. It is an existential state of being for most Palestinians and 'is central to their social history and collective identity' (Masalha 2012: 7). It remains at the 'heart of Palestinian's collective memory, national identity and the struggle for collective national rights' (2012: 208). Herein lies the importance of bringing the Nakba into our discussion. The intention here is not to reinvent the wheel. There is already ample literature describing the Nakba and the devastation it brought upon the Palestinians (for example, Khalidi 1992; Pappe 1988, 2001; Morris 1988, 2001; Said 1979; Flapan 1987; Lentin 2010; Kimmerling 2003; Masalha 2005, 2012; Sa'di and Abu-Lughod 2007). In fact, recent literature has even begun to draw comparisons and parallels between the Palestinian Nakba and the Jewish *Shoah* (the Holocaust), removing the exclusivity of the term genocide to the Jewish experience (Lentin 2000; Masalha 2012).

What concerns us here are the gender aspects of the Nakba: the differential ways Palestinian women experienced it; the vital role women have played and continue to play in keeping it alive in the memory of Palestinians; and the political role the Nakba plays, namely, as a driving force behind Palestinian women's struggle and resistance. The gendered impact of the Nakba was expressed in various ways. To begin with, the loss of the land of Palestine had a different effect on women than on men. For Palestinian women, the overwhelming majority of whom were peasants until 1948, the land served as a social and cultural space in addition to being their primary source of survival. For example, during certain agricultural seasons, such as *mawsem al-zaitoun* (the olive-picking season), women and children, who often did most of the work, would spend days in the field socializing with other peasants, sharing their stories and lives with others. It was the same with *mawsem al-burtuqal* (the orange-picking and packing season). Recognizing the fact that the olive tree is a potent symbol of Palestinian nationalism, it is important to note that women had a primary role in developing this culture, for example, through making olive oil soup, pickling the olives for sale, using oil as medicinal cure, and so on (Abdo 2011b: 71–72). The loss of land during the Nakba has deprived women of a major part in their social, economic and cultural lives. The nostalgia around this loss occupies a major part in women's narratives of the Nakba, as will be seen in Chapter 3.

Moreover, women's bodies and sexuality were particularly targeted during the Nakba. As Ilan Pappe and Benny Morris, among others, have claimed, during 1948 many massacres of women and children took place and dozens of women were raped. In a 2004 interview with *Haaretz*, Benny Morris addressed the occurrence of 'about a dozen' cases of rape in 1948. According to him:

> In Acre four soldiers raped a girl and murdered her father. In Jaffa, soldiers in the Kiryati Brigade raped one girl and tried to rape several more. At Hunin two girls were raped and murdered. There were one or two cases of rape in Tantura; one case of rape at Qula; at Abu-Shusha, there were four female prisoners; one of whom was raped a number of times ... Usually more than one soldier was involved [and the event] ended with murder. [We] have to assume that the dozen cases of rape that were reported ... are just the tip of the iceberg.
>
> Quoted in Galleymore (2009: 89)

In his *Birth of the Palestinian Refugee Problem*, Morris also suggested that the expulsion of Palestinians was premeditated; concrete expulsion orders were given in writing, with some traceable directly to Israel's first Prime Minister David Ben Gurion (Ash 2004).[18]

Elsewhere I have accounted for the sexual atrocities committed against Palestinian women in the massacre at Deir Yassin, which took place on 9 April 1948 and where, of the 250 people murdered, '25 pregnant women were bayoneted in the abdomen while still alive, 52 children maimed in front of their mothers, then slain and beheaded; their mothers were in turn murdered, their bodies and sexual organs subsequently mutilated; 60 other women and girls were killed and mutilated' (Abdo 2011b: 51). Targeting women's bodies and sexuality has been a consistent policy of the Israeli state. Sexual torture of Palestinian women was practiced by the state's armed forces during the 1948 Nakba as discussed elsewhere (Abdo 2011b), it was – and continues to be used in Israeli prisons against women political prisoners – as will be discussed in greater detail in Chapter 4.

The development of oral history based on women's narratives as research methods used by Palestinian feminists, especially over the last decade or so, has produced extensive data on the gendered nature of the Palestinian history and nationalism, especially around the Nakba. Masalha devotes an important section of his recent *The Palestine Nakba* to discussing such developments in Palestinian feminist scholarship (Masalha 2012: 216–17). In addition to the pioneering work of Rosemary Sayigh mentioned above (1979; 1998), he lists the important contributions of Sayigh's recent project, *Voices: Palestinian Women Narrate Displacement* (2005). This project, according to its website,

> is a digital book in which [one] can hear the voices of around 70 Palestinian women, as well as a few men, currently living in Gaza, the West Bank, Jerusalem and Israel. They were recorded between 1998 and 2000 telling about their different experiences of displacement.
>
> Sayigh (2005)

In the introduction to this project, Sayigh relates her own experience with Palestinian women refugees in Lebanon's camps. She explains the impact of camp living conditions on Palestinians: the absence of employment and consequently absence of most men – except for older ones – from the camp, with camp women largely left alone – with their children – in these camps. Herein lays older women's important role in transmitting Palestinian history and culture to the next generation (Sayigh 2005). To these works should be added the edited work of Ahmad Sa'di and Lila Abu-Lughod's *Nakba: Palestine, 1948, and the Claims of Memory* (2007) as well as Fatma Kassem's *Palestinian Women: Narrative Histories and Gendered Memory* (2011). Kassem's work is especially interesting as it focuses on the stories and voices of Palestinian women citizens of Israel, part of the Palestinian society that was for quite a long time neglected or undermined by Palestinian and other academics. This new genre of research has undoubtedly challenged the existing masculine Palestinian national story; it also represents a challenge to the Israeli myth of the 'purity' of its army, demonstrating the masculine nature of their powers (Lentin 2000).

In this context, it is important to note that several progressive Israeli feminist scholars and activists established Zochrot (remembering), an NGO whose purpose is to document the voices of Israeli soldiers who took part in the Nakba of 1948. According to its website, Zochrot, which was founded in early 2002, aims to bring knowledge of the Palestinian Nakba to Jewish-Israeli people. It considers the Nakba as the 'ground zero' of the Israeli–Palestine conflict. Among the organization's activities are tours for Palestinian and Jewish children of destroyed Palestinian villages, tours that are to bring 'memories which often compete with the common, Zionist memory of the place'. An innovative part of a given tour is the production of a special booklet in Hebrew and Arabic for each tour. These booklets reflect Zochrot's process of learning. They feature testimonies by refugees, photographs of the village being toured, and historical background from different sources. It is Zochrot's ambition to recreate the Nakba in Hebrew – in other words, to 'enable a space where the Nakba can be spoken of or written about in the Hebrew language'. The name of the organization is significant, in that it is grammatically female in form:

> We are often asked why Zochrot and not the masculine, Zochrim. The masculine form of remembering, as presented in the Zionist discourse, is violent and nationalistic. Zochrot aims to promote another form of remembering, an alternative form that will enable the expression of other memories that are often kept silent. In addition, Zochrot makes an effort to create a space for the memory of women in the Palestinian Nakba. The name 'Zochrot' insinuates to all of these.
>
> Zochrot (2012)

In addition to its activities expressed above, the research conducted by Zochrot has become an important source of information. Ronit Lentin, for example, has based her recent *Co-memory and Melancholia: Israelis Memorialising the Palestinian Nakba* (2010) on information provided by Zochrot. Other Israeli and Palestinian academics and political activists have also consulted Zochrot documentation. More recently, in a new documentary called 'Seven Deadly Myths', former Israeli settler and journalist Lia Tarachansky, sheds light on the collective amnesia of Israelis when it comes to the fateful events of the Nakba years. She follows the transformation of four 1948 Israeli-Jewish veterans as they uncover and challenge decades of denied memories. She then returns to her own settlement, in the heart of the occupied West Bank, to uncover a landscape of denial and a history of erasure (Tarachansky 2013). The stories of the veterans in Taracharansky's documentary are taken from Zochrot mentioned above.

Whether it is the work of Zochrot, the research of Rosemary Sayigh or the writings of Fatma Kassem, among others, Palestinian oral history – produced largely by women – has undoubtedly contributed to the development of a new genre of literature: Palestinian history of the Nakba, of national and anti-colonial resistance written from a gender, or rather feminist, perspective. This history being brought back to life from a gender and feminist perspective will undoubtedly serve as a rebuttal to both the Orientalist and imperialist feminist perspectives on Palestinian women. It is also the history and memory which served as a driving force for women's involvement in the armed struggle as will be seen in Chapter 4. This, together with the ongoing Israeli settler colonial rule over the Palestinians is finally, what old and new imperialism as well as Orientalist and imperialist feminists have ignored and continued to ignore.

3

Colonialism, Imperialism and the Culture of Resistance

The contradictions between the indigenous culture of the colonized and occupied, which encourages and fosters resistance, and that of the imperialist culture, which, among other things, criminalizes anti-colonial and anti-imperialist struggles and resistance and transforms the latter into terrorism, is best exemplified by the Palestinian case. The long history of Palestinian national and anti-colonial resistance, beginning in the early 1920s has produced a remarkable culture of resistance, manifested in among others, in *adab al-muqawama* (resistance literature), in *shea'r al-muqawama* (poetry of resistance) and thus *shua'ra al-muqawama* (resistance poets), as well as in *adab al-sujoun* (prison literature). This culture formed the larger body of revolutionary literature at both the regional and international levels. It also played a vital role in Palestinian women coming to be involved in the national and anti-colonial struggle as well as in their commitment and determination to partake in the armed struggle. Throughout our conversations, women of both generations emphasized the impact of *adab al-muqawama* on their activism: they saw themselves as an integral part of this culture.

The experience of colonialism and imperialism has produced a history of anti-colonial resistance expressed in different forms, including the social, cultural and physical. Anti-colonial resistance literature has emerged throughout the world, in Latin America, the Caribbean, South East Asia and the Arab world, including among Palestinians. Revolutionary artists have also emerged, from Chile's Pablo Neruda to the Caribbean's Aimé Césaire and Edward Kamau Brathwaite and to Cuba's Nicolás Guillén and Palestine's Mahmoud Darwish; the themes and ideologies of these artists have been transmitted to and became very influential on many other committed political resistance writers and poets throughout the world. While differing in context, the majority of these authors have been concerned with documenting the devastating effects of colonialism, imperialism and fascism, expressing their resistance to all forms of oppression and their hope for a better future based on justice and human dignity. The names and sometimes images of revolutionary national leaders such as Che Guevara, Ho Chi Minh, Mao Tse-tung and General Giap have become international icons and role models, particularly during the 1960s through to the 1980s. The Palestinian resistance movement and women's involvement in the armed struggle was heavily influenced by local, national and international struggles and the cultures of resistance which accompanied such struggles.

The historical specificity of the long and continuing Palestinian struggle and the experience of the Nakba have produced a political culture historically known as *adab al-muqawama* (resistance culture): a culture which emerged in the early twentieth century and was further developed after the Nakba (1948); it was largely composed of poetry, prose and novels, with poetry being dominant. The term *adab al-muqawama* was first coined by Ghassan Kanafani in his *Adab al-Muqawama fi Falasteen al-Mohtalla* (Resistance Literature in Occupied Palestine) to describe Palestinian literary production under Israeli colonialism (Kanafani 1977a).

Kanafani, an internationally renowned Palestinian literary critic, paid special attention to oral culture and the predominance of various forms of folkloric expressions. He provides extensive evidence of folkloric songs sung in the form of *zajal*, *a'taba*, *mawwal*, *sahja* and so on, produced spontaneously on social and political occasions such as weddings, funerals, births and public protests – all of which express a critical stance and resistance to the oppression the people find themselves under, especially since 1948. Some songs were against Arabs (Palestinians) who joined Zionist political parties; others were against land confiscations and against Israeli brutality (Kanafani 1977b: 36–47). The simple words used in these and the repetitive nature of the music makes it easy for the crowds to recite, memorize and reproduce their messages for the generations (1977b: 46).

This said, Kanafani specifies the works of various Palestinian poets in 1948 Palestine, especially that of Mahmoud Darwish, Tawfiq Zayyad and Samih Al-Qasem, as being resistance poetry par excellence. In his introduction to Kanafani's book, Mahmoud Darwish states that he considers Kanafani a *fidai`* (freedom fighter) for announcing the presence of resistance literature in 1948 Palestine, saying: 'We who were writing what Ghassan termed "resistance poetry", did not know we were writing "resistance poetry'" (Kanafani 1977a: 20). Resistance literature, which is born among people under colonial oppression, military rule and the like, expresses commitment against all forms of oppression and the hope for liberation. It also expresses the love of the homeland and the responsibility for and the meaning of steadfastness. Differentiating between Palestinian poetry produced in the occupied homeland and that in exile, Kanafani writes: 'Poetry in the occupied lands is not about crying, weeping, sobbing or despair; it is rather revolutionary and full of hope.' (Kanafani 1977b: 58)

Resistance literature is produced by committed authors who seek justice and humanity, and detest power and hegemony. These are often nationalists under occupation, colonialism and oppressive rule. In her *Resistance Literature* (1987), Barbara Harlow, while acknowledging the role of Kanafani in developing the concept of resistance literature, says that resistance literature is 'invested in people's actual lived and memorialized history and is written as a political weapon for the oppressed to use in their struggle against the oppressor. She sees resistance literature to 'represent an essential arena of struggle' (Harlow 1987: 77).

Building on Kanafani's concept of resistance literature, Harlow borrowed the concept and developed it into a full theory, suggesting it as a conceptual framework to understanding literary and oral forms of resistance voiced by the oppressed. To poetry and novels as forms of resistance expression, Harlow added diaries, especially political prisoners' diaries and narratives. These forms, she maintains, are true expression of resistance and revolution (Harlow 1986a: 102, 1987).

Before going into further detail on Palestinian resistance culture in general and resistance literature more specifically, where I will be focusing on, although not exclusively, three male cultural or literary resistant producers, Ghassan Kanafani, Mahmoud Darwish and Tawfiq Zayyad, the issue of female resistance literary producers must be addressed. The period which this book focuses on, namely the late 1960s to the late 1980s, and so prior to the First Intifada (1987–1992) represents a special phase in the history of Palestinians. These were the first three decades after the Israeli occupation of the West Bank and Gaza Strip (1967); it was also the period of intense Israeli oppression of 1948 Palestinians who until 1966 were placed under Israeli military rule. Such conditions have intensified patriarchy within the Palestinian traditional culture, limiting, among other things, women's representation in the public realm. The accentuation of patriarchy through military occupation and settler colonial rule, in other words, widens the gender gap, leading the relationship between gender, textuality and orality assuming particular forms, where textuality becomes the male tool of expression while women's voices, words and contributions are expressed in oral forms. In Chapter 2, we discussed the role of orality in maintaining and reproducing the Palestinian history, especially through the Nakba, which was largely women's domain. It is no surprise, therefore, that textual or literary production was not women's domain. In fact, throughout this book, we have been arguing that women's resistance including their participation in the armed struggle has remained largely in the realm of oral history rather than the written official one. It was not until the late 1980s, partly due to women's increased education and partly due to women's massive participation in the First Intifada (1987–1992) that female resistance literary production began to emerge, with contributions by authors such as Fadwa Tuqan, Liana Badr, and Sahar Khalifeh to name a few.

Liana Badr who lived a diasporic life began her production with *A Compass for the Sunflower* in 1979 which is a general novel describing Palestinian fragmented lives and scattered families, an attempt to make sense of her and other Palestinian diasporic lives. Her second novel *A Window on the Fakhani* in 1989 is largely concerned with the 1982 Israeli invasion of Lebanon and the experience of Palestinians in Beirut. Nationalist but not necessarily resistance or militant literature and yet it comes in a different time and location than occupied Palestine. Fadwa Tuqan's experience and literary production is somewhat problematic and complex in the context of anti-colonial resistance. Critics of Tuqan have rightly pointed out that most of the poet's production was focused on her personal life and feelings of oppression in her patriarchal upper-class family. For example, Anna Ball, while theorizing Tuqan's poetry as a form of 'invisible feminism', recognizes that the poet did not see herself as gender aware or as a feminist. Still, Ball found the poet's most important emphasis to be placed on her own life experience of social-familiar oppression, the 'interior struggle' in the poet (Ball 2012: 52–60). It is true that Tuqan's upper-class origins were partly responsible for her feelings of seclusion and oppression in Nablus, a city historically known for its class contradictions and social conservatism. Although this reality did not impede the emergence of *munadelat* (women freedom fighters) – several of the women interviewed came from Nablus, and some also came from the upper class as well – family patriarchy was used by Tuqan as a centre for her poetry.

It is not unlikely that alongside family patriarchy and class, there were other 'subjective' or personal reasons which perhaps distanced Fadwa Tuqan from being involved with immediate and important political events between the late 1960s and, say, the mid-1980s. This reluctance on the part of Tuqan to be involved in political resistance, for example, with the meaning and plight of female political detainees, was noticed by some of the female political detainees in our conversations. Aisha Odeh in particular both in the interview and in her book expressed dismay at the distance of Tuqan from the political scene. While in prison along with many other women fighters challenging Israeli harassment, colonial oppression and their sentences of life imprisonment, Aisha read a very pessimistic poem by Fadwa Tuqan and became upset – 'How dare she be so pessimistic when we are resisting all of this oppression?' – and decided to write to her (Odeh 2012: 204). In response, Tuqan wrote a poem, 'A Small Song of Pessimism,' published it in a newspaper and dedicated it to the 'prisoner Aisha.' When Aisha read the poem, she responded with dissatisfaction: 'I was pinched [hurt] by the dedication, "to the prisoner". Aren't we *munadelat*? Did [she] forget the difference between the two?' (Odeh 2012: 205).

The emergence of female Palestinian cultural resistance artists, especially in the genre known as the spoken word (poetry, rap and other word performances) have emerged in a strong way in the past two decades or so. Some of these will be mentioned, especially film directors and producers. However, our concern with the historical period in which our case study is located, which is before the First Intifada, is the rationale behind focusing on Palestinian classical resistance literature acknowledged as *adab al-muqawama* (resistance literature) and *adab al-sujoun* (prison literature), a literature that was primarily produced by males who both experienced prison and fought imprisonment in words.

In her *Resistance Literature* (1987), Harlow devotes considerable space to discussing Palestinian literature of resistance, focusing on, among others, Ghassan Kanafani, caricaturist Naji Al-Ali and Mahmoud Darwish. She also devotes a special section to prison literature, emphasizing the importance of oral histories and political prisoners' narratives as constituent elements of resistance literature. Harlow's special emphasis on women's (and men's) oral history, especially political prisoners' memoirs, are further developed in her *Barred: Women, Writing and Political Detention* (1992) where she examines ex-political prisoners' memoirs, including those of Palestinians, as forms of resistance to oppression and colonialism.

It is such narratives, as the following chapters will show, which constitute the bases of Palestinian women's resistance and revolutionary culture.

International and Regional Struggles: Impact on the Palestinian Revolution

Resistance culture expresses the materiality of the struggle itself through the fighters and leaders themselves who become icons and models of revolutions and radical change. The era of the 1960s through to the 1980s throughout the world produced an impressive list of such leaders, whose acts and achievements became symbols of and role models for resistance for most revolutionary movements internationally. The Palestinian revolution during those decades, being itself a part of the international struggle for justice and against colonialism, was heavily impacted by this international revolutionary culture.

The international aspect of the Palestinian struggle was expressed in a myriad of ways. Revolutionary literature, including the works of Marx, Lenin and Mao as well as others such as General Giap, Ho Chi Minh and Che Guevara, were used as educational material during the training of female (and male) Palestinian fighters, especially among those belonging to the left within the PLO.[1] During our conversations, many women took pride in how their political awareness and consciousness was impacted by world revolutionary ideology. During the training phase of the armed struggle, women attended political courses at which time they read and discussed world struggles and revolutions, from Algeria to South Yemen, Vietnam, China and Cuba. They also learned about world revolutionary leaders including Castro, Che Guevara, Mao Tse-tung and General Giap. The trainer in her military camp, Aisha writes, 'would fill our training camp with revolutionary books and insisted that we read them, saying, a gun without knowledge can turn us into mercenaries and turn our struggle into *bunduqiyya maajoura* [something motivated only by money] ... we considered ourselves part of Jabhat Al-Nidal Al-A`lamiyya [the international resistance movement]' (Odeh 2012: 138). Itaf, Amne, Ghada, Mariam and Sonya, as Chapter 4 will show, emphasized the role of theoretical training they received. Others who were not organized spoke about their autodidactic political education and their exposure to revolutionary culture on their own.

The internationalism of the Palestinian revolution was also expressed in the support given and solidarity expressed by groups and individuals, support and solidarity that poured in from various parts of the globe; some of these joined the PLO training camps and fought alongside the Palestinians, while others smuggled money and/or weapons to the Palestinians in the Occupied Territories. In her account of Palestinian political prisoners, Soraya Antonius mentioned several names of women who were detained by the Israelis on charges of aiding and abetting Palestinian resistance. These include Edith Borghalter (60 years old), a Parisian fighter charged with bringing explosives to Israel. She spent eight years in prison. Other people, such as Marlene Bradly and Nadia Bradly from Morocco and Terry F. Leena from the United States, were charged with aiding Palestinian resistance and were imprisoned by the Israelis (Antonius 1980: 71). In her *Thamanan lil-Shams* (For the Sake of the Sun) (2012), Odeh reaffirms Antonius's findings, discussing in detail a group of non-Palestinian *fidai`yyat* (female freedom fighters) who joined them in prison. These included French Moroccan Nadia Bradly, a group commander, and her sister Marlene, along with a group of French women such as Evelyn Bourg and Edith Borghalter and husband Pier who was in his 70s at the time (Odeh 2012: 166–70). Antonius, while mentioning most of these people, added a large number of names of women from various other countries, including the United States, France and Holland, who in one way or another had joined the Palestinian armed struggle (Antonius 1980: 72). This type of solidarity has undoubtedly reinvigorated women's struggle in general and political prisoners more specifically, leading to strengthening further their resolve to resist.[2]

An internationalist culture of revolutionary expressions was celebrated among various sectors of the Palestinian population, especially among the 1948 Palestinians (that is, those who remained in Palestine and became citizens of Israel) who are also known as 'internal refugees' (Masalha 2012: 231–232; Abdo 2011b: 40; Zureik 1979). Until the early 1970s, 1948 Palestinians, while pushed (by force or choice) into joining the Zionist parties, were prevented from having their own political party or legally associating with Palestinian political parties or organizations outside of Palestine/Israel. The only legal anti-Zionist party present at that time was the Maki (Communist Party of Israel, CPI), one which many joined and which others on the left – especially nationalists – refused to join, as they desired alternative Palestinian parties.[3] Among these Palestinians, especially since the mid-1970s, groups of university students would express their political commitment through study groups and public meetings in which they would discuss the Palestinian struggle as well as other struggles and revolutions across the world. This author, for example, was a member of such a group in which, in addition to the frequent political discussions and debates we would frequently have, we would also paint posters and copy the image of Che Guevara onto T-shirts to distribute or sell for a nominal price to other members of the community.

Internationalism as a material force, as a movement, played a central role in the making of the Palestinian revolution through the leadership strategies of that revolution and through the cultural implications for other struggles and revolutions of the Palestinian one. Palestinian resistance literature, including poetry, must be viewed in this international context of revolutionary culture, a culture which addresses the themes of oppression, agitation and resistance. The following excerpts from Pablo Neruda's powerful testimony of Franco's fascist rule in Spain and the Spanish Civil War is a case in point. In his remarkable poem 'I Explain A Few Things', a poem which signals the transformation of Neruda from the poet of love and nature into a resistance poet, he writes:

You are going to ask: and where are the lilacs?
and the poppy-petalled metaphysics? [...]
I'll tell you all the news.

I lived in a suburb,
a suburb of Madrid, with bells,
and clocks, and trees. [...]

My house was called the house of flowers [...]

And one morning all that was burning, [...]

Come and see the blood in the streets! [...]

And you'll ask: why doesn't this poetry
speak of dreams and leaves
and the great volcanoes of this native land?

Neruda (2007: 29–34)

Chilling images of a burning homeland, children's blood in the street, of horror and terror and the ruin and destruction of nature and the environment, are not uncommon to various homelands subjected to colonial and imperialist wars and to occupation. For this poet, and in fact other poets as well, love turns into the love of the homeland, of humanity, children and against destruction. Historically we have seen this in Vietnam and Algiers, among others, and more recently in Iraq, Afghanistan, Libya and Syria. All have been the direct and indirect victims of imperialism. Moreover, the destruction of homes, uprooting of trees, mass expulsion of people from their homeland, and the bombing of schools, hospitals and infrastructure, are all familiar acts of Israeli colonialism in Palestine.

In addition to the role international resistance movements and cultures have had on the Palestinians, the latter were also heavily impacted by the regional (Arab) movements and literary forms of resistance that emerged either in resisting foreign colonialism or as direct critique of many Arab regimes seen then (as now) as tools of imperialism. Relevant in this context is Mudhaffar Al-Nawwab, the well-known Iraqi poet, whose sharp criticism of imperialism and of Arab regimes have led to his exile in Syria for most of his life. In 'Al-Quds' (Jerusalem), Al-Nawwab's most famous poem, he writes:

Jerusalem is the bride of your Arabism
Why did you send all the rapists into her room
And you stood, silently, behind her room,
listening to her cries as she was being raped ...

Al-Nawwab (2008)

Also among Arab resistance artists are Lebanese lyricists and singers Marcel Khalifeh and Ahmad Qa`bour, who composed and then sang much of Mahmoud Darwish's poetry and whose songs remain very popular among all Arabs, and especially among Palestinian youth, and the Egyptian duo of poet Ahmad Fouad Nijm and composer and singer Sheikh Imam, both of whom have spent many years in prison, producing there some of their best work.[4] One of their famous poem-songs sung by Arab students and workers throughout the Arab world, especially by Palestinians, is 'Ya Falastiniyya wil-Bunduqani ramakum bil-Sohyouniyya ...,' which contains the lyrics 'Oh Palestinians – my hands are bursting – my hands accompany you – to kill the snake – to end Hulagu law [i.e. end the law of the conqueror].' Because of the difficulty of translating this Egyptian colloquial duo's work, loosely translated excerpts will be presented:

O Palestinians, the exile has lasted too long,
The desert has seen too many refugees and victims,
The earth calls its peasants,
Revolution is our aim, victory is our first stage
O Palestinians, the victory of Vietnam, she woke up after hundreds of
thousands of bombs, the candle is lit and the Americans are retreating
in defeat, hope this will be your future too.

Sheikh Imam, n.d.

Almost all Arab resistance literary and other artistic producers have made
Palestine, the Palestinians and their struggle as a focus for their work.
The call for resistance, for saving humanity, the hope for freedom from
oppression, colonialism and imperialism expressed in this literature is part
and parcel of resistance literature worldwide. Arab resistance literature has
characterized different stages in the history of Arab national development.
It became an important force of agitation, resistance and hope sung or
recited during demonstrations, sit-ins, social gatherings and student
activities among Arabs in general and Palestinians more specifically.
The orality which is characteristic of Arab, including Palestinian culture,
is an important force explaining the close relation between the people
and literature. In the early twentieth century, Philip Hitti addressed this
issue claiming:

Modern audiences in Baghdad, Damascus and Cairo can be stirred to
the highest degree by the recital of poems, only vaguely comprehended
by them, and by the delivery of orations in the classical tongue, though
it be only partially understood. The rhythm, the rhyme, the music,
produce on them the effect of what they call 'lawful magic' (*sihr halāl*).

Hitti (2002: 90)

Another historical regional factor with significant impact on
Palestinian resistance was the re-emergence in the late 1950s of the
Harakat al-Qawmiyyeen al-Arab (the Arab Nationalist Movement –
ANM),[5] which sought to establish Arab unity and free Arab countries from
Western imperialism and colonialism (Tibi 1997). Among the very strong
supporters, and the first leader of this movement was the Egyptian leader
Gamal Abdel-Nasser, with his constant call for the unification of the
Arab peoples in order to create a strong front against Israel. Abdel-Nasser
became a symbol of and for Arab resistance and unity and an important

force in the Palestinians' anti-colonial liberation struggle. Throughout our conversations, many women expressed their deep regard for Abdel-Nasser; they stressed his concern for Egypt's sovereignty and independence, his concern with Arab unity, and his resentment of US and Israeli imperialist intervention. They had memorized many of his speeches, and several were keen to recite one line he delivered after the 1967 War: 'Ma ukhidha bil-quwwa la yustaradd illa bil-quwwa' (What was taken by force can only be regained by force).

International and regional (Arabic) resistance literature constitutes one trajectory within the larger context of the cultural production of resistance literature produced by Palestinians, strengthening further the ideological bases of the Palestinian armed struggle, and functioning as a further incitement for struggle and resistance. To all this, we add the wealth of the Palestinian culture of resistance which, during the historical period discussed in this book, was largely expressed in poetry and novels and facilitated by Palestinian oral traditions – a literary force which has travelled freely among Palestinians in historic Palestine and beyond its borders, cementing their history and identity. In fact, a whole genre of resistance literature, including novels, theatre productions, films, caricatures and more, has also developed. Still, it is the initial forms, namely, poetry and novels, which have had a specific impact on the Palestinian struggle in general and on women in the armed struggle more specifically.

Palestinian Resistance Culture: A Historical Context

The first Palestinian uprising of 1929 arose as a protest against British policies that acknowledged the Zionist demand for establishing a Jewish home in Palestine. It was also sparked by British taxation policies and the imprisonment of people unable to pay taxes, its extra-judicial measures, and the intensification of its brutal colonial policies. The Royal Commission Report of August 1929, also known as the Shaw Report, along with the detailed 1930 report by Sir John Hope Simpsons, document the deteriorating conditions of the Palestinians as a result of British pro-Zionist policies (Shepherd 2000; Masalha 2005; Sayigh 1979; Abdo 1989, 2002, 2011b).

Continued British oppression against Palestinians, the crack down by the former on the leaders of the 1929 revolt and the further appropriation of Palestinian lands by European (Jewish) settlers all further aggravated Palestinian lives and resulted in the emergence of the Palestinian armed struggle. As a measure for controlling Palestinian uprisings, in June 1930 the British colonial government executed Muhammad Jamjoum, A`ta Al-Zir and Fouad Hijazi: three national leaders who had been imprisoned for their participation in the 1929 uprising. The execution of these anti-colonial fighters, considered by Palestinians at the time to be national heroes, sent a wave of shock and anger across all of Palestine. These fighters remain national heroes for Palestinians to this day.

The early twentieth-century resistance in response to the brutal policies of British colonialism, which had culminated in the execution of political activists, marked the beginning of the development of *thaqafat al-muqawama* (the culture and consciousness of resistance), even if it was not called that at that time. This culture was and still is based on the strong oral history tradition of the Palestinians. Thus, during the execution of the martyrs Jamjoum, Al-Zir and Hijazi, their mothers, who had been denied permission to bid their sons a last farewell,

> stood in front of Acre prison, and at the top of their voices shouted words of encouragement to their sons inside, urging them to be steadfast and brave. Then they began singing patriotic songs to them. Nobody remembers the names of the mothers, but the people have continued singing those same songs.
>
> Al-Hout Noueihed (2012)

During the funeral procession, the following lyrics were chanted by the crowds:

> A funeral procession took off
> from Acre prison, for Muhammad Jamjoum and Fouad Hijazi
> Oh my people, punish the High Commissioner and his folks ...
> A`ta says: Yousef, my brother, I trust you will take care of mother.
> You sister, never mourn after my death
> I sacrificed my blood for the sake of this 'watan' [nation]
> For the eyes of Palestine.

> Their bodies rest in the soil of the homeland
> Their souls are in the Paradise of Pleasure
> Where there is no complaint about tyranny

Where tolerance and forgiveness overflow
Their souls will not request pardon from any but Him, He is the God
He holds the world in his hands
His greatness is mightier than that of all who rule over land and sea.

McDonald (2006: 13)[6]

Although the author of these lyrics is anonymous, this folkloric song has entered almost all Palestinian homes and has been recited by several generations up to the present time. Palestinian nationalist poet Ibrahim Tuqan named the day of execution of these three martyrs 'Red Tuesday' in remembrance of their deaths; 'Red Tuesday' is also the title of the poem Tuqan wrote in June 1929 after the execution of the three heroes. Tuqan's poem serves as a clarion call for Palestinians to continue the struggle for freedom and independence (see Abdullah 2002: 82).

A`ta's statement about 'sacrificing his blood for the sake of this *watan* [homeland], For the eyes of Palestine,' occupies a significant place in the Palestinian history of struggle. It accentuates the value of martyrdom as a positive trait and a commitment to defending the homeland. The three men – two Muslims and one Christian – became *shaheeds* (martyrs): they were killed because of their nationalist anti-colonial resistance, for the freedom of their homeland. The terms *shaheed* and *shahada* were used by Ibrahim Tuqan himself in the early 1920s in the context of his writings. These terms reflected the high value of self-sacrifice for the liberation of the homeland.[7]

Speaking about the Palestinian resistance, including the armed struggle, Ibrahim Tuqan in his poem '*Mawtini*' (My Homeland) wrote:

The sword and the pen
Not talking nor quarrelling
Are our symbols
Our glory and covenant
And a duty to fulfil it
Shake us
Our honour
Is an honourable cause […]

The youth will not get tired
Their goal is your independence
Or they die

We will drink from death
But we will not be slaves to our enemies
We do not want
An eternal humiliation
Nor a miserable life
We do not want
But we will return
Our great glory
My homeland.

Jayyusi and Tingley (1977: 285–87)

This poem became the de facto national anthem of the Palestinian National Authority (PNA) in 1993 and was adopted by Iraq in 2003 as the country's official national anthem.

The establishment of the state of Israel in 1948 and the resulting Nakba has ruptured the lives and culture of Palestinians. Although this literature has two provenances – in the occupied homeland (particularly inside Israel) and in the Diaspora (particularly in Lebanon, a country with a large population of Palestinian refugees), the rupture in the lived experiences of Palestinians was in fact reconstructed through resistance literature.

Harlow's important contribution to the development of the theory of resistance literature, as argued above, lies in her insistence on the role of oral history, narratives and diaries as important constituents of resistance literature, and we may add, resistance culture in general. Orality, diaries and narrative to reiterate, carry a special value within the Palestinian context, as the contribution of Palestinian women to their history of resistance and revolution, more specifically their participation in the armed struggle, remains largely in the realm of oral rather than written or official history.

The experience and memory of the Nakba has in fact been carved in the minds and hearts of all women interviewed in this project. It served as the primary reason for their determination to join the armed struggle. Other memories which also partook in shaping women's determination to struggle and resistance included the emergence of the PLO in 1964, the 1967 Naksa (Arab defeat in the 1967 War) and the humiliation experienced living under Israeli colonialism and occupation. These are the same events and forces which lay at the heart of Palestinian resistance literature; events feed Palestinian political consciousness and struggle. Women, not unlike their male comrades, have always joined the resistance of their own volition; they need not be forced to do what they already want to do, and they chose the path of resistance freely and without coercion. The importance for women's narratives cannot be overemphasized.

Women, Memory and History

The scars, the trauma and the memories of the atrocities against and the torture and humiliation of the colonized have persisted through the many decades and have been transmitted inter-generationally, from generation to generation. The Armenian people are yet to receive recognition and apology from the Turkish government for the genocide of their people in the 1920s; the Blacks in the United States and the native peoples in existing settler societies remain in a similar situation, given the historical wrongs committed against them. In his 'Jean Ziegler: "This World Order is not just murderous, it is absurd"', Siv O'Neall (2008), the former UN Special Rapporteur for the Right to Food, who served on the advisory committee of the board of Human Rights of the United Nations (2008–2012), discusses what he calls 'the injured memory of the Arabs under colonialism,' who went through 'slavery, killing destruction and imprisonment and so on.' (O'Neall 2008) In particular, Ziegler refers to the Algerians under French colonialism, recalling, among other things, the visit of French President Sarkozy to Algeria to sign an agreement for gas and oil. According to Ziegler, Algeria's President Bouteflika demanded an apology from France for one of the massacres (Sétif) which claimed the lives of over forty thousand Algerians – all were killed by the French colonial army in 1945. Sarkozy refused the Algerian request. This position has further soured the relationship between the ex-colonized and the ex-colonizer. Potential trade agreements between the two countries were cancelled, and Bouteflika's scheduled visit during 2009 was also cancelled.[8] In December 2012, the French President François Hollande, who had just paid a visit to Algeria, was quoted as saying that Algeria suffered under the 'profoundly unjust and brutal system' of colonialism, but he stopped short of apologizing for French rule of the North African state (in Alpert 2012). Colonialism, imperialism and occupation, in other words, may no longer directly intervene in the lives of the colonized, but their memories of trauma linger on, as the case of Algeria shows.

In the following, I would like to shed some light on Palestinian history through narratives gathered from female camp refugees who lived and experienced the Nakba first hand. The following narratives are original stories retrieved from videos of an oral history project conducted between 2007 and 2009 by PalestineRemembered.com.[9] Their oral history project collected information from both women and men. What is particularly telling about women's narratives are the vivid pictures they drew of their homes, lands and the trees surrounding their homes; they also reflected on their ordeal under British colonialism, but placed especial emphasis on the Nakba. For example, Huda Hannah (born in 1918), from the village of Rama in the Galilee, recounted what she refers to as 'the famous olive trees' in Rama. She describes the scenery of the 'plains of olive trees' she used to watch from her home, saying: 'You could not see the end of the grove.' In the 1940s, Huda and a friend from Gaza were studying in Jerusalem, and they both took part in resisting the Zionist settlement. She proudly recounted one incident when, 'with a friend of mine from Gaza, we burnt the house of a settler in the city!' The testimony of Fatema abi A`qlain (born 1918) from Kokab Al-Hawa, district of Beisan (currently in Israel), also brings to life the material map of Palestine. She recounted the beautiful landscape of her village and remembered the trees, her home, the *wadi* (valley) and the wells from which she and the other village women used to draw the water.

Hamda Al-Bishtawi (1916), a Bedouin woman from Um Saboun, Beisan district, vividly remembered and was proud of her work at the time, such as rearing chickens, working in the wheat field, fetching water from the two wells around her village, building the home from scratch (the tent was made from lamb wool), milking cows and goats, and making ghee, milk and cheese. She was well aware of what happened to her village during the 1936–39 revolution. She talked about British troops burning their homes, ordering men out of the houses, and spilling oil on wheat and otherwise ruining their food during house searches. She also remembered how all the village inhabitants were driven out of the village by force and subsequently became refugees in Jordan as a result. Similar accounts, especially around the 1936–39 revolution and the 1948 Nakba, were voiced by others, for example, by Souad Andrawus (born 1922) and Marie Andrawus (born 1932) from Tabariyya (Tiberias). This notwithstanding, the one principle that all of the refugees shared with deep hope and great enthusiasm, was that of return to the homeland, despite all of the odds confronting the materialization of this dream.

For Palestinian refugees, memory of the past represents the fuel for their survival and acts as a force in maintaining and reproducing their claim as the rightful owners of the physical/material space called Palestine. It serves to keep them and their identity intact, and feeds their hope for a just future. It also cements the material/geographical map of their homeland. This shared memory of the Nakba generation has formed a solid basis in Palestinian culture of resistance in all its forms and content. This is particularly true in the case of resistance poetry, as will be seen in the following section. This culture, in its material, moral and emotional power, had a significant impact on women's determination to join the armed struggle, as conversations demonstrate in the next chapters.

Adab Al-Muqawama (Resistance Literature)

As defined earlier, the term resistance literature concerns a form of cultural production that recognizes the sufferings and ordeals of the colonized, a form that allies itself with the oppressed and is aware of the colonizer's policies – policies that are based on ignoring the natives, silencing them, and discrediting their right to live in their homeland. Resistance literature has no geographical boundaries, and no force can prevent it from travelling across borders and penetrating people's hearts and minds. One needs to remember here that resistance literature expresses ideas or words only while it is still under production; the moment the word leaves the pen or the desk of the writer, it turns into a dynamic force for change.

Palestinian cultural resistance production includes various forms of creative expression, the most important of which, at least until the 1980s, were *adab al-muqawama* (resistance literature) and *adab al-sujoun* (prison literature). These genres of literature are embedded in the history, geography and politics of the Palestinians; they express their past and present and provide hope for their future.

Memory and collective memory more specifically informs people's history and identity; a nation without memory and without culture is a nation without history (and so in fact not a nation at all). For Palestinians who after the creation of the state of Israel became a people of refugees and of exile, resistance literature has functioned as a driving force in their commitment to survive and struggle for justice and against colonialism, as well as their hope to return to their homeland. Resistance literature, as Aisha, Ghada, Kholoud and most women relayed in the interviews, formed the fuel which kept their revolutionary spirit thriving. Aided by a rich literature which keeps the memory and history of Palestine the homeland alive, the Palestinian struggle is not an ideological struggle or a struggle of ideas alone: it is a materialist struggle as well. Palestinians struggle for regaining a homeland carved in the memory of the Nakba generation as well as for the generations that followed and for those to come. Amilcar Cabral has aptly captured the meaning of people's struggle. In his 'Tell No Lies, Claim No Easy Victories', Cabral says:

> Always bear in mind that the people are not fighting for ideas, for the things in anyone's head. They are fighting to win material benefits, to live better and in peace, to see their lives go forward, to guarantee the future of their children.
>
> in Turok (1980: 204)

While the memory of the Nakba has never left the hearts and minds of Palestinians, mini-Nakbas continue to befall those who live under the ongoing settler-colonial control of Israel. Israel has not only erased the map of Palestine from the world's geography; it has also attempted to erase the memory of the Nakba from the Jewish mind and has used its institutional and legal power to erase such memory (Masalha 2012: 9). As mentioned in the earlier chapter, the Israeli organization Zochrot was established for this particular reason: rekindling Jewish memory of the Nakba. Israel's policies concerning the erasure of the Nakba are a continuing process. Official Israeli insistence on ignoring and denying the Palestinian Nakba has never stopped. The legal ban on Nakba commemorations by Palestinians through the Nakba Law of 2011 is just one example.

The visit by Israeli President Shimon Peres to Nazareth in March 2012, mentioned in the earlier chapter, had a very important message. In a speech he gave to Palestinian high school students, he said:

> Don't concern yourselves with history, with the past ... what happened, happened, and is not important ... History is irrelevant ... Technology and high-tech represent today's wide world: all who want to learn Arab history can go to the internet.
>
> Lappin (2012: 2)

His utterances in the speech were only one part of the insult. The utter arrogance of Peres resides in the fact that his speech was given at Mahmoud Darwish Cultural Centre, which is located in a neighbourhood in Nazareth known as Tawfiq Zayyad village – both being spaces built to commemorate the lives and struggles and revolutionary contributions of these two most famous resistance poets. To claim that 'land and borders are of the "old world"', while that of the 'new world is one of science and technology' is yet another attempt by Israel to dismiss the Palestinian catastrophe.

In fact, any attempt made by Palestinians or even by critical and conscious Jews (Israeli or otherwise) at remembering Palestinian history has been violently attacked by the state. An example here is Eyal Sivan's documentary *Izkor: Slaves of Memory*, produced in France in 1990. This documentary was banned in Israel simply because it speaks about what Palestinians remember (the Nakba) and what the state wants all to forget (Hayward 2006: 492).[10] Israel has banned various other cultural productions critical of its aggression towards Palestinians, such as its massacre in Jenin. Mohammad Bakri's 2002 film 'Jenin, Jenin' was banned in Israel and the film-maker was charged with defaming the state, but found not guilty. The significance of Sivan's '*Izkor*', which in both Arabic and Hebrew means 'remember', lies in the very message of memory and remembrance of the Nakba and the history of Palestinian oppression and expulsion by Israel, a history which the Israeli state has been aggressively trying to suppress (Hayward 2006: 492). The attempt of the colonial state at erasing the colonized memory of history or devaluing it received special attention from Frantz Fanon, according to whom

> Colonialism is not satisfied merely with holding a people under its grip and emptying the native's head of all form and content. By a kind of perverted logic, it turns to the past of the oppressed people, and distorts, disfigures and destroys it.
>
> Fanon (1965: 168)

The position of the Israeli state on the Nakba is also shared in official Western quarters. As George Bishara once said: 'No ethical person would admonish Jews to forget the Holocaust ... yet in dialogues with Israelis, and some Americans, Palestinians are repeatedly admonished to forget the past, that looking back is not constructive,' and so on. 'Ironically,' he adds, 'Palestinians live the consequences of the past every day – whether as exiles from their homeland, or as members of an oppressed minority within Israel, or as subjects of a brutal and violent military occupation' (Bishara 2007).

Palestinian Culture: A Genre of Resistance

It is no exaggeration to suggest that the Palestinian genre of resistance literature, whether expressed in films, documentaries or theatre, were largely woven around the Nakba, its memory, meaning and symbolism. For example, within the hundreds of feature and documentary videos and films that contain the spirit of resistance culture, one finds a particular set of themes, all of which revolve around the questions of refugeeism and exile, of valuing the homeland, the symbolic meaning of the citrus orchards and the olive trees, and the centrality of the various material/ physical space Palestinians call homeland – the memorized material space of the Palestinians. This form of resistance culture occupies a special place in the Palestinian psyche, as most documentaries, for example, are based on oral history: interviews with women and men who either continue to fight against their dispossession or with those in exile and refugee camps whose knowledge of the homeland is based on their remembered experiences.

Of these, it is worth noting Sahera Dirbas's 2009 documentary *A Handful of Earth*, which is particularly relevant as it examines the role played by oral history in maintaining the bond between Palestinian refugees and the homes from which they were driven in 1948. The title of her documentary was taken from the handfuls of earth from their original villages that many still keep. In fact, all of Dirbas's documentaries explore the oral traditions that have spanned the generations, sustaining the links between exiled Palestinians living in Jordan, Syria, Israel and the West Bank and their shared homeland and histories. Another key documentary is Eyal Sivan's 'Jaffa: The Orange's Clockwork' (2009), a film based on a political essay excavating the entwined visual and political histories of that famous citrus fruit originating in Palestine and known worldwide as the 'Jaffa Orange'. Although Jaffa oranges along with most of Jaffa land has been confiscated and appropriated by the Zionist enterprise and the state of Israel, for Palestinians Jaffa oranges remain a powerful symbol of the loss and destruction of their homeland: a loss expressed in Kanafani's story *Ard al-Burtuqal al-Hazeen* (The Land of Sad Oranges) (Kanafani 1987). In this list of films, it is important to mention Kassem Hawal's 1982 'Return to Haifa', which is an adaptation of Ghassan Kanafani's famous novel of the same title. The title and of course content and message of this film emphasizes the strong bond between the Palestinians and their material culture. All the documentaries speak directly to all Palestinians under conditions of colonialism and occupation, and more specifically to the exiled and to the refugees. As Tawil-Souri has put it, in enduring repression, annihilation, control and silencing, 'the task of Palestinian culture has become the negotiation between the everyday and the extreme, between the continuation of normalcy and a battle against all eradications' (Tawil-Souri 2011: 473).

Caricature drawings or cartoons as a form of political resistance have also emerged, especially with the work of renowned critical cartoonist and cultural satirist Naji Al-Ali. 'I am a man who carries his tent on his back and my people are the poor' is the main theme throughout Al-Ali's work. Internationalist in his vision as he criticizes US imperialism, Israel, colonialism, all Arab reactionary and corrupt regimes and all other forms of human oppression, Al-Ali has made the Arab condition in general and the Palestinian ordeal in particular his primary cause. Al-Ali is most famous for the way he signs his cartoons, using the figure (*Handhala*): a caricature which features a Palestinian boy who is depicted wrapped in the *kafiyya* and whose hands are tied behind his back, with his back turned to the viewer. *Handhala* is a rendering of the cartoonist at the age of ten, an age at which Al-Ali decided to remain until such time as he could return to the homeland. *Handhala* the caricature represents the bitter life Al-Ali and most Palestinians endured in refugee camps.

Naji Al-Ali considers the role of caricature drawing to be a political tool used by the artist in critiquing oppression, subjugation and injustices everywhere. In her 1994 'Writers and Assassinations', Barbara Harlow writes that for Al-Ali, caricatures present life bare, spreading life on strings in the open air, on the street, capturing life wherever it is found and taking it to the surface for the world to see the way in which there is no opportunity to hide the gaps and flaws of life: 'Caricatures to al-Ali,' she adds 'preach hope, revolution, and the birth of a new person' (Harlow 1994: 167).

Al-Ali's resistance caricatures were used as a basis for the documentary titled *Naji al-Ali: An Artist with Vision* (Abid 2000). This documentary reflects his life and also documents his assassination in London in 1987. In other words, resistance of the status quo and the hope for a better future based on justice and human values remains at the core of all forms of resistance culture. This is most true in the case of resistance poetry, as will be seen in the following pages.

Palestinian Icon of Resistance Literature: Ghassan Kanafani

Loyalty and commitment to the cause, to the struggle for justice and against colonialism and occupation and for the independence of the homeland, constitute the main pillars in resistance literature. In the quote cited in Chapter 2, Edward Said is reiterating Kanafani's definition of committed intellectuals, of Palestinians with a cause as he calls them in several of his novels. It is to the work of the world-renowned and pioneering resistance intellectual, novelist and literary critic Ghassan Kanafani that we now turn.

Kanafani's significant contribution to world literature resides in his development of the philosophy of resistance literature, wherein he establishes a strong relationship between the voice and physical movement and between resistance as a concept and actual resistance on the ground. In his non-fiction work *Al-Adab al-Falastinin al-Muqawem tahtal-Ihtilal 1936–1968*, Kanafani argues that 'militant and literary forms of resistance complement each other: resistance constitutes "dissent" and is in adherence to one's roots and stances' (Kanafani 1977a: 23). Resistance for Kanafani originates from the will and commitment for liberation. Kanafani concedes that Israeli policies of silencing Palestinian intellectuals, along with its policy of political assassinations, has in fact enriched their literary productions and inspired them to become even more committed and aware of their social and political realities; hence he defines them as resisters (Kanafani 1977).

Kanafani's emphasis on the close relationship between literary resistance and practical resistance, including armed struggle, has been further elaborated on by Barbara Harlow. In her *Resistance Literature*, Harlow elaborates on the theoretical framework of resistance culture articulated by Kanafani and suggests that 'neither armed struggle alone nor cultural resistance by itself can provide the necessary resources for resistance … Armed struggle and resistance literature go hand in hand.' 'Kanafani,' she adds 'identifies poetry as a pioneering force in spreading the call for resistance, since it can easily be memorized and spread mouth to mouth without printing or publication' (Harlow 1987: 626).

In his literary work, Kanafani recognizes the strong relationship between the social, the economic and the political in the making of peoples' histories. For him, Palestinian living conditions furnish the grounds for their political stance and provide resistance intellectuals with the necessary material for their revolutionary voice. It is no surprise, therefore, that terms like *sumoud* (steadfastness), *manfa* (exile), *lujoua*` (refugeeism), *hisar* (siege) and *muqawama* (resistance) constitute a central theme throughout his literary work. The experience that these terms represent, experiences which Kanafani and the majority of the Palestinian people have lived through, represent the ground on which he bases his testimony, reflecting the public sentiment of Palestinians.

In his famous novella *Rijāl fīsh-Shams* (Men in the Sun), Kanafani (1980a) employs a class analysis to explore the trauma of life in exile. Three Palestinian protagonists from three different generations who were looking for an escape from their poverty and destitution decide to go to Kuwait in the hope of finding better life opportunities. These men had not known one another prior to this; they found themselves together through an intermediary who had promised to smuggle them into Kuwait. Employing metaphors and symbolism, Kanafani delves deeply into the hearts and minds of these men on the road, describing their hopes and dreams for a better future for themselves and their families. Although the term homeland itself was not used by Kanafani in the men's conversations, the spirit of home and the hope for return was always present.

The vehicle used by the smuggler to transport the three men was a large water tanker lorry used by him to carry water from Palestine to Kuwait. After spending several days in the burning desert and having reached the border, the driver leaves the lorry with the men inside and goes to settle his entry papers with the border guards. The time spent at the border with the three men in the empty, oven-like water tank brought an end to the dreams, hopes and aspirations of these men; upon his return to his vehicle, the driver found all three dead (Kanafani 1980a).

Kanafani was among the very few Palestinian intellectuals who were gender conscious and paid special attention to women's voice. Women characters were present in most of his novels. Still, his novel *Umm Saa'd* stands out as a true representation of his commitment to accentuating women's role and voice in the Palestinian history and struggle. *Umm Saa'd* is made up of nine short stories; each one is entitled according to a line or idiom spoken by Umm Saa'd. Kanafani dedicates these stories to Umm Saa'd, whom he describes as an actual woman he knew well and who was a member of his family. For Kanafani, Umm Saa'd was 'the people and the school' from which he drew his information and to whom he dedicated his life (Kanafani 1980c: 241). The one outstanding short story in this collection is the one titled 'Khaima a'n Khaima Tifriq' (one camp is not the same as another). Umm Saa'd explains the difference between the misery of the refugee camp in which she spent most of her life and raised her children, and the *fidai`* (freedom fighter) training camps where the Palestinian freedom fighters live as members of the armed struggle.

In this short story, Umm Saa'd comes to the Kanafani house to inform him that Saa'd, her son, has 'gone' to join the *fidai`yyeen* (freedom fighters). A long discussion ensues between the two, wherein she says that she is not upset about him leaving, but wants to visit him in his training camp and take care of him and the others there. After this discussion, Umm Saa'd becomes convinced that her son is mature and that what would please him would be to do what he wants: fight or partake in the armed struggle. At that point she looked at Kanafani and said:

> I tell you what, you go to his [her son's] commander-in-chief and ask the latter to not upset Saa'd. I know my son, he is a good boy; but if he wants something and cannot get it, he will become upset ... Please ask him [the son's commander-in chief] – to give my son what he wants ... If he wants to go to war, why not?
>
> Kanafani (1980c: 266)

Umm Saa'd represents the ordinary Palestinian victim of the Nakba, the refugee, but more importantly she is the strong woman who defies the camp's victimization and rebels against its social and political norms. She is the mother who understands the meaning of sacrifice for the return of the homeland.

Kanafani's last published novella, *A'aed ila-Haifa* (Returning to Haifa) (1980b) also had a direct political message, albeit one framed in a different historical and ideological context. The story tells of a refugee couple, Safiyya and her husband Said, who decide in 1967 – immediately after the Naksa – to return to Haifa and search for their infant son who they had left behind in the midst of the terror, confusion and panic during the Nakba of 1948. After a long search, they found their home in Haifa occupied by a Polish Jewish family, Miriam (a holocaust survivor), and another occupant who was the widow of Yifrat Kushen; both Miriam and Kushen's widow were refugees from Nazi-occupied Poland and arrived in Palestine in March 1948. They were given Safiyya and Said's house by the Jewish National Fund (JNF), which controlled most of the land and homes of Palestinian refugees. Safiyya and Said also discovered that their son had been adopted by Miriam and raised as a Jew. He had been given the Jewish name 'Dov' and had enlisted in the Israeli army. The couple were let in by

Miriam, who told them she knew who they were and had been waiting for their return!

At the beginning of Said's discussion with 'Dov' (his Arabic name was Khaldoun), 'Dov' rejected his biological parents, blaming them for abandoning him; but the end of the conversation remains incomplete, and so a large question mark, awaiting 'Dov's' decision to reconcile or not with his biological parents. The context for this story is not only the Nakba and the feelings of despair among Palestinians, many of whom after the Naksa (1967) had become refugees for the second or third time, it is also the context of new forms of struggle, including the armed struggle. The PLO, it should be noted, adopted armed struggle between 1967 and 1969 – the time Kanafani wrote his novel (Kanafani 1980b).

The plot in this novella lays in the discussion between the father Said and Dov the son – Safiyya, while central to the story, did not take part, as the discussion was in English. During the discussion, Dov – in his military garb – stood in the middle of the room and told Said: 'The human being, after all, is not about flesh and blood, but rather is a cause … and you are on the other side' (Kanafani 1980b: 400). Astonished and humiliated, Said found himself in defence of his very pride and existence as he realized that Dov was not interested in 'dialogue'. Talking to himself, Said began to ask: 'What is the nation? I am searching for the true Palestine. A Palestine that is larger than memory, larger than a son …' (1980b: 404). It is also at this point that Said realized that Palestine 'the cause' is only achievable through the armed struggle. Kanafani, who as a member of the Marxist-Leninist party the PFLP wrote the PFLP charter and so the organization's vision in the late 1960s, has successfully employed the notion of historical dialectics in this story. This was clear in his last words to Miriam, who asked him to not leave until they settled the question of 'their son'. On his way out, Said looked at Miriam and said:

There is nothing more to say. For you this might seem like bad luck, but history is not like that; when we came here we were against history, and now, I admit, we were also against history when we left Haifa, but all of this is temporary. You know something, my Lady? Every Palestinian will pay the price. I know many who paid with their children, and now I know I too paid with my son in a strange way … That was my first share, and this is difficult to explain.

Kanafani (1980b: 413)

A`aed ila-Haifa* (Returning to Haifa), which was staged as a play in various countries, including Israel/Palestine and the United States, was perhaps the most controversial of the novels written by Kanafani. Yet the controversy is rather one-sided. It was interpreted by Israeli intellectuals as a balanced story that told of two losses and two catastrophes. This is based on the first encounter of Said and Miriam. The story ends with Said expressing a strong commitment to the armed struggle, as he realizes the asymmetrical relationship between the two: the colonizer and the colonized. Kanafani's strong voice of resilience, resistance and his insistence on the 'right to return' in his work was not lost to the Israelis. On 8 July 1972, Kanafani was assassinated in Beirut through a bomb planted in his car; his niece was in the car with him, and she also was killed. Kanafani was just 36 years old. His assassination confirmed that Israel's enemy is any and all forms of resistance, even if those were expressed in words.[11]

Adab Al-Sujoun (Prison Literature)

Prison literature may very well be a unique feature of Palestinian culture, primarily because of the longevity of the Palestinian struggle and the brutal Israeli reaction to it and given the incarceration of hundreds of thousands of Palestinians throughout the years.[12] This form of literature was born among committed intellectuals who remained in the homeland and became citizens of the state of Israel. The context for the rise of prison literature, which is primarily expressed in poetry, goes back to the establishment of the state. The imprisonment of hundreds of thousands of Palestinians, especially but not exclusively since the occupation of the West Bank and Gaza Strip in 1967 just for being Palestinian, demanding the right to live as human beings and for being intent on keeping their identity alive, has undoubtedly been a major reason for the emergence of prison literature. As a sub-set of *adab al-muqawama*, *adab al-sujoun* was particularly strong among 1948 Palestinians, at least until 1967 – on account of their long resistance to the structure and policies of the Israeli state towards them, especially the ones aimed at their cultural genocide. While the term *shua`ra al-muqawama* (resistance poets) will be used here to refer to two authors of resistance, there are several other resistance poets whose contribution to resistance poetry and prison poetry has been invaluable, including Ibrahim Tuqan (mentioned earlier), his sister Fadwa Tuqan, Hanna Abu-Hanna and Samih Al-Qasem, among various others.

Prison poetry is largely written by authors who themselves have experienced incarceration, humiliation and torture in the Israeli prison system. Most such poetry expresses defiance of prison, and speaks of the rejection of prison and colonial control; as such, it constitutes revolutionary incitement. The political power of prison poetry, including its power to incite, are quite strong: the prisoner's poem, as Hanna Abu-Hanna wrote, can be more powerful than the prison itself:

> They are defeated, they couldn't imprison my song
> Instead, they fuelled the fire of my poem
> A flaring fire that cannot be shackled with chains
> Fire, turned into hell for the oppressors
> It is an honour for my poem to be able to disturb
> The ultimate enemy in his sleep
> Be proud of a poem
> Stronger than the prison which is surrounded
> With soldiers and barriers
> Forever, my son.
>
> In Kanafani (1977a: 79–80; author's translation)

As we saw earlier, Mahmoud Darwish, Tawfiq Zayyad and Samih Al-Qasem have been identified by Kanafani (1977) as *shua' ra al-muqawama*; these poets have spent time in Israeli prisons on account of their words and voices. Of these three, we will examine the poetry of Darwish and Zayyad only.

Resistance for Hope and Healing: Mahmoud Darwish

Israel's cultural genocide of the Palestinians, along with the inhumane treatment of political detainees, has understandably furnished the grounds for the emergence of this specific form of poetry. Resisting, as renowned poet Mahmoud Darwish asserts, is a means of healing. It is intended to assure 'oneself of the heart's health ... the health of your tenacious disease: the disease of hope' (Darwish 2004a: 181). In his *A State of Siege*, Mahmoud Darwish opens the poem with words stressing the meaning of hope in resistance:

Here, where the hills slope before the sunset and the chasm of time
near gardens whose shades have been cast aside we do what prisoners
do
we do what the jobless do
we sow hope.

Darwish (2004a: 184)

A crucial dimension of resistance literature in general and prison
literature more specifically is the commitment of the authors to
their people and their cause. It is also their determination to keep the
Palestinian cause alive and their resistance to colonialism on the agenda;
this is a characteristic feature of resistance culture, as its role is to function
as an agent for resistance and change. National anti-colonial resistance
intellectuals use their poetry and prose as a form of struggle against
colonialism and imperialism. These intellectuals, to put it differently, are
committed intellectuals: persons who know what it takes to speak truth to
power and are willing to say that which is before us, as Edward Said says
(Barsamian and Said 2002: 39).

Resistance poetry finds welcome reception in oral cultures such as that
of the Palestinians. Many poems, especially by Mahmoud Darwish, Samih
Al-Qasem and Tawfiq Zayyad, have been turned into popular songs, which
as we noted above are recited and sung. Moreover, resistance literature
in general and poetry more specifically have been included in the school
curriculum of most Palestinian students outside of Israel, especially
among refugees; this literature has also been integrated into the school
curriculum of the Palestinian Authority (PA) in the West Bank and the
Gaza Strip. For Palestinian citizens of Israel, where resistance culture,
especially poetry, emerged, the situation was and remains rather different.
Israel has always forbidden any mention of Palestinian identity in its
institutions, especially in its schools, and this literature has no place in the
Israeli school curriculum. For many years even drawing the Palestinian flag
was taboo in Israeli schools and was considered punishable.[13] During the
last Labour government (1997–2001), two Israeli ministers of education,
Yossi Sarid and Shlomit Aloni, who are considered on the left of Zionism,
attempted to introduce Mahmoud Darwish's poetry into government
schools, but to no avail; their efforts were annulled soon after Labour lost
and the Likud formed the government (Abdo 2011b: 153–154).

Israel's suppression of Palestinians, its repression and silencing of their
critical voice and resistance, has dialectically produced counter-resistance

forms expressed in resistance literature and visual arts. Thus, despite its violent reaction to Palestinian resistance, whether through imprisonment, exile or assassination (such as was the fate of Ghassan Kanafani and Naji Al-Ali), the Palestinian genre of resistance continued to thrive and affix its identity in the memory of the colonized people.

Shea`r al-Muqawama (Resistance Poetry)

Mahmoud Darwish, who in 1988 wrote the Palestine declaration of independence and died in 2008, is considered one of the most influential poets of the human condition; he was a world-renowned resistance poet, being known as Palestine's '*Shea'r al-Muqwama*' (Palestine's resistance poet), and is also known as a revolutionary poet. Darwish wrote extensively on issues of love, defiance, longing, hope, struggle, memory, identity and revolution. Born in the village of Al-Birweh, Akka (Acre) district, Darwish experienced the Nakba as a young boy, fleeing with his family to Lebanon. When they returned to Al-Birweh, their village, they found no homes or trees left standing; as was the case for hundreds of other villages, it had been turned into ruins and erased from the map of Palestine. They subsequently moved to Dair Al-Assad, another village in Northern Palestine.

Darwish's testimony and voice were seen as a threat by the Israeli state; he was constantly harassed, and he spent time in an Israeli prison. In 1971, he left Israel for Lebanon. Then, after Israel's invasion of Lebanon in 1982, he moved to Tunis, remaining there up until the late 1990s, at which time he returned to Palestine – to the Occupied Territories. However, he was prevented from reuniting with his family in 1948 Palestine. It is no wonder, with this history, memory and the experience of exile combined with Darwish's sharp intellectualism and literary talents, that he became the voice of struggle and resistance.

One of his famous poems, which turned into a very popular song is '*Ila Ummi*' (To My Mother). This poem was written in prison, after a visit by his mother, who brought him a '*rakwa*' (coffee pot) which was confiscated by the prison authority. The words were written on his cigarette pack (Ayyoub 2010):

I yearn for my mother's bread [...]
And I love my life,
For if I died

I would feel shame for my mother's tears
Take me, if I ever return,
As a veil for your lashes
And cover my bones with grass
Baptized in the purity of your heel
Tie me to you
With a lock of your hair [...]
Perhaps, I would then become a god [...]
If I touched the depths of your heart.

Darwish (1980: 160–62)

In a poem describing his treatment in prison, Darwish expresses how they:

Fettered his mouth with chains
tied his hands to the rock of the dead and said: You're a murderer
They took his food, his clothes and his banners,
And threw him into the well of the dead.
They said: You're a thief.
They threw him out of every port,
And took away his young beloved.
And then they said: You're a refugee.

Darwish (1980: 20–22)

Similar to Kanafani's concern with and hope for a just Palestinian future, as seen throughout his writings, Darwish's longing for a just future is also central to his literary work. He explores the complementary relationship between people's resistance and resistance literature through his poetry. An eloquent example of this relationship can be gleaned through his poem, *The Rose and the Dictionary*:

So be it
For me, it's essential
Essential for the poet to have a new toast
New songs.
***
I carry the key of legends, the relics of slaves
And pass through a vault of incense [...]
And I see history in the form of an old man
Playing backgammon and sucking in the stars.

So be it
For me it's essential to reject death
Even though my legends die
I am searching in the rubble for light, for new poetry
Oh, did I realize before today
That letters in the dictionary, my love, are stupid?
How do all these words live?
How do they increase? How grow up?
We still nourish them with memories' tears
With metaphors – and sugar!

So be it
For me, it's essential to reject the rose
That comes from a dictionary or a volume of poetry
Roses sprout from a peasant's arm, a worker's grip
Roses sprout on a warrior's wound,
On the forehead of a rock.

In DeGenaro (2011)

Popular resistance movements, as Darwish says, grow from the arms of the peasants ... the fists of the labourers, and the wounds of the warrior.

These 'peasants' and 'labourers', it should be noted, were also women, whose material culture and daily survival was based on a particular geography containing land, olive trees, fruits and other agricultural products. It is only natural, therefore, that when women (and men) tell their stories, their testimonies carry the weight of their (historical) materiality. A large number of documentaries based on oral history conducted with and among women who lived through the ordeal of the Nakba has been and continues to be produced around the memory which turns the lost material culture into live stories.

As with most resistance literature, Darwish's poetry and prose themes are about the land, the olive trees, Jaffa oranges, return, and resistance to injustice and hope, themes that we have seen as occupying the memories of most of the Nakba generation, especially women. In *Memory for Forgetfulness*, a prose poem written during the Israeli invasion of Lebanon in the form of a narrative in 1982, Darwish says:

I am not solely a citizen of Palestine, though I am proud of this affiliation and ready to sacrifice my life in defending the radiance of the Palestinian fact, but I also want to take up the history of my people and their struggle from an aesthetic angle that differs from the prevalent and repeatable meanings readily available from an unmediated political reading.

Darwish (1995: xxvii)

During the period of the 1960s through to the late 1980s, Darwish was heavily invested in recreating the Palestinian identity, affixing it to Palestine (both the real and the imagined). In one of his famous poems, *Identity Card*, written in 1964, Darwish speaks about the importance of Palestinian identity against a colonial state that has been and continues to deny such identity. In this poem he challenges Israeli's denial of Palestinian identity and the Israeli vision of Palestinians as a 'demogaphic threat', saying:

Write down
I am an Arab
and my I.D. number is 50,000
and my children are eight in number
and the ninth
arrives next summer
Does this bother you?

He goes on to talk about Palestinian roots in Palestine and expresses pride in his Arabic features:

and color of hair: jet black
and color of eyes: brown
distinguishing features: on my head a camel-hair headband
over a kaffiya
and my palm is solid as a rock
scratching whoever touches it.

Darwish ends this poem saying:

However
if I am hungry
I will eat the flesh of my usurper.
Beware ... beware ... of my hunger
And of my anger.

Wedde and Tuqan (1973: 24–25)

Although Darwish's primary cause was Palestine and the Palestinians, he has been recognized as a world-class poet on account of the complexity of his poetic and literary writings. As Carolyne Forche wrote, while Darwish 'is known the world over as the poet of Palestine ... he is indisputably among the greatest of our century's poets' (Darwish 2011: back cover). Iraqi poet and novelist Sinan Antoon, who translated several books by Darwish, points to the significance of Darwish's work as a Palestinian resistance poet who brought the Palestinian tragedy to a world level (Antoon 2007). Mahmoud Darwish's poetry about the human condition, exile and identity is truly international and global (Goodman 2008). An example is the poem he wrote in honour of the late Edward Said, where he emphasizes the compatibility of the two thinkers (Said and Darwish), saying: 'If the past is only an experience / make of the future a meaning and a vision.' This poem speaks to the dilemma of refugeeism and exile which many people including Palestinians experience. Quoting Said, Darwish says:

I am from there, I am from here
but I am neither there nor here
I have two names which meet and part ...
I have two languages, but I have long forgotten
which is the language of my dreams.

The poem also talks in general about identity as a constructed or 'self-invented' one, and that the real commitment is to the 'victim' who needs solidarity wherever one might be (Al-Ahram Weekly 2004). The expansionist nature of the Israeli settler society has created a major hardship for Palestinians in terms of 'border crossing', between for instance Palestinians from the West Back to Israel or to the Gaza Strip, but mostly for 1948 refugees who were prevented from returning to their homes. Borders and military checkpoints became a point of frustration and a reason for their further alienation from their lands and people. It is no surprise that borders became a prominent topic in Darwish's cultural production. In his famous 'Waqqafouni A`lehdood' (They Stopped Me at the Borders), which became very popular all over the Arab world, Darwish details the humiliation Palestinians go through on the border. He writes: 'They stopped me at the borders ... and asked for my ID card. I told them it's in Jaffa ... hidden by my grandmother [...] in Palestine.'

His response angered the Israelis who deny the existence of Palestine, let alone Jaffa which they occupied and turned into part of Israel. As a response, 'They divided me into two halves: One-half stayed at the borders ... and the other on the lap of my grandmother.' He continues by explaining how the Israelis want to bury his ID and erase it from the world. He ends his poem by threatening the Israelis that he will return to Palestine even through clouds which could carry bombs and rain 'on them' (author's translation).[14]

Halat Hisar (A State of Siege) remains among the most powerful resistance poems Darwish wrote. He wrote this poem as he and the rest of his people were under the 2002 Israeli siege of Ramallah: 'The martyr encircles me every time I live a new day / And questions me: Where were you?' He then goes to talk about resistance:

The siege will last in order to convince us we must choose an enslavement that does no harm, in fullest liberty!
Resisting which means assuring oneself of the heart's health,
The health of the testicles and of your tenacious disease:
The disease of hope.

Darwish (2004a: 177–249)

Darwish's critical and revolutionary spirit in this poem goes much beyond his criticism of Israeli colonialism and the military siege of the Palestinians. His popularity among many, especially Palestinians, is also because of his critical stance on the Palestinian national leadership, as he believes that after Israeli colonialism is over, the Palestinians will have many differences among themselves and will quarrel:

We are standing here. Sitting here. Always here. Eternal here. We have only one goal: to be
After that we differ on everything: on the shape of the national flag [...]
We also differ on the words of our new national anthem [...]
We also differ on women's responsibilities.

[About the latter he says]:

you will do good, my people, if you choose a woman to head the national security.

(Darwish 2004a: 216)

Still, Darwish's strongest critique of Israeli colonialism, written in 1988 during the First Intifada and which is seen as the poet's sharpest message, is titled, *O Those Who Pass through Fleeting Words*, where he says:

O those who pass between fleeting words [...]
Carry your names, and be gone [...]
Steal what you will from the blueness of the sea
and the sand of memory [...]
Understand [...]
That which you never will:
How a stone from our land builds the ceiling of our sky. [...]
As for us, we have to water the martyrs' flowers [...]
live as we will [...]
leave our country [...]
Everything, and leave the memories of memory.

Al-Jabiri (1991)

These lyrics have angered the Israeli establishment as well as many Israelis who consider themselves on the left. In 1987, Yitzhak Shamir, then Israel's Prime Minister, cited the poem in the Knesset as a sign of 'Palestinian hatred and their evil thinking of throwing the Jews into the sea.' Amos Keinan, Israeli author and critic of Israel's policies was particularly opposed to this poem and considered it as a call for war between the two peoples (Mahmoud 2010). Finally, Darwish's emphasis on the value of memory for Palestinians and the fear this memory generates among the Israelis is worth noting here. After all, the issue of memory, especially the Nakba memory, plays a crucial role in the Palestinian national resistance and among the women in our conversations. In his *We Have on This Earth What Makes Life Worth Living*, a repeated theme for most women in the conversations, Darwish writes:

On this land there is what's worth living [...]
the aroma of bread at dawn/a woman's point of view about men [...]
the beginning of love, [...]
mothers living on a flute's sigh and the invaders' fear of memories [...]
the hour of sunlight in prison [...]
the people's applause for those who face death with a smile [...]
mother of all beginnings and ends.

She was called Palestine. Her name later became
Palestine […]
We love life whenever we can.

Darwish (2007)[15]

Both the poems *We Have on This Earth What Makes Life Worth Living* and *O Those Who Pass Through Fleeting Words* speak to and express Palestinian women's determination to remain steadfast, to persevere, hope but also struggle and resist. Resistance through the word or through the pen, as Kanafani attests, is no less powerful a tool than resistance through sword or arms: both forms of resistance complement each other and express each other; they also anger the colonizer and occupier and leads it seek means to silence both.

Tawfiq Zayyad: The Voice of His People

As in the case of Mahmoud Darwish's resistance poetry, Tawfiq Zayyad's poetry also represents a powerful voice against Israeli colonialism and occupation, with an emphasis on Israel's treatment of Palestinian political detainees or the voices of resistance. Living in Nazareth all of his life, elected by the Nazarenes to be their mayor for two terms (the second of which he did not complete because of his sudden death), Zayyad's poetry became the voice of the immediate and the present. *Somoud* (steadfastness), rootedness and remaining in the homeland constituted major themes in Zayyad's poetry. As he wrote about Nazareth, Sakhneen, Kufur Qasem, Dair Yassin and many other Palestinian villages and cities which had witnessed traumatic events such as massacres and brutal treatment by the Israelis and so on, Zayyad's work became an important resource for Palestinian history and memory. In *Huna Baaqoun* (Here We Shall Remain, also translated as 'The Impossible'), Zayyad writes:

As if twenty impossibles we are
In Al-Lid, Ar-Ramleh and the Galilee
Here … on your chests, staying as a wall
Remaining we are
In your throats […]
And in your eyes […]

Hungry we get … naked … we challenge … Chant poems […]
Fill prisons with pride
Produce children … a revolting generation …
after generation.

Zayyad (1994d: 133–135)

Challenge and resistance in this poem were expressed in words like 'If thirsty we squeeze rocks and if hungry we eat soil'. He finishes the poem as follows:

Here we have a past
A present
And a future.

Zayyad (1994d: 133–135)

Zayyad's powerful words express the strong national sentiment which is the foundation of Palestinian culture including women's struggle and resistance. Like Darwish and other national resistance poets, Zayyad was jailed for his defiance and resistance; being a member of the Israeli Knesset (the Israeli parliament) and a member of the Israeli Communist Party did not provide him immunity from arrest and torture. Zayyad was incarcerated several times and for different periods; his family was harassed and his house was targeted and raided by the Israeli police during several cultural events, especially after the first and second commemorations of the Day of the Land in 1976 and 1977 (Masarwi 2009). In fact, there is a well-known saying about his sharpness in defying and challenging the Israeli establishment. At the time when he became a member of the Knesset, his Hebrew was not good, as he had never studied it in school. One of the Knesset members shouted, 'Where did you study Hebrew?' Zayyad's response was: 'In your prisons.' Zayyad's response to his oppressors and torturers was equally strong. In *Khalfal-qudban* (Behind Bars), Zayyad defied prison authority by telling them, 'The chain is weaker than my wrists.' He emphasizes the role of 'will-power' and the love of 'resistance and steadfastness', which characterize Palestinian resistance (Zayyad 1994b: 11, author's translation).

Zayyad's loyalty and love for his people and the homeland and the extent to which he went in sacrificing himself for his people was unwavering. In his *Ashuddo a'la-Ayadeekum* (I Press on Your Hands), he wrote:

I press on your hands
kiss the ground under your feet ...
I sacrifice myself
And give you as a gift
the light of my eyes
and the warmth of my heart.

Zayyad (1994b)

He then turns to his people affirming that his 'tragedy' is his share of
'their tragedies'. Zayyad finishes the poem by saying: 'I did not humiliate
myself in my homeland .../ I did not lower my shoulders / I stood facing
my oppressors / orphaned, naked, and barefoot' (Zayyad 1994b: 40–41,
author's translation).

The lyrics of this poem which was turned into a very popular song
among all Palestinians and many Arabs, was also sang by many of the
women in our conversations. During one of his periods of imprisonment,
when he was incarcerated for two years on account of his pen and voice,
Zayyad wrote several poems that were smuggled out of the prison. His
revolutionary voice of challenge and resistance to colonialism and
occupation was best expressed in his very powerful poem *Fal-Tasma'a
kulled-Dunia* (Let the Whole World Hear). This poem was among 39
poems censored and banned for many years in Israel, and almost all were
smuggled out of prison. As he himself writes, the poems were distributed
in the thousands in Nazareth. In his introduction to his book *Sujana'
al-Hurriya* (Prisoners of Freedom) *and Other Forbidden Poems*, Zayyad,
referring to the 39 poems in the book, said: 'These are forbidden poems
I could not publish before because of Israel's very sensitive democracy,
which cannot even tolerate singing, but remains our fate in our land; this
is why it had to wait several years to see the light' (Zayyad 1994a: 5). The
following is an excerpt from the poem, *Fal-Tasma'a kulled-Dunia* (Let the
Whole World Hear): We shall never submit to the power ... the phantom
[...] the canon / We shall starve / go naked / sliced into pieces / And we eat
soil / [...] But will never surrender.'

He continues his defiance by declaring that he shall write 'everywhere
in Palestine' that Palestine 'was occupied / It became free / And the
occupier, usurper ... was / It became a memory. (Zayyad 1994a: 13–14,
author's translation)

On 30 March 1976, Tawfiq Zayyad, while occupying his official posts as mayor of Nazareth and member of the Knesset, led the first mass demonstration for what is known as Land Day (celebrated by all Palestinians) in protest of Israel's policies of racism and land confiscation, and more specifically against the Judaization of the Galilee. On that day, six young men and women citizens of Israel were shot dead by Israeli soldiers who had entered villages and cities in their armoured vehicles. Since then, on 30 March of every year, the Land Day is celebrated with a mass protest by Palestinians both in historic Palestine as well as in the exilic refugee camps. The Land Day has become another marker in Palestinian culture of resistance and a further incentive for the Palestinian struggle.

The relatively long quotes in this chapter taken from Palestinian resistance poetry were selected to demonstrate the strong 'soul' of Palestinian culture, so to speak, a culture which embraces multiple forms of resistance, details the contradictions between the colonized and the colonizer, encompasses Palestine's history and keeps its memory alive. This resistance literature, and especially resistance poetry, represents a significant resource for Palestinian women political detainees. It has served and continues to serve as a major resource for their ideological commitment to their just cause, and a force of agitation to resist Israeli colonialism and occupation. Palestinian women (and men) take special pride in their national culture and the solace it provides. There is hardly a Palestinian household without at least one member who does not know the works of Mahmoud Darwish, Ghassan Kanafani, Tawfiq Zayyad or other great resistance authors. This is particularly true for political activists. Belief in their just cause reaffirmed by powerful words, voices and testimonies has undoubtedly encouraged and strengthened women's resilience and insistence in partaking in the arm struggle against the colonizer. The tremendous impact of Palestinian resistance literature, which accompanied the Palestinian struggle from the 1960s through to the 1980s, was particularly expressed by the women during our conversations. As our conversations will reveal in chapters 4 and 5, the women recognized their resistance culture as a major force in their struggle.

In fact, there was hardly a woman in our conversations who did not know by heart at least one of the poems chosen above; there were hardly any women who had not read Ghassan Kanafani's work or who were not aware of Naji Al-Ali's drawings. In fact, most of them quoted at least one – if not all – of the above resistance poets and novelists in their testimonies and stories, as the following chapter will show. The strength of Palestinian oral tradition, expressed, among other things, in poetry, songs and stories, has remained an undeniable fact in the life of Palestinian resistance to colonialism and occupation. Palestinian rich culture of resistance, along with the wealth of regional (Arab) and international literature of struggles and revolutions have undoubtedly served as the context and resource from which Palestinian women involved in the armed struggle have drawn.

4

Political Detainees and the Israeli Prison System

In February 2012, the UN General Secretary Ban Ki-moon made a visit to Gaza. At the Beit Hanoun (Erez) checkpoint, he was met by a large number of women and other family members of political detainees in Israeli prisons; they came to greet him and plead with him to intervene on behalf of their family members who were undergoing torture there. Ban Ki-moon refused to meet with them or listen to their pleas. Expressing their frustration, women (and men and children) showered his vehicle with their shoes. In protest against his decision, dignitaries, NGOs, and human rights' and women's organizations in Gaza refused to meet with him.[1]

The deafening silence on the part of this international body and its top official, a silence similar to that of the United States, Europe and various Arab countries, and its refusal to side with the victims of Israeli colonialism demonstrates the degree of international complicity with the violence of the Israeli state. It also, albeit indirectly, encourages and further strengthens Israel's flagrant disregard of international laws and human rights, and its consideration of itself as above the law.

Silence is manifested in different shades and forms. One shade, discussed in Chapter 3, relates to the reluctance or refusal to speak up against the atrocities of the state or of colonialism or imperialism and the injustices which accompany such regimes. This silence represents the voice of complicity and renders those who are 'silent' as allies of or participants in the atrocities – a tacit agreement with colonial injustices. Another form of silence, discussed in Chapter 1, namely, the silence of the victims of injustices, in our case, women political detainees who find it personally painful to reveal their experiences of imprisonment and torture. Both forms of silence do speak, although in different languages: the language of the oppressor and that of the oppressed. Here we are more interested in the second type of silence, the silence of the victim and the oppressed. In Chapter 1, several reasons for this type of silence were discussed, and all were related to the personal agony felt by women whose experiences in prison were too traumatic to reveal, and for them the best way of continuing to survive and cope was through forgetfulness and not remembering. Here I would like to add another important reason for this kind of silence, which the author herself has also experienced that is, the concern about being placed behind bars just for speaking out. This is something unique to the experience of Palestinian women and the context of the Israeli prison system, however, as in many cases of detention among the women subjects of this project, these women have been threatened by a given prison authority to not speak about their experiences of prison or 'else'. Moreover, in the Palestinian case, many political detainees, including some of the women in the case study, have been expelled from their homeland and alienated from their families, loved ones and their social environment. Aisha, who was arrested in 1969 and handed two life sentences plus ten years, along with various other women whom I interviewed, was in this category; she, like the others, returned to her homeland after many years in exile, through special arrangement such as, for example, prisoners exchange deals between the PLO and Israel. At the outset, I would like to mention that all women in our conversations are from the West Bank and occupied Jerusalem. While almost all were initially taken to the main interrogation centre, the Moscobiyya in Jerusalem, all were later transferred to Israeli prisons.[2]

As I have just said, I have shared in this type of silence; for about 25 years I was reluctant to talk or to write about my experience in an Israeli prison for all the reasons discussed here. If I forget, I kept telling myself, I would live a more productive life, with less agony and pain caused to myself and my family. To the degree the prison experience is traumatic, it also eats away at one's soul. It fosters forgetfulness and renders ex-detainees incapable of recalling certain prison experiences. Sonia's experience is perfectly apt here, for although she spoke extensively about her detention experience, she lamented the fact that she could not remember times or dates or various periods while in detention camp. During the focus group, as we were listening to Rawda relating her experience and recounting important dates, Sonia relayed: 'I wonder … [a pause,] did I divorce the prison from me? I do not remember even the date of my court hearing, dates for me are meaningless'. With a pause and a puzzled look on her face, she added: '[D]id I lose dates because the prison has left my memory or because it is deeply engraved in me?'

By 2007, when our first focus group discussion took place, a relatively long time (between 10–15 years) had passed since most of the women had been released from prisons. Still, we must remember that for some of them, these discussions represented the first public event for airing and sharing their experiences. More importantly, as noted in Chapter 1, these discussions were particularly significant as this was the first time that most of these women had had the chance to meet with old friends, friends they had met and bonded with during the period of detention both as older veterans already with many years of experience and as newcomers who found in the former the support, direction and protection they needed in their isolation.

Rawda, from Nablus, one of the veteran ex-political detainees who spent over eight years in prison (1977–85), expressed her feelings thus: 'This is a very important event for me as it positions me among friends I haven't seen since my release 12 years ago.' Like most Palestinians, Israeli military checkpoints between cities and villages as well as within them have obstructed people's movement and made it almost impossible to go from one place to another. Restricted mobility has led to a situation whereby women who had been imprisoned had difficulty keeping in touch with one another. Sonia, from Ramallah, shared Rawda's gratitude for being reunited with old friends she also had not seen over the many years since her release. Similarly with Kholoud, from Jerusalem, who said: 'Although I joined Aisha during her last days in prison, as she was preparing to leave, I never had a chance to meet with her [again] until today'.

Life Before Detention

Chapter 2 provided an account of Western neoliberal/imperialist feminist constructions of Palestinian women *munadelat* (freedom fighters). It argued that Palestinian *munadelat* have been painted in very dark colours through depictions as terrorists, as ill-educated, as a burden on their families, and as women who committed shameful acts, and further that their participation in the armed struggle – the so-called suicide bombings – was simply intended to cleanse the family name. The point which needs to be emphasized here is that not one of the imperialist feminists is familiar with Palestinian history and culture, or they intentionally ignore this history and culture of resistance to make their point. Hamas and Islamic Jihad, referred to in every piece in that literature, were supposedly a new phenomenon in the Palestinian culture of resistance. Hamas in particular, which was first supported by Israel as a counter-front to the secular PLO and especially Fatah (the latter having come to rule the Occupied Palestinian Territories [OPT]), became an arch enemy of the state of Israel – a story familiar to all who have followed US policies for the last two decades or so. Another example is the creation of al-Qaeda, which was heavily funded and armed by the United States to fight Soviet rule in Afghanistan: 'we created al-Qaeda', Hillary Clinton once observed (Chossudovsky 2013: 1). The USA, as current events in the Middle East show, still maintains a strong relationship with al-Qaeda and its offshoots, by supporting them in its war against Syria; the USA also supports various Islamist tendencies in Egypt, Tunisia and Libya (Ahmad 2009; Ali 2008).

There is no intention here to equate al-Qaeda with Hamas – quite the contrary; throughout the years Hamas, while traditional and socially conservative, have proved to be a strong force of resistance to Israel. Still, it is important to remember that Hamas was never and still is not a member of the secular PLO. It emerged during the First Intifada, in 1990, partly due the failure of Fatah to deliver as the national government in the OPT, and partly due to the total isolation of the Gaza Strip from the West Bank. This isolation has undoubtedly ruptured the cultural, economic and social cohesion among Palestinians as an entity. Although a traditional society that had moved from peasantry to urbanization, Palestinian cultural traditions, which emphasized strong and close family relations among other things, was still characteristic of this community at the time of the First Intifada. For the majority of Palestinians who were Muslims, their religion, while preserved and followed, was never an obstacle to their struggle and resistance. Also, religion was never an issue for the women fighters or the hundreds of thousands of women who took part in the First Intifada. Until the Second Intifada (2000), most women political detainees were secular whether belonging to the left parties (e.g. the Popular Front for the Liberation of Palestine – the PFLP, the Democratic Front for the Liberation of Palestine – DFLP or the Communist Party), or even to Fatah.

By the early 2000s, and due to the welfare services (social, health and education) it provided to the destitute masses of refugees in the Gaza Strip (over 80 per cent of Gazans live in refugee camps), Hamas was able to rise as a major political power in the Gaza Strip. Many Palestinians considered Hamas to be 'cleaner' than Fatah, less corrupt and more principled, a fact which resulted in the former's impressive victory in the elections of 2006. At the time it was reported that many secular Palestinians (both Christians and Muslims) had voted for Hamas for those reasons. In fact, Ali Abunimah makes this clear when he states that 'Hamas election was a vote for clarity' (Jeffery 2006; Abunimah 2006; Bahour 2006). This victory came despite the Second Intifada, which used armed struggle against Israeli colonial occupation and was heavily criticized and attacked not only by the West and Israel, but also by Palestinian feminist intellectuals (Johnson and Kuttab 2001: 23).[3]

My conversations with the women, all of whom were arrested on charges related to organization and armed struggle activities and who unanimously described themselves as *munadelat*, defy Western feminists' perceptions of Arab/Palestinian women as terrorists or villains. Such perceptions fail to appreciate why Palestinian women would chose resistance as a path in their lives, and how they managed and survived detention/prison. To begin with, almost all of the women in the conversations and in the individual interviews demonstrated strong personalities. While, as will be seen later in this chapter, they were highly active in the political sphere, their social consciousness and awareness of and sensitivity towards gender equality and struggle for equal relations with their male peers had preceded their political involvement. These women were very proud of themselves. They all spoke highly of their academic achievements, of their grades at school and of how much they were appreciated by their teachers. While some were helped by their open-minded families, others had had to fight for their rights. Even so, all cherished education, knowledge and self-empowerment. In other words, political consciousness for these women did not come incidentally, by accident or by force. The foundation for their willingness to join the resistance had already been present. It is not surprising, therefore, as will be clear throughout this chapter, that when they decided to join the PLO in one form or another, the decision was taken independently and not under external pressure from friends or family.

Without exception and regardless of their class and religious background, all of the women interviewed spoke highly of their relationship with their parents, with an emphasis by some on the close relationship that they had with their fathers and brothers. They also spoke proudly of their own agency and the respect they commanded at home and from their community. Aisha, who was sentenced to multiple life sentences, was released through the first prisoners exchange between the PLO and Israel in 1979.[4] She spent ten years and 14 days (1969–1979) in prison, and when released, was immediately deported to Libya; she then moved to Syria, then to Lebanon and finally decided to go to Jordan to be close to her hometown. She spent 14 years in exile and only returned to the homeland in 1994 after the Oslo deal. The following is Aisha's account of her life before detention:

> I lived with my family, which consisted of my parents, two sisters, and one brother. We were peasants living off our land. At the age of five my father passed away and my brother took very good care of us, especially me as I was the youngest and spoiled sibling. I was the first girl from my village [Deir Jrir – Ramallah district] to complete elementary school and the first girl to leave the village to Ramallah to continue my education and live there on my own. When I graduated from high school, I joined the Teachers' College in Ramallah as a maths and sciences teacher. My brother and I were close friends. We both would visit people's homes to convince them not to leave the homeland and stay [i.e. where they were]. Together with my brother and other friends, we began to organize resistance cells against the occupation.
>
> Aisha

As for the question of how her mother accepted the fact that her daughter was living alone and away from home, she responded:

> My mother was also *munadela*, in her own ways; our house was '*Beit munadeleen*' [a home for Palestinian freedom fighters]; we used to hide and protect *fidai`yyeen* [martyrs] from Jordan. However, social pressure put on my mother from various women in the village, who blamed her for leaving her daughter alone and without protection, made my mother uncomfortable. She used to say, 'Why should I, a widow, send my daughter to the city to continue her education while the *mukhtar* [village head] with all his power and financial well-being does not do the same for his daughter?' She began to put pressure on me. In grade nine, when I went home to visit, my mother kept me at home and refused to send me back to Ramallah. She kept me at home for 18 days, during which time I would sit in my room and cry with my books in front of me. After this period and as a result of the intervention of various members of the community and especially the principal of the village elementary school who insisted on my seriousness, good behaviour,

and most importantly the fact that I was the best student throughout elementary school my mother gave in and I was back in Ramallah. My other siblings never went to school; when my brother left for Brazil to work, he would send me letters to read to the family and money which I distributed with wisdom. I became the 'man' of the house.

Aisha

A relationship of trust and respect was also characteristic of the relationship between Ahlam and her father. Ahlam lived with her parents, eight brothers and two sisters. She came from a very poor family. Her father worked in a gas station and she was his right hand, helping him by cleaning car windows and receiving pennies at the end of the day. She was a good student and loved learning, but could not continue her education as she was arrested at the age of 15 while sitting for her final exams.[5]

During our conversation, Ahlam started crying. When I asked why, she responded:

I had a very close relationship with my father; he adored me and I respected him a lot. But the fact that I stole gas from his workplace to prepare explosives, which resulted in him being fired from his job and in his inability to take my detention and my being away from home, affected him. He died at the age of 51, just one year after my detention. I feel I killed him ... You know, my father used to raise birds. In the morning both of us would go and change their food. We put boiled eggs as food for the robins and other birds and put the cages back on the trees. I was my father's right hand. When my mother would tell him that she would send his lunch with one of their sons, he would respond: 'No, send it with Ahlam'. He welcomed my assistance in his job in Nablus. In other words, I was *hassan-sabi* [a tomboy]. On his deathbed, he asked my mother for pardon if he had ever bothered her and pleaded with her to take special care of me. After my release – six months after his death – I discovered that he had sold his wedding ring and with its price bought a piece of gold in the shape of a small golden tank and asked my brother in-law to buy a sheep and serve it at my release. I got the message ... It was not the usual verse from the Quran usually given as a gift, but a tank. He basically was telling me to continue my struggle against occupation. My friends in prison knew about his death but did not tell me, knowing how strong our relationship was.

Ahlam

The situation was not very different for Ameena, who was proud of the great support she received from her family and especially from her father, who was also a fighter in 1948. Ameena described her family support as very strong despite their refugee status and the oppression, hunger and cold they endured under Israeli occupation. Haleema 'F.',[6] who was detained at the age of 15 in 1979 and was released after six years in prison, also shared the same sentiments regarding her relationship with her family, especially her father, saying:

> I was the favourite kid of my family. I was the youngest of my three female siblings. After the death of my mother, people used to tell my father, why not marry again, you can have male children. He would respond: 'To me a girl is worth a million boys'. My relationship to my father was excellent; we were close friends. My father was leftist. He was detained under the British and his cousins were killed in 1948. I lived the era of Abdel Nasser [Egypt's Arab national socialist leader at the time], during the peak of the Arab national movement. At the age of eight, I used to join my father with a group of other men, listening to the Egyptian radio and the nationalist calls for resistance. I remember that in Jordan [where West Bank Palestinians lived between 1948 and 1967], we were not allowed to listen to Egyptian nationalist commentaries and the punishment for doing so was the prison. I remember how close I was to my father as we both were glued to the radio at low volume so no one could hear it.
>
> Haleema 'F.'[7]

Rawda had a slightly different story to tell. A Christian girl from Nablus, at the age of 15 she moved to study in Jerusalem and lived with her father and brother. He father treated her very well. He himself attended a Christian school and was a teacher there. As a child, she missed her mother a lot and was not happy to be far from her. She did not have a close relationship with her mother, as the latter was forced to marry her cousin (Rawda's father), and she did not love him, let alone want to marry him. But Rawda understood her mother's inner bitterness, which she did not show; her mother had to raise her three other children by herself, which added to her bitterness. The testimony of Rawda is fascinating at both the social and the political levels, as well as at the feminist level of analysis, as will be demonstrated here and in Chapter 5.

As for the political affiliation of the women, the majority belonged to the leftist parties and a few were members of Fatah and one belonged to Islamic Jihad; a small number were independent. For example, Aisha was a member of the PFLP before her detention and switched to the DFLP in prison. Ahlam was independent and did not belong to any political organization, as with Haleema 'F.' Ameena was a member of the PFLP, as was Haleema 'A.', while Munia, Itaf and Rawda belonged to Fatah. After Oslo, the United States, Israel and Europe considered the PLO to be the legal representative of the Palestinians, but did not recognize all of its political factions. Only those who accepted the Oslo Accord, namely Fatah, were legalized, while the other organizations were deemed illegal. During the early half of the 1990s, the DFLP was divided into two parts: FIDA, with leader Yasser Abed Rabbo accepting Oslo and joining the quasi-government; the other faction, led by Nayef Hawatmeh, retained the DFLP name, rejected the Oslo deal and remained in Lebanon. As for the PFLP, it adopted what it considered to be a pragmatic or practical policy: strict resistance and constant criticism of Oslo at the central location of the organization in Beirut. Committed members living in the occupied territories adopted what they consider political or pragmatic policies: critical of Oslo, yet participants in the Palestinian Authorities. Some, for example Khalida Ratrout-Jarrar (PFLP), was and still is a member of the Palestinian Legislative Council (PLC). As for Hamas, and despite its popularity, it remains outside of the PLO.

Why Do Palestinian Women Join the Armed Resistance?

All women in the conversations, whether interviewed individually or as part of the focus group, commonly shared two kinds of characteristics that led to their participation in the armed struggle: commitment to the national cause and love for the homeland. Women joined the resistance and struggle not because they wanted to live in heaven, but because they wanted to live on their land in freedom and without occupation and oppression. For them, the homeland was a worthwhile struggle; as Mahmoud Darwish once said: 'a` la haadhil-ard ... ma yasstaheqqul-haiat' [on this land there is something that makes life worth living] (Darwish 2007). Still, each participant expressed her response to this issue differently. Ameena, for example, had the following to say about why she joined the armed resistance:

What led me to take the path of armed resistance against Israeli colonialism and occupation is my belief that the Israeli enemy occupied my homeland and expelled us from it an event that caused us a lot of suffering. Also, I was totally convinced about the righteousness of the political and military position of the PFLP. What I did was intended to send a message to the world about the injustices afflicting my people, I participated in the resistance because I wanted the world to know that there is a homeland and an occupied people that have been suffering from killings, oppression, and humiliation carried out by the Israeli state. What I did is the result of my strong conviction that what was taken by force can only be reclaimed by force.

Ameena

It is worth noting that unlike most of the women in our conversations who were charged with attempting to deliver weapons, or attempting to and/or succeeding in placing explosives in Israeli military outposts, Ameena was involved in a plane hijacking in 1968. While all the limelight was focused on Leila Khaled as the first Palestinian 'terrorist' who hijacked two aeroplanes, Ameena, who also belonged to the PFLP, was in fact the first woman to take part in a plane hijacking – an act which requires some qualification because it involved civilian passengers. When asked about the fate of civilians in the plane, she responded: 'We intended no harm to the civilians', adding:

In prison, we were not defending ourselves as individuals, instead we were defending our cause and our people and our land, so the whole people will learn about our land which is occupied by the Israelis. We wanted the Western world who have been supporting the Zionist movement to hear about us. They [Western media and public] were asking who is this young dark-skin woman who would sacrifice herself, she could have been killed and why would she do such a thing ... these questions made the Swiss people ask about the reasons for doing such a thing.

Ameena

Similar words were in fact uttered by Leila Khaled who in one of her interviews said:

They hijacked our homeland, nobody asked. Nobody asked why the Israelis did so, why the Zionists did so. Why they were supported by the West and the Americans in particular. We had to ring that bell and we rang that bell and it was effective ... I regret absolutely nothing ... In addition to tell the world who we are ... we wanted to release our prisoners from Israeli jails.

Jajeh (2013)

Responding to the question of civilians involved in the plane(s), Khaled said: 'We had very strict instructions: do not hurt the passengers. Only defend yourself' (Viner 2001). No one was killed by Palestinian women hijackers. In the case of Leila Khaled's missions, her colleague was shot by Israeli commandos. Similarly in the case of Ameena's, where shooting was erupted by an Israeli secret agent who had been placed in the plane.

Leila Khaled's insistence on the rightfulness of her deeds was constantly echoed in her autobiography (written by George Hajjar 1973), in the movie made about her (Makboul 2006) and in *Leila Khaled: Icon of the Palestinian Liberation* (Irving 2012).

Ameena's testimony echoes the historical significance of the Arab national movement and the place of Palestine within it. Her statement, that 'what was taken by force can only be reclaimed by force' constituted a line taken from Gamal Abdel-Nasser, the former president of Egypt, for whom liberating Palestine was an important concern, one repeatedly reiterated by him in many of his public speeches. His influence and impact on women resisters will be discussed further in the following section.

Most women interviewed were heavily influenced by Palestinian political and resistance culture, especially by the poetry of Mahmoud Darwish and Tawfiq Zayyad. Ameena needed to 'let the world know about the just cause of liberating Palestine', echoing Tawfiq Zayyad's poem *Faltasma'a Kulled-Dunia Fultasma'a* in which he wrote: 'Let the whole world hear / We shall starve, go naked, be sliced into pieces / But we shall never submit' (Zayyad 1994a). It was the same for Itaf who, on her way to the court for her trial, was chanting: '*namoot waqifeen wa-la narka'a ma dam lana tiflun yarda'a* [We shall die standing tall, and will never surrender]'. This is again another verse in the same poem by Zayyad: 'as long as we have one suckling infant left, we shall never surrender ... we shall die with our heads up'. (Zayyad 1994a)[8]

Ghada voiced her rationale for partaking in the resistance in this way:

There are many things that human beings cannot tolerate and should not tolerate. Resistance is not just about carrying weapons, but also about their love of their people and the urge to help them. I always believed that the weapons of the fighter are her humanity. When a person decides to take up the path of resistance to defend her people, she does this because she refuses to see her people enduring all the suffering, killing, starvation, and oppression they undergo living under colonial occupation. In fact, neither I nor my family had to face direct oppression by Israeli colonialism, yet when I saw my people undergoing so much pain, I decided to become a *munadela* and rid my people from the cruelty, harassment, and repression they have been experiencing at the hands of Israelis.

Ghada

The right to defend Palestinian human rights and resist the inhumane Israeli treatment of the Palestinians was echoed by most participants. For Ghada, resisting colonialism and occupation is a human right that needs to be embraced by humanity. Ghada's humanist approach to the armed resistance and Ameena's need to send a message to the world about the Palestinian ordeal were two essential reasons for Aida Said's determination to join the armed resistance. As Aida put it:

I did not intend to kill; I did not want to kill. I was young and humanity meant a lot to me. My goal was not to kill. My goal and intention was to let the world, especially the Arab world, know about our ordeal and feel our oppression ... I wanted them to feel the meaning of living on rations and the charity of the UNRWA [United Nations Relief and Works Agency for Palestine Refugees in the Near East]. I wanted them to come and free us from Israeli occupation and oppression.

Aida[9]

Itaf shared a similar humanistic approach regarding her mission as a militant resister:

We never, ever deliberately targeted civilians in our resistance. I never in my life thought of killing, nor at the time did I develop a clear vision or idea about the implications of my acts. All I was concerned with was executing my mission ... All that occupied my thinking at the time was that Israel was occupying us, dehumanizing and killing us daily.

No country, Arab or Western, seemed to care about us. If we cannot harm the occupation, we should at least create chaos in their midst. *Ma behikk jildak ghair difrak* [if you do not help yourself, nobody else will help].

Itaf

Aisha's reasons for participating in the armed resistance against Israeli colonial occupation were heavily influenced by the memory of exile and repression afflicting her people since 1948 – which is to say, the memory of the Nakba. This is Aisha's voice on her joining the armed resistance:

At the age of four I became a witness to my people's suffering. I remember the day when my aunt's family fled from their home during the Deir Yassin massacre. I remember when the news of this massacre reached my mother, how terrified she was about the whereabouts of her sister. When she heard the news, she ran from Deir Jrir, our village, to the Mazra'a Sharqiyyah, her family's village – a very long distance – to enquire about her sister. I remember seeing a lot of women fleeing their homes while still in their sleepwear and barefooted. Everyone was crying; it was a total catastrophe. As a little child, I would sit with the people in my village listening to the horrendous stories they told about the Deir Yassin massacre. These stories were sealed in my memory, and my biggest dream since then was to see them returning back to their homes and lands. At the age of 17, I learnt about the Arab nationalist movement and its aim to liberate the Arab people. I became a member of the movement in 1963 and participated in the demonstrations against Israeli colonialism. In 1965 I became very active and took part in the resistance movement which at the time, in Jordan, was an underground undertaking. During the same time I was studying at the teachers' collage in Ramallah. At that time the PLO had an office in Jerusalem and I was elected as a member of its management team. The theory was that we did not know how to get to the Israelis; in 1967 they got to us and we needed to fight them. When the Arab national movement turned into the PFLP, I joined as member. Together with my comrades we were convinced that what was taken by force can only be reclaimed by force. We were trained in using weapons. Together with Lutfiyyeh and Sulafa [two other female political detainees in the same prison], we started organizing for civil disobedience.

Aisha

The inspiration of Abdel-Nasser's path and his commitment to free the Arab land from Zionist settler colonialism and occupation was glaringly clear in most interviews. Aisha, Ameena, Haleema 'F.' and Doris were clear on this issue, and so were Aida Said and Ittaf Alian, who expressed their feelings more publicly. Here is what Aida had to say about the influence of Abdel-Nasser on her decision to join the armed resistance: 'During that time Abdel-Nasser was my inspiration and the cause of my people; my community and my family were the legitimate grounds for all acts of resistance against Israeli military occupation'.

For Ittaf Alian, Abdel-Nasser was also her National Hero:

Abdel-Nasser was our only hope for liberation from the Zionists and for Arab unity. As a teenager I participated in one of the demonstrations held to mourn the death of Abdel-Nasser. The next day I went to school in mourning wearing black and found out that all my female classmates were wearing black too.

Alian (2011)

It might be noted here that the death of Gamal Abdel-Nasser became an-all Arab event. The author herself left school with some of her classmates and partook in a large demonstration held in Nazareth which mourned the death of this leader.

Women's Voices, Personal Experiences

In addition to the love for and loyalty and allegiance to the national homeland, our conversations revealed that a number of the women had personal experiences that were catalysts for their decision to participate in the armed struggle. Here is Ameena again:

I strongly believed, and still do, that *man la watan laho, la karamah lahu* [those who have no homeland have no pride]. Our enemy is colonial, a murderer and oppressor, and must be resisted. As a child, I lived in Gaza and witnessed the brutality and malice of this enemy as it administered all kinds of torture against my people. For, in addition to the massacres in Deir Yassin and at the Lidd's Mosque, where the refugees used to hide from the violence and vicious attacks of the Israelis, between 1956 and 1967 Israel continued to commit collective murders, targeting all

Palestinians. In 1956, I was eight years old when the occupation lifted the curfew in Gaza and we were allowed to go to school. While at school, the curfew was reinstated. We – all the children – started to run in the streets as gunfire was all around us. When we reached the qala'a [castle], we found that a group of Palestinians between the ages of 16 and 45 had gathered there and had been shot to death by the Israelis. We continued to walk towards our homes with our feet deeply covered in our people's blood. This is a very short account of the horrendous deeds of the Israeli colonizer.

Ameena

Haleema 'F.', who was a child[10] when she was arrested, provided the following painful experience which drove her to carry weapons and become a militant resistant.

I did not pursue this path accidentally. An experience I had one day while on my way to school was a determining factor in my decision. In May 1979, as I was walking to school, I saw a large crowd close to our house. Some were talking about the presence of the Israeli army, while others were mentioning Khader, my brother. I stated running towards the crowd. When I was close to the chaos, about 15 metres, I saw my brother with the army as they were announcing a curfew in the area. I kept running towards my brother and our house where the army was while the soldiers kept shouting at me, 'beitak, beitak [Ashkenazi Arabic for go home, go home]'. I understood and did not understand at the same time. 'What's wrong with my brother', I asked myself. I was conscious but unable to understand what was going on. I was only 15 years old at the time. I started running faster, and saw the army surrounding Jabal el-Tour, in an area called Ras el-Ayn, where our house was. I kept running towards my brother and the house, while the soldiers kept beating me and screaming 'Roukh min houn' [Ashkenazi Arabic for 'off from here'] … 'What do you mean, roukh min houn?' At about 12 metres away from the scene, I saw my brother with the skin of his hand torn and his blood flowing all over the place. His white shirt was not white, but dark red, soaked in blood. They took him to the detention camp and instead of sewing back his skin they amputated this hand. When I visited him there, I noticed his left arm was in a cast and it [i.e. his left hand] was much shorter than his other hand. He had already lost a lot of weight during the interrogation. Seeing my brother like this was a big shock to me. This experience taught me the meaning of occupation, the value of Palestine and the brutality of the occupier.

Haleema 'F.'[11]

Rawda's decision to become a *munadela* was an educated one:

When I decided to become *munadela* I was mature and fully responsible for my acts. In 1968, when I was a student in grade nine at the Ma'mouniyya school, we would organize demonstrations that would leave our school and go to the graves of the martyrs. I remember vividly how the soldiers used to beat us, especially during demonstrations. I still remember the blood flowing from my nose. I remember the first Land Day in 1976, the murder of the *shaheeda* [martyr] Leena al-Nabulsi[12] and *shaheeds*, Abdallal-Hawwas and the Kurdi. I was a teacher at the Schmidt's school in Jerusalem. Every day on my way from Jerusalem to Beit Lahem and back, I would be body searched three or four times each way by Israeli soldiers. I would be ordered to leave the bus and would undergo humiliating body searches conducted by the occupying forces. I am a human being and this is my homeland, how dare the soldiers humiliate me like this every single day?

I was only 15 when they arrested Aisha and tortured her. She was my female role model. Her struggle and resistance left a great impact on me. Aisha's house was in front of ours. I remember vividly when they bulldozed her family house; that did it for me. I could not keep silent, sit and watch any more. I had enough ... I felt I must do something. I started to be active and began volunteering in Jerusalem, collecting money and sending it to the PLO for three years, and then I decided to join the armed struggle.

Rawda[13]

For Ghada, the decision to join the armed resistance was mediated through her father's experience. Here how she related such experience:

In 1967, I was five years old, but still remember how they pushed all of us into one room as they [i.e. soldiers] started to search the house. My father was hiding for almost a week. Before going into hiding he went to his office; he was working at the Jordanian Ministry of the Interior and burnt all important information. The whole neighbourhood, including my father's office, was surrounded by tanks. We were sure my father was killed. My mother was crying and I was lying on her lap asking her constantly if my father had come back home. My father climbed the mountain and hid in a house. We had no phones at the time. Four days later, someone came to the house and told us that my father was still alive and hiding in the mountain. But throughout this week, we were acting as if he had been killed. The old town [Nablus] where we lived was surrounded by tanks; gunshots were heard all over the place; it was a terrifying scene that I shall never forget!

Ghada

The women had and continued to have agency, will-power and the determination to effect changes in their own and their people's lives. The women in the conversations were well-versed in Palestinian resistance culture and exposed themselves to a large body of the world's cultures of resistance. Except for the very young ones who were arrested as children and taken from school and who were not able to continue their higher education after prison – such as Ahlam, Itaf, and Haleema 'F.', for example – the rest, who made up the majority of the participants in the conversations, had completed their higher education; some were still in college and university, as was the case with, for example, Salwa, Sonia, Aisha, Doris, Ameena and Kholoud.

The national cause and the consequent military struggle and resistance to Israeli colonialism and occupation, lay at the heart of the detention of all the women in our conversation, both those with whom I conducted face-to-face interviews as well as others who participated in the focus group. During our focus group, the question emerged of women who after the Second Intifada were detained for reasons other than national resistance. Munia observed that she met two such women, who knifed Israeli soldiers for social reasons, but warned that this was not representative of the women's armed struggle at the time and that it was wrong to use them as a pretext to distort women's struggle. The fact that both women mentioned were from Jerusalem explains the sort of social breakdown which was developing within the Palestinian society, especially in Jerusalem which suffered high rates of poverty, family breakdowns, absence of social services and alienation from the rest of the Palestinians. Munia's observation supports the claim about the intended distortion of Palestinian women's struggle adopted by imperialist (Israeli and Western) feminists as discussed in the earlier chapters.

From Arrest to Interrogation to Detention

> *There are moments which pass like a lifetime.*
>
> Mostaghanmi (1993)

The moment referred to by Mostaghanmi in the epigraph to this section refers to the actual arrest. As most of the conversations revealed, the timing of an arrest was not accidental. Most arrests of women (and men) suspected of being, or considered to be, a 'security risk' would take place after midnight.[14] This timing is chosen by the authorities because it ensures that the 'suspect' was at home. It is also adopted by the police or the military in order to minimize the likelihood of neighbours' intervention. Most importantly, however, raiding homes during midnight is intended to serve as yet another method of terrorizing the individual and her family. Most night raids it should be noted end up with arrests. In most cases of arrests, a female soldier joins the male soldiers in the night raid. While the male soldiers begin to search the house for 'illegal' material or any 'evidence' that might help in preparing their allegations or in fabricating the case, the female soldier keeps a close eye on the woman suspect as the latter gets ready to leave the house. The search itself turns into an act of terror for the whole family as rooms are ransacked. In my discussions with the women, there was hardly any case mentioned in which the search turned up arms or any military equipment. In my personal experience, the 'evidence' taken from my room – which I shared with my sisters – consisted of books of poetry and others on Palestinian political culture. Although the period of time it takes for an arrest is actually short, for the family the trauma of the event makes it seem like a long time.

Haleema 'A.' expressed her experience of being arrested in a night raid as follows:

> I had just gone to bed and fallen asleep when I heard heavy banging on the door and on the rooftop. I did not think of being arrested at the time. I thought there were robbers around the house. Having turned on the lights and from the peephole in the door, I noticed an army jeep pointing a large searchlight directed at the door. They said: 'Army, army, open the door!' One of the soldiers said in Arabic: 'Is it you, bitch?' I responded, 'Is it you, son of a bitch?' I was still in my short sleeping gown; it was summer time. I asked him to wait till I changed ... All of a sudden I saw a huge number of soldiers, about thirty to forty of them

along with one female soldier, who forced their entry into the house. They started searching every corner of the house. My mother was still sleeping. After turning the house upside down, they stood in front of my mother's room. The Arabic-speaking soldier said in a loud voice: 'Go put your clothes on, you are coming with us', and turned to my mother and said, 'Do not worry, *hajja*' [honorific used for older women], my mother was aware of *qissti* [my story – political involvement] 'we will take her for a couple of hours and she will be back soon'. I hugged my mother and kissed her. Leaving my mother alone was the most difficult thing for me. I am the only one she had. When I stepped outside, I saw the whole street surrounded by the army with tanks and by intelligence personnel. I turned to them and said, 'Allahu Akbar [God is Great]; if I intended to destroy the whole country you would not have brought all this military force' (i.e. the display of force was out of proportion to the situation). I was shocked. They asked me to 'Shut up', cuffed my hands behind my back, tied a black blindfold around my head, and took me immediately to the Ramalla compound and then to the Moscobiyya[15] in Jerusalem. Only then did they remove my handcuffs and removed the blindfold.

Haleema 'A.'

Aisha's experience was doubly painful as her house was raided twice: first, when her house was raided at midnight on the night preceding the arrest, and second during the actual arrest on the next day. Her testimony concerning this moment was most chilling, therefore my decision to present it here in full:

At 1am I heard heavy banging on the door, with army searchlights directed at my house. My thoughts started going everywhere: did they see us last night as we were cleaning the weapons? Was someone watching us? Who could that be? I then thought this was my fate and that I should meet it bravely and faithfully. Everyone in the house woke up terrified at the banging on the door. My mother – who used to sleep in the room close to the main door to protect me, came close to me and said: 'Wake up, *qarouta* [one orphaned of both parents], these are Jews'. As she was walking towards the door, she looked back at me and ordered me to stay in bed. Nijmeh, my sister-in-law, came close and whispered to me to quickly give her anything suspicious so that she could hide it.

After opening the peephole in the front door, I shouted in a daring voice mixed with fear: 'Who are you and what do you want? There are no men here; we are only *hareem* [women] and children.'

The banging stopped and one of them said, 'Do not worry, *hajja*; we just want to ask you a question.'

I immediately responded: 'Why not ask from your place?'

Soon after, one of the soldiers kicked the door with his boots. I felt the door was about to break, and he [the soldier] said: '*Iftach* [Ashkenazi idiom for the Arabic term "open"] or we will kick in the door.'

As soon as I opened the door, a large number of soldiers barged in and shone their guns' laser sights into every corner of the house. With their fingers on their triggers, they surrounded the house. My mother, sister-in-law and I were frozen in place, with my mother's eyes moving between me and the soldiers!

After the terror and havoc they created in the house, their commander asked for my name and the name of my sister-in-law, but not my mother's name. Then he looked back and asked, 'Who is Aida?' My tension eased a bit and I responded: 'We have no Aida in this house.' He then asked to see my ID, saying: 'Do you know Rasmiyya?' I answered, 'No'. 'Are you active in Ina'ash al-Usra [a charitable organization based in Ramallah]?' I said 'No'. He apologized for the 'inconvenience' and ordered his troops to leave.

My mother began to pray, asking God to help her against the oppressors, as she always called them, and then she showered me with all kinds of questions. I wanted to comfort her; I denied everything and pretended to be very sleepy so as to escape her anger. At that moment many thoughts came to my mind: How did this happen? Was there an informer who told about me? What should I do? Should I hide or choose confrontation? If I fled or went underground, where would I go? How could I live my life? How would I ever confront my fear? Would I have to hide in Jordan as my brother and friend did? But when my brother hid from the Israelis for three months, he faced a harsher life than he would have had in prison – fear, always suspecting that he was being followed, the danger of the army destroying the house he was hiding in, in retaliation. My sister, whose husband is detained, had her house demolished after hiding one *fidai`* [martyr]. I decided not to hide … Many thoughts of steadfastness, confrontation and resistance came to my mind, and I decided to confront and resist: a beating which does not kill you can only empower you!

The next day was Al-Adha Eid; my mother was walking in with the hot bread she was carrying from the *taboon* [stone oven placed outside the house]. I could not face her. Then she started asking me about all the names the soldiers had asked about the previous night ... I denied any knowledge of them.

At eight in the morning a woman came to me and told me about the arrest of Rasmiyya and asked that I take care, and left. As I was having my tea at the neighbour's house, my cousin, terrified, barged in, saying that the army with soldiers and tanks were surrounding Omar's house (it was 100 metres from ours) ... 'Do not go home!'

I decided to go home. On the way, a male stranger approached me holding a photograph and asked if it was of me. I responded positively. He then said: 'You see, we caught you easily. You are a suspect and should come with us.' I kept walking to the house, feeling like a hero. From the bottom of the stairs of my house, I heard my mother saying: 'God, destroy their state and turn fate against it as it destroyed our houses and turned them upside down. My God, I am *waliyya* [a helpless woman] and from a simple family. Do not disappoint me.'

I arrived home to find soldiers throughout the house with their fingers on the trigger, watching my every movement. Other soldiers entered my room, emptied my drawers and threw my clothing all over the floor. As soon as my mother saw me, she said: 'What brought you here, *qarouta*?' I felt like laughing at my mother's words, but the seriousness of the situation restrained me. Their commander gave me a paper to sign. I refused, saying, 'I do not read Hebrew!' Then he said, 'We are taking you with us for some questions.' I started picking through my clothes, looking for my pants. One soldier screamed at me and said, pointing to the only female soldier with them, 'She will take care of your pants!' The woman soldier entered the bathroom with me to watch me put on my clothes while they refused my sister entry to bring me the rest of the clothes. I was ordered to walk with them. My mother was furious when one soldier looked at her and told her, 'Do not worry, *hajja*; a couple of questions, and your daughter will be back with you.'

Donned in her white headdress, my mother said: 'Take me with her.' I asked her to not be afraid and said that I would be back soon. She insisted: 'No! I want to come with you.' One soldier came close to her and wanted to separate her from me. She pushed him away and said: 'I will not allow my daughter to go with you alone.' A large number of male soldiers surrounded me, rushing to their armoured vehicles. My mother went crazy; she pulled herself away from the soldiers holding her, saying: 'I will not allow her to go with you alone.' To me she looked like a lioness defending her baby. I was sandwiched into one of the vehicles with soldiers surrounding me and their fingers tight on the trigger. I noticed my sister-in-law restraining my mother and taking her back home. She pulled herself away, going around the place, with her hands up to the sky, crying: 'Oh God, bring horror to their daughters and sons the way they do to us. Listen to me, God. This is the state of darkness. Where are you God? Are you watching?' The scene of my mother haunted me during my ride to detention.

Aisha

Aida and Itaf also went through similar experiences during their arrests, with tanks, armoured vehicles, and many soldiers and searchlights directed at their houses. For other detainees, having to leave their small children alone, especially their babies, was their utmost worry at the time of arrest. This was the case for Alian, who was separated from her 18-month-old daughter Aisha, despite her repeated pleas to take her with her to prison. She held a six-day hunger strike demanding that they bring her daughter to her. With the involvement of the Red Cross, her daughter was brought to her, but when the child turned two years old, they took her away and sent her to live with Alian's mother-in-law. (Alian 2011: 186)

The 'suspect' in most cases leaves her home with some immediate things on her mind: on the one hand, the thought of her terrified family, the crying mother and, in many cases, the idea of leaving young siblings behind; and on the other, she is faced with the question of how to confront an unknown future. These thoughts, especially the image of the family during the raid, were certainly the ones that most hounded me during my ride to the detention camp. I still remember my mother's and sister's horrified faces, my little niece and baby nephew crying, while my father was pleading with the security police to take him instead of me, or at least to take him with me, but to no avail. Theoretically, a search warrant or an arrest warrant are legal requirements in such situations, but in the case of the OPT, which is under military rule, this law is often ignored.

Transit to the detention prison, which usually occurs in an armoured vehicle with the detainee either handcuffed or positioned between two male military police officers, is the beginning of the mysterious path awaiting her. For Palestinians from the 1967 Occupied Territories, especially the West Bank which is the source of all our examples, the first place she 'visits' is often the Moscobiyya in Jerusalem for the interrogation, or at least part of the interrogation; she is then moved to a prison in Israel. Although the Moscobiyya itself was often referred to by Palestinian prisoners as a prison or detention camp, in fact it was primarily used for interrogation. Transferring political prisoners from an occupied territory to the territory of the occupier represents a flagrant violation of international humanitarian law and the Geneva Convention (Sfard 2011: 192). Political prisoners who are citizens of the state of Israel are taken directly to a prison. The identity and location of their detention camp or prison is never revealed to her beforehand. Regardless of how short or long the distance from home to the first detention camp proper, the woman detainee – although physically with other people – is mentally and psychologically in a different world, thinking of ways she will act and how she will respond to and/or resist her interrogators. Upon arrival at the destination, each detainee is thrown into an isolation cell until interrogation begins.

Detention, including 'administrative detention', is divided into two phases. The first phase is the phase of interrogation, which could last from ten days up to three months in duration, and sometimes much longer, such was the experience of Munia, who spent nine months in the Moscobiyya. The second phase is that of the actual incarceration, which begins with the sentence passed by the military court order. These are two very different phases. The first, interrogation phase, as will become clear in the following, is believed to be the harshest experience a Palestinian woman goes through perhaps in her entire life. But it is also the phase in which women political detainees gather and use all their powers, agency and resiliency to confront and resist such treatment. The second phase, of detention, while also characterized by bitter and harsh treatment on the part of the prison authorities, is utilized by the detainees for starting their new life: one of struggle and resistance (B`Tselem 2013).[16]

The women with whom I had conversations were handed sentences ranging from three years to multiple life. In most cases, the length of time spent in Israeli detention camps was arbitrary. The story of Iman, who became religious while in detention, is particularly significant here. Iman was arrested and charged with weapons possession, but in the absence of any proof to that effect, she was sentenced to two years in prison. But that was not the end of it. Here is her story:

While in the cell, one prison guard assaulted me, she hit me ... I responded by hitting her back. As you know the prison guard has right to beat detainees, but the detainee has no right to respond or retaliate. For this episode, I was given an additional sentence of three-and-half years. All together, my sentence became six years.

Then, on our way to the military court my friend and I were both handcuffed. It was winter and we were asked to wait outside the courtroom in the cold. We were very cold. So we started stomping our feet, partly to warm up and partly out of anxiety. The female soldier who accompanied us demanded that we keep silent. When we refused and kept making noise, she started insulting us, saying, 'This is not your country. You have 22 Arab countries, why don't you go and live there,' and she started beating us. I jumped on her, with my hands cuffed, beat her face and pulled her hair. As a result, my friend and I were charged with attempted murder. I was given another ten years in prison. Altogether, I was sentenced to fifteen-and-a-half years in prison. I spent ten years in prison and was released in an exchange deal in 1997.

Iman

Walid Fahoum, the Palestinian lawyer from Nazareth who represented many women political detainees, among them Iman, agreed with her observation about military prisons. During an interview I had with him, he said: 'The prison authority and guards are always right, while the detainee is always wrong ... They lie!' (March 2007). The 'lie' in Fahoum's statement was in reference to the soldiers' claim about how the fight began.

Interrogation: Where it Hurts Most

> There are grey mornings that have no relation to the fall.
>
> Mostaghanmi (1993)

Upon their arrival at the first detention camp or prison, female detainees (like their male counterparts) were thrown into an isolation cell to await their interrogation, which invariably took place in the early hours of the morning. The *zinzana* (isolation cell), where the detainee was held throughout the interrogation period, was invariably described as filthy, tiny, malodorous, infested with mice, cockroaches and other insects, dark with no windows, and lacking beds, with only filthy torn mattresses lying on the ground. Salwa, for example, who was interrogated for 45 days in a cell at the Moscobiyya prison, described her cell as 'one metre long and half-a-metre wide. I went through a horrifying experience, but one which proved a learning experience for me. During the 45 days of interrogation, I was in this dungeon, 11 stories underground – no light, you don't know if it was day or night.'

Neither Haleema 'A.' nor Salwa nor Haleema 'F.' were able to sleep during the period of interrogation. Both said they would sit and try to close their eyes in the hopes of getting a little bit of rest before the second bout of interrogation.[17]

Describing the cell she was placed in for over a month during interrogation, Haleema 'F.' said:

Oh, these cells are unbelievable. My cell was very tiny … No more than one metre by one metre, no beds or mattresses, but a small ripped and reeking blanket was placed on the floor. In the corners of the cell there were the remains of food that rotted and was full of worms, and a small Arabic-style bathroom [basically a hole in the floor], which was disgustingly filthy with big blue ants crawling all over, a plastic cup which was black from dirt, and a rusty pipe dripping water. I used to drink from this rusty pipe, despite my sensitivity and neatness. This was one form of psychological terror which I and other detainees were exposed to.

Haleema 'F.'

Not all isolation cells had toilets or running water. In the case of this author, a lack of running water in the cell and the filth of the 'public shower', which was open and exposed to all who passed by, made me refuse to have a shower for 13 days until the time when I was released. In my cell, instead of a bathroom or even 'a hole in the ground', to use Haleema 'F.''s words, there was a bucket for urination, which was full at my arrival and which stunk up the entire cell. Unable to enter the room because of the stench, I requested the removal of the bucket from the room. I was locked in for several hours until one prison guard came and emptied the bucket.

Haleema 'F''s description of the prison cell was not unique to the Israeli detention camps or prisons. Prison isolation cells seem to be similar throughout the world. In his *Tilka al-Atmah al-Bahira* (The Brilliant Darkness), Tahir Ben Jalloun (2001) described the unbearable filth of the

Moroccan prisons in which political activists were held: they were filled with cockroaches, mice, rats and snakes that the prison authorities would bring at night into the cells, leading to the death of one inmate during his detention (Ben Jalloun 2001). Munia would recognize this method very well, as she said:

> The mice and cockroaches they place in the rooms were terrifying. After a while you start to communicate with them and make them into friends. We had one cockroach in the room with his antennae just peeping out of the toilet pipe. After two weeks, I noticed the cockroach's antennae had disappeared. I ran to the other girls in the room and told them: 'Guess what, the cockroach is walking!'
>
> Munia

She resumed:

> Have you ever seen large mice walking between the arches of the ceiling? I swear to God, their mice were, like their rats well trained and highly advanced, they could walk on the arched ceiling.
>
> Munia[18]

Isolation, solitary confinement, humiliation and ill treatment of female inmates were not unique to the Palestinian case. Malika Oufkir's narration of her experience in the Moroccan prison demonstrated similar methods of torture (Oufkir and Fitoussi 2001). Equally important in terms of the torture methods used against political prisoners, which also characterized the Palestinian case, was the use of sexuality and women's bodies as forms of torture oriented specifically against women as will be discussed further in this chapter. The rationale in most such methods of torture, it should be noted, had been and continues to be a means to obtain information, to break down the prisoner, to destroy a victim's sense of self-esteem and to intimidate those close to her or to him. The Israeli methods of torture have been and continue to be aimed at 'punishing the suspect, as well as acquiring information about Palestinian political and military organization, obtaining a confession as primary evidence against the accused, and warning and frightening others from further political activity' (Punamaki 1988: 83). This rationale was corroborated by almost all the women during our conversations.

Physical Torture

Not unlike their male comrades, Palestinian women political detainees confronted all types of physical torture. These included beatings, black hooding and manacling, forcing detainees to stand many hours at a time over several days, exposing naked women to cold water and depriving them of food, sleep and access to medical facilities, for the latter especially in the case of menstruating women. All women political detainees were beaten in prison; the difference in women's experiences was one of quality (e.g. how, where and with what means) and quantity (magnitude, frequency and severity of the beatings).

For example, Ahlam was 15 at the time of her arrest. Her school was raided and she was taken from the school grounds. Ahlam was repeatedly beaten and her nose broken. She relayed the following:

> One day four female soldiers barged into our prison room, which included political detainees as well as criminals. They held Rawda and started beating her hard. I could not take their cruelty. I climbed on top of the door and held one of the soldiers. After I did that, they stopped beating Rawda. They removed all the women from the cell, closed the door tight and started beating me. One prison guard punched me on the face several times until the blood was pouring from my nose. Only then, they stopped beating me and took me to the prison hospital and brought me back to the cell after a couple of hours.
>
> During interrogation, he [i.e. her interrogator, Abu-Ali] kept calling me names, and I kept throwing ones back at him. He beat me on the face with his huge fist. I grabbed a chair and threw it at him. He started hitting me with his fists and boots and shouting *sharmouta* [whore], and I kept responding: 'I am a Palestinian *munadela*.' He kept telling me: 'I want to show you, *munadela* – you are not *munadela*, you are *sharmouta*.' He grabbed my hair, started pulling it and pushing my head onto the wall.
>
> When he got tired of beating me, he brought in six other male soldiers and all of them were taking turns in beating me with their fists and boots, tossing me from one to another like a ball. They were trying to force me to admit I was a militant in prison and to tell them about who organized me [i.e. introduced me into an organization]. At the time, I was not organized nor had any connection to any organization. I did not give them what they wanted.

> Ahlam

In her 'Experiences of Torture, Means of Coping, and Level of Symptoms among Palestinian Political Prisoners' (1988), Raija-Leena Punamaki refers to the pressing of lit cigarettes onto detainees' bodies as one technique of torture used by the Israelis against Palestinian prisoners. This means of torture appears to have been practised more against male detainees. One horrifying scene this author witnessed while in detention occurred when they took me to the cell of one young political detainee as a means to pressure me to admit things which I knew nothing about. When I arrived at the cell, I saw three prison guards surrounding the man as he was on his knees. One guard pushed five lit burning cigarettes into the mouth of the detainee while the latter was on his knees with his hands handcuffed behind his back, and another guard pushed the detainee's head down. They (and I) waited for about five minutes as the smoke of the cigarettes penetrated the detainee's eyes, ears and throat until he coughed and the cigarette butts were dropped from his mouth. Then they asked him: 'What is your name?' He did not answer at first; another guard kicked him in the back and asked the same question loudly: 'What is your name?' The detainee muttered something in a low voice. 'Speak louder', the guard demanded. 'Poodle', he said. Having me witness this was a tactic to scare me into compliance the guards were showing what could happen to me if I did not co-operate.

Having female detainees watch the torture of male detainees in order to frighten them and force them to collaborate was not unusual in the experience of many. Israeli prisons' techniques of torturing Palestinian political prisoners included '*Shabeh*' and '*kees*' among others. The term *mashbooh*, or *mashbooheen* for the plural refers to detainees who are bound to either a chair or the wall, with their hands tied behind their backs or on top of their heads. The actual act is known as *shabeh*. The term *kees*, used by various interviewees refers to a black hood placed over the head and shoulders and often reeks of urine smell. Here is what Haleema 'A.' relayed about her experience:

> When I arrived one female security guard took me to a cell and demanded I take off all my clothes, including my underwear. She took my clothes with her and left me naked for a whole hour, hoping I would harm myself. After one hour they came back with my clothes; I put them on while one of the guards ordered me to carry a chair ... I refused. He picked up the chair and walked towards a corner in the corridor which to me sounded like a slaughter house. From that corner,

I would hear the screams of men undergoing torture, while walking towards my cell I also saw two men *mashbooheen*, with the *kees* which reeked of urine smell covering their heads then they entered another corner, one of them put the chair on the floor and demanded I sit down. Then he cuffed my feet, tied them and hung them through a hook on the wall, and placed the *kees* on my head, it had an awful stench, and the smell of urine was suffocating. I could hardly breathe.

Haleema 'A.'

The torture methods of *shabeh* and the *kees* were also used against Ghada, Salwa, Haleema 'F.' and Rawda. Here is Rawda's testimony in this regard:

They tied my hands and feet to the chair and used my body as a rag sweeping the floor with it. I felt so humiliated, I started crying hard. I woke up in the hospital and found myself totally naked. I was then brought back to the cell with the doctor's gown on my body; according to the doctor, my pants had been ripped and he told me that that was why he covered me with his gown. When I left the Moscobiyya to be taken to prison, I had already lost 13 kilos.

Rawda

Amne's experience of *shabeh* was particularly long and painful.

After 25 days of interrogation in the Moscobiyya, I was sent to al-Khalil prison [Hebron prison which was for men only]. There I went through another arduous experience. Once, I was *mashbooha* [the act of *shabeh*] for 72 hours, except for five minutes once in a while when I was allowed to go to the bathroom. They used to interrogate me for six to eight hours every day for the whole time I was there. They all spoke in one language: 'This is not the Moscobiyya; here there is only one thing, *salekh* [skinning]; here there is one thing, *dabeh* [butchering]. We do not spoil terrorists here!'

Amne

The intention behind placing the body in a painful position, as the method of *shabeh* does, is to inflict the most severe bodily harm on the detainee. It is known to ruin the spine, impair one's movement, and affect the joints and can lead to paralysis; hence its frequent use against political detainees.

Nonetheless, what was and still is specifically different about Israel's colonial methods of torture used against Palestinian political detainees is the cultural context within which the prison authorities frame their techniques of torture, a means, as will be seen in the following, believed to be most demeaning and damaging to the women political detainees, their families and their communities. These techniques were designed to work on the psychology of the detainees. Most women in our conversations were strongly convinced that the Israelis knew a great deal about their traditional lives, the importance of the family, the importance of female chastity to both the family and the community at large, and the value of the mother figure in Palestinian culture. Ahlam put it this way: 'They understand how we feel – one of the interrogators [Abu-Ali] knew Arabic. They understand our psyche and our traditional ways of life.'

Drawing on the conversations we had and on my own experience, I find this aspect – thinking your enemy knew all about you – to effect most harm on the detainee. And this is why, as most of them stressed and as I agree, the interrogators would hammer on the traditional and cultural issues and use them as additional psychological pressure against female detainees.

In almost every case of interrogation, the detainees reported the presence of at least two interrogators: one of Ashkenazi background, who is often described as blond, with white skin, relatively calm and civilized – the 'good cop'; the other of Arab origin (mostly Moroccan, Iraqi or Egyptian Jew), described as the 'bad cop'. The latter is described as dark, fat, and sporting a black moustache; he speaks Arabic, swears in Arabic, and exhibits his 'expertise' in and knowledge of Arabic culture and tradition. According to Munia, 'One of the interrogators appeared as the nice guy, while the other one, Abu Amin, of Arab origin was always bad.' Haleema 'A.' had the following to say about this issue: 'One day they took me to the head of the interrogators; his name was Abu-Nihad. He was an Iraqi Jew who spoke good Arabic and knew Quranic verses and "the sayings of the Prophet ..."'

Haleema 'F.''s description of her interrogator who was of Arab origin was particularly interesting. 'His name was Shawqi, and he truly looked like Fareed Shawqi.' The latter is a well-known Egyptian actor: dark hair with a moustache, a large body and rough hands. He would often play the role of the cruel monster, the giant, the man who would often brawl. He was nicknamed *wahshel-shasha* (the monster of the big screen) on account of his [i.e. Fareed Shawqi's] overwhelmingly physical roles in his movies. The description of the interrogator of Arab Jewish background as cruel, rough and disgusting was common among the detainees. All Jewish interrogators of Arab origin were called *abu* (father of), a common honorific character used in Arabic to indicate respect for a man by calling him not by his first name, but instead as the father of his oldest son. A similar honorific applies to women, who are also known as *um* (the mother of so-and-so). Elsewhere I provided a detailed analysis of this phenomenon in prison, which I identified as racism within the Jewish citizens in Israel (Abdo 2011b).

Psychological Torture

Humiliating acts directed against detainees' nationality, religion, culture and traditions, the deprivation of food as well as sleep, and the threats directed against members of their family, especially mothers, were experiences commented upon by most, if not all, women during our conversations. Also common to most women's experiences, especially but not exclusively, during interrogation, was the deprivation of food and the denial of medical facilities and family visitations. During Salwa's 45 days of interrogation, visits by her family were totally banned; during Rawda's eight years in prison, her family was not allowed to visit her.

On the other hand, interrogators attempted to intimidate several of the women by threatening to bring family members to the prison. In Ghada's case, her cousin was actually brought to prison while he was on his way back from his university in Damascus:

> One day they brought my cousin to the interrogation room to see me then they let him out, but kept him in a cell near mine, they tortured him. He used to call my name and say in a pained voice: 'I have nothing to do with this. Why am I here?' I felt terrible for him, knowing that I caused his agony.

Ghada

A particularly painful experience in this regard was when the mother of the detainee would be brought to prison to put pressure on her daughter, as Salwa experienced:

> They brought my mother to prison and put her in a cell beside my cell in order to put pressure on me and make me work or cooperate with

the interrogators. Instead of doing this, my mother was encouraging me to remain steadfast and resist. They kept my mother in prison for three days she could only talk to me, but I was prevented from seeing her.

Salwa

Rawda revealed she was very emotional and felt a lot of pain when one week after her arrest, they called her father and told him to 'bring a coffin', saying: 'God knows if you will find her alive or dead.' In her presence, they told him: 'We found her yesterday with men.' 'Embarrassed as he was, my father looked at me and said: "I wish you were dead"; this event pained me a lot.'

In Aida's case, the prison authorities brought her brother in and tortured him in front of her:

They brought my bother and tortured him in front of me. They used very cruel psychological and physical torture against him; exposing him naked. Worse yet, they brought my mother to a cell next to mine and made me hear her screams and pain. Still, they could not break me.

Aida

Other detainees spoke of threats made by the interrogators against their mothers, fathers and children. Interrogators threated Amne, for example, by saying that they would bring her mother, father and daughters to prison. When she responded positively, saying 'So be it, at least I can see them', the interrogator was furious and started striking her with his hands and boots.

Concerning one of the bouts of interrogation and torture, Aisha reported the following:

One day, an interrogator passed by my cell with a truncheon in his hand and screamed at me: 'You do love your sister-in-law, don't you?' He was not really asking me a question, but stating what he suspected was a fact. Then he shouted at some men in the other room, saying: 'Go bring her mother and sister-in-law and hang them from their breasts, so she will hear them screaming in pain.' Then he left.

Aisha

One Hundred Eyes Cry, But Not My Mother's

The Arabic proverb *meet ain tibki wa-la ain ummi*, which means one hundred eyes cry but not my mother's, was often spoken by interrogators in the presence of political detainees, along with a similar proverb *alf ain tidma'a wa-la ain ummi* (one thousand tears but not my mothers'). These proverbs play on the close family ties within Arab culture, especially the relationship between mother and daughter, and were used to exert more pressure on the women – another technique of psychological torture. Often, before threatening to bring the mother, sister-in-law or sister to prison, the interrogator would utter one of these proverbs and leave. In some cases, they combine the proverb with statements like 'What will your mother do if you become mentally ill? What if a kick to your head blinds or paralyzes you?' Or, 'What if you were raped and lost your honour?'

Expressing her feelings at that time, Haleema 'F.' said: 'I swear to God, he would carry me like this [she stood up and re-enacted the scene; he was tossing her in the air!] and say: "*alf ain tidma'a wa-la ain ummi*".' This proverb was used against Salwa twice: the first time just before they brought her mother to prison and incarcerated her for three days to put pressure on her daughter; the second time involved a death threat, with the claim that they would report that she had committed suicide. Haleema 'A.' was threatened by Abu-Nihad, her interrogator, who said that if she did not co-operate, that her mother would suffer. The proverbs were used to undermine women's resistance by telling them that their mothers (standing in for their families) would not be upset at their deaths, because they have shamed the family. In one of the interrogation sessions, Abu-Nihad began a session by using the one thousand eyes cry proverb, adding: 'You slept with all those married men and none of them married you.' The frequent use of this technique was intended to exert the utmost psychological pressure on Palestinian women in order to force them to confess.

The strong presence of Palestinian women in the resistance movement and the detention of thousands since the 1960s, as mentioned in Chapter 3, was a cause of alarm for the Israeli authorities. It is no surprise that the intent to humiliate detainees through attacks directed against Palestinian nationality was rampant in Israeli detention camps. While all detained suspects were treated as terrorists, women had their own special share of humiliation. The use in Israeli prisons of techniques that dehumanized and degraded Palestinian nationals mimic the attitudes of the Israeli establishment and its institutions in general. Israeli prison authorities refuse to admit that Palestinians are a nation, hence the denial of their identity. Instead, Palestinians both within Israel and in the Occupied Territories have been and continued to be referred to by the general term

'Arabs'. Also, at other moments they differentiate between 'Arabs' and 'Christians', insisting that only Muslims can be called Arabs.[19] As Kholoud said, 'the Israelis recognized Muslims only as Arabs. In this way Doris and Rawda for example [both being Christians] were excluded from their classification.' This does not mean that Christian political detainees were treated better than Muslims. It only shows how Israel, even in prisons, tries to exploit religious differences in an attempt to create frictions among Palestinians. In this context one understands the recent statement by a senior Israeli lawmaker that 'Christians are not really Arabs' (Abunimah 2014), and in this context we could also explain Israel's recent attempts at enlisting Palestinian Christians in its army, albeit with little to no success.[20]

Equally bad if not worse was the humiliating, belittling and dishonourable way in which interrogators referred to highly respected Palestinian national leaders such as George Habash (PFLP leader at the time) and Abu-Ammar (Yasser Arafat, PLO leader at the time). Haleema 'A.', a member of the PFLP, recalled one of her interrogation sessions in which this tactic was used:

In one of my interrogation sessions, Shawqi, my interrogator, came in, pushed me onto a chair, chained one of my hands to the chair and chained the other around my neck ... At that time I had my period and was very smelly, as they had refused to give me sanitary napkins. Shawqi looked at me with disgust and said: 'So, Haleema? Is George Habash the only man allowed to fuck you? I want to fuck you too, and right now ...'

Haleema 'A.'

Haleema 'F.' who, as mentioned earlier, was a child when arrested recalled the following painful bout of interrogation:

One day in the interrogation room, one interrogator came, held his hand in front of my eyes, and said: 'Do you know who severed my fingers? They were your terrorists. Abu Ammar! How many times did Abu Ammar fuck you?' I was a child and did not understand what he was talking about. Then he came near me and kicked me with his boots and threw me into the corner. I was beaten so much that I lost consciousness several times. One interrogator would finish his beating bouts and leave the cell, only for the next one to come and start anew. I understood nothing of what they were telling me: 'How many times did you sleep with Abu-Ammar?' 'You the terrorists severed my fingers'

… How in hell would I know Abu-Ammar? How dare he say that I slept with Abu Ammar? Where is Abu-Ammar and who am I? I am still a schoolgirl, I kept telling myself. What do I have to do with his fingers?

Haleema 'F.'

It is important to emphasize how the prisons' authorities related to the detainees' families. As discussed above, family members could be brought in, even during interrogation – a period deemed as most important by prison authorities – in hope of pressuring the detainee into submission. In other words, they were brought in to serve the interests of the military establishment. With the exception of when this technique was used, detainees for the most part were not allowed to see their families, especially during periods of interrogation – which could last up to three months or longer – but also during incarceration.

Although a total ban on visits was effected in 2007 concomitant with the building of the Apartheid Wall and the heavy restriction on movement placed on Palestinians both in Gaza and the West Bank, movement restriction on Palestinians in these territories has always been part of their living conditions, making family visitations very difficult. With the transfer of Palestinian detainees from the occupied land to the territory of the occupier – Israel 'proper', an illegal act according to the International Humanitarian Law – family visitations became almost impossible. Ben-Ari and Barsella observe that it is illegal to transfer people under occupation to the territories of the occupier, adding that: 'the Universal Declaration of Human Rights (UDHR) in particular insists on the recognition of the dignity, human rights, and fundamental freedoms of people under occupation' (Ben-Ari and Barsella 2011: 201).

Not only families were banned from visiting; detainees were also deliberately separated from their children as a matter of policy. Amne had three children when she was arrested; the oldest was eight while the youngest was only three years old. Upon her arrest she was separated from her children and despite her pleas the prison authorities refused to allow the youngest child to join her. Detainees were also prevented from seeing their parents on their deathbeds. All these were additional forms of torture undergone by detainees. As for the death of her father while she was in detention camp, Amne relayed the following:

My father died just several months before my release in late 1993; earlier that year there had been another prisoners' swap and I was instructed to get ready to be released, as the remaining period for my incarceration was just a few months away. My husband and three daughters were waiting for me at home ... But I was not released. One month after the release of the earlier swap, my father died. The authorities refused to give me permission to leave the prison so that I could go and tell him that I loved him.

Amne

Theoretically, with a proper permit, families from the West Bank can visit detained family members. However, having to go through the excruciating process of applying for three instead of one permit to be allowed to cross into Israel has turned the theoretical assumption of possibility into the impossible, deterring people from their right to see their family members. In his 'Devil's Land: The Transfer of Palestinian Detainees into Prisons within Israel', Sfard elaborated on the three permits as follows:

> With all the checkpoints, the fences, the monstrous bureaucracy requiring three permits – a permit from the military to enter Israel, a permit from the Civil Administration to pass through the Seam Zone [the area enclosed between the separation fence erected by Israel inside the West Bank territory and the Green Line demarcating it], a permit from the Israeli Prison Service (IPS) to hold the specific visit, and the involvement of the General Security Service (GSS) and the Israeli Police.

Sfard (2011: 188)

Intimidation and humiliation directed against the detainee's religion was not unusual in Israel prisons either. Iman, who became religious and donned the veil in prison, was often harassed and ordered to remove her veil. Alian went through a similar experience:

> The interrogators abused the fact that I was religious in order to desecrate me; they called me names and violated me. I remember that one of them had forcefully removed my veil and tore my traditional *jilbab*, and threatened to molest me sexually.

Alian (2011: 184)

The line separating physical from the psychological torture is often blurred. Isolation, solitary confinement, denied seeing their families, torturing detainees while calling them names, as well as various other forms of torture, some of which are discussed above, cannot be classified under one category as either physical or psychological. For most participants, interrogation included physical, psychological and sexual abuse. The following voices and experiences illustrate this.

Denigrating Arab Culture and Values through Sexual Language

Denigrating Arabic culture through the use of sexualized language was a normal practice of torture used by prison authorities against Palestinian political detainees. While all political detainees were referred to as 'terrorists', almost all of the women were treated as prostitutes and as lacking integrity, and were accused of sleeping around with men in their political organizations. Many of the women were called *sharmouta, qahba* and *manyouka*; the three terms are synonyms for 'whore'. The use of these terms is deemed in Arabic culture as absolutely taboo, and women would not use such terms, nor do they expect to be called these names. Such slurs were used against most if not all of the women, as our conversations revealed, and for many of them these instances were the first times in their lives that the slurs had been used of them – hence the shock and disbelief felt by most. Sometimes, when I insisted on hearing the exact words used, they would either say the words with a shy smile, or wait for me to say the words first and only then they concur, saying: 'Yes, those ones!'

It is true, as discussed earlier in the chapter, that women who decide to join the resistance in whatever form value the freedom of their homeland even more than their lives. It is also true, as our conversations revealed, that many of them (perhaps not the children like Haleema 'F.' and Ahlam) were well read and informed about Israeli methods of torture in prison and at least psychologically were prepared at some level for what they encountered. Nonetheless, these fighters and resisters remain the product of a particular culture, one that is largely traditional and patriarchal with a strict set of norms covering female behaviours, especially sexual behaviour. In this culture, women are highly respected as the protectors of their own and their family honour, and the terms of abuse would never be directed against them or even uttered in front of them, let alone be smeared through the use of such terms publicly.

A deeper understanding of the dynamics of interrogation, which included falsification of evidence and the extraction, by force, of confessions, especially from child detainees, reveals a great deal about the extent to which Arab culture and traditions have been targeted by Israel's prison authorities. Several women in the conversations expressed concern about prison authorities trying to frame them. Several women interviewed said their interrogators threatened to tell their brothers or other male family members that they were sexually deviant and slept around. Munia, for example, was particularly alarmed at the fact that in Telmond prison (in Israel), she along with other political detainees was placed in a room next to a group of *jinaeyyat* (Jewish women criminals, charged with murder and dealing drugs):

> I remember vividly their screams. How they used to come to our door, look through the door opening and ask us to come in. During meal times, they would put us together in the same dining room. One morning as we were having breakfast I saw Mercedes (the name of a Jewish Israeli inmate) put her hand in her pocket and pulled out scissors, but before she could do anything, I shouted at her and everybody in the room surrounded our table to see what was going on. They did nothing to her. Instead, they punished us all and prevented us from leaving our room for a whole week.
>
> Munia

Placing female political prisoners with Jewish criminals, especially drug dealers was raised during our round-table discussion as a real concern. Women explained how fearful they were whenever placed with Israeli Jewish criminals. They particularly expressed concern about the potential occurrence of '*isqat*': a defamatory mechanism used by the military or prison authorities to intimidate women and force them to submit. This mechanism involves seducing and drugging a women and placing her naked in a sexual pose. Her photos are then presented to her as 'evidence' to extract information by force, or forcing her to collaborate.[21]

Psychological Torture, Sexual Abuse, Threat of Rape and Rape

Most political detainees (males and females) experienced physical and psychological torture and heard threats related to the bringing of their mothers or sisters to prison. In many cases physical torture also contributed to psychological sufferings. A 2013 report on torture of Palestinian political prisoners (including women) in Israeli prisons found that '95 percent of Palestinians who had been imprisoned in Israel had been beaten; 89

percent were deprived of sleep for long periods; 82 percent were forced to stand in difficult positions for long periods; 55 percent were subjected to extreme hot and cold temperatures' (Ferwana 2013).

The above forms of torture, which could be classified as physical, undoubtedly leave their psychological impact on the detainee. Still, the impact of psychological pain caused by sexual torture remains particularly painful. To begin with, it is important to note that rape and attempted rape are considered crimes against humanity and stand in flagrant disregard of international humanitarian law. Unfortunately however, Israel's open rejection of most UN decisions and declarations often makes it seem above international laws. It is noted that Israel has ignored many UN resolutions. According to Paul Findley's *Deliberate Deceptions: Facing the Facts About The U.S.–Israeli Relationship*, between 1949 and 1992 Israel was the target of 65 UN resolutions, all of which it ignored (Findley 1995: 192–94). What the Israeli establishment is more concerned with when enacting laws and implementing policies against Palestinians, whether its own citizens or those under its military occupation, is how to advance its own interests at any cost, even if this meant causing the utmost harm to the indigenous Palestinian population.

It is true that there is less information about male sexual abuse, especially attempted rape and rape, among male political detainees. One story that drew international attention was that of Sheikh Mustafa Dirani, who was abducted from his home in Lebanon in 1994. Dirani testified that he was sexually assaulted twice in Israeli prisons: once as he was raped by a prison guard and a second time when he encountered an attempted rape through the use of a truncheon (McGreal 2003).[22]

This said, female Palestinian political detainees experience sexual abuse, molestation, threat of rape and even rape more frequently than do men. Playing on their own imagined stereotypes of Arab culture, especially the traditional norms concerning sexuality, Israeli military officers and prison authorities deliberately target Palestinian female political detainees and victimize them sexually. In my conversations with the former detainees, there was hardly any woman who was not sexually harassed or threatened with rape.

When Haleema 'A.' voiced her experience about one interrogation session, she described it as 'the most excruciating form of torture.' Here is what she said:

During one of the interrogation periods, I refused to answer their questions. One of the interrogators slammed my head against the wall several times and another one held my breasts tightly. I was resisting both interrogators. I never cried and stayed steadfast throughout ... I was unable to find sanitary napkins nor did I have any extra underwear ... I asked the interrogator for sanitary napkins. He said, 'You talk, we will get you some.' He [the interrogator] put one of his legs here [she stood up and demonstrated the scene for us]; he pushed one of his legs between my legs and wrapped his other leg around me ... I knew they were exploiting Palestinian social or traditional norms. I wanted to give him the message that he will not scare me by this pressure he is putting on me. He looked at me and said: 'You are smelly and filthy. Fuck off.' He kicked me with his boots and said, 'you disgust me ... you *sharameet* [plural of *sharmouta*] always move from one man to the next in the PFLP.'

Haleema 'A.'

Ghada's experience of sexual assault was voiced thus:

I was beaten very frequently, on all parts of my body. There was a lot of psychological terror and threat of rape. They kept saying: 'We will sleep with you now if you do not answer our questions ....' I went through *shabeh* many times. One day, several interrogators entered my cell as I was defecating in my cell. They would take me to interrogation, then to the solitary confinement. I spent five weeks in solitary confinement. After two months of my detention, they moved me to a room with other women and I stayed there for 20 days; the room was very tiny. It had a bathroom and one tap that dripped all night. I was sleep deprived throughout my detention. I lost eight kilos during interrogation.

Ghada

The use of sexuality, especially in the form of attempted rape, as a method of torture of Palestinian political prisoners was rather widespread in Israeli prisons. Qahira al-Saadi, who was released after ten years of imprisonment in Israeli jails in the January 2012 prisoners exchange with Hamas, said that she had been held for interrogation for three-and-a-half months at the Moscobiyya, then transferred to Ramla (Ayalon) prison. Referring to her incarceration, she said that Israeli guards mistreated and tortured her during the interrogation; the guards 'threatened to rape me and to mistreat my children if I refused to co-operate with them.' She added that the guards also used the ugliest form of verbal and physical insults against her during the interrogations: 'Then they brought my husband and threatened him in order to encourage me to make confessions by saying that they would rape me in front of his eyes ... I quite remember well that my husband begged my interrogator, Colonel Kohen, not to touch me' (Al-Saadi 2002).

Still, actual rape was not unheard of either in Israeli detention camps. During my frequent visits to Palestine I tried to get in touch with Rasmiyya Odeh whose experience of rape became an international issue discussed by the Red Cross, her lawyers and *The Sunday Times* London in 1979 but to no avail. Since her release, Rasmiyya has become very ill and has spent many years in treatment in Jordan and abroad. However, based on the existing literature (Antonius 1980; Langer 1975; Fahoum 1980) and the testimony of Aisha who was with Rasmiyya in the detention camp and who witnessed Rasmiyya's torture, the following account demonstrates the cruelty and savageness of the Israeli prison torture methods. Rasmiyya, who was sentenced to life imprisonment, spent ten years in prison and was released in a prisoners' exchange deal, was tortured beyond imagination. In one bout of her interrogation, and in order to put pressure on her to collaborate, they brought her father to the interrogation room. They used the method of *shabeh*, as she had been fixed to the wall naked; they then ordered her father to rape her. When he refused, they inserted a wooden rod in her vagina until she bled and fainted. Watching this, her father also lost consciousness and was removed from the scene.

The rape experience of Aisha Odeh was no less dramatic and painful and one of fierce resistance on her part. After an excruciating bout of physical beatings, showers with cold water, and the loss of consciousness, the next day, as Aisha explained, the unexpected happened:

> They opened the door. I saw them dragging a big bag, then I saw the body of Ya'aqoub Odeh [a PFLP prisoner who died in prison under torture]. He was dead ... They killed him and dragged his body. I immediately thought, 'That's it ... my turn to die. If it has to happen, I will die a *shaheeda*. The interrogator, Uzraeel, tall, pale and looking like the angel of death with glasses without earpieces [i.e. a pince nez], came very close to me. In the middle of the room stood a short man with a thick black moustache and a big belly. A few moments later, a tall blonde woman wearing a military uniform stepped in. Uzraeel began issuing

his orders: 'Take off your clothes.' I placed my hands over my chest for protection. He did not give me any time, and asked the others in the room to undress me. I resisted but it did not help as I was lying on the floor naked, with my hands cuffed behind my back, I was thrown on the floor. The cuffs were pressing on my spine and it was painful. The short interrogator placed his both ankles on my belly. The tall one – Uzraeel – opened my legs using a wooden pole, and the woman held my head in place with her foot. The one who was holding me with both ankles started brushing my breasts with his huge hands, while Uzraeel started pushing a wooden pole into my vagina. They kept crushing my breasts, and trying to penetrate my vagina with a wooden pole, but could not do it … I resisted fiercely.

Aisha[23]

For all female detainees, the moment of attempted rape, of harsh physical and psychological torture, passes like a lifetime. Aisha put it succinctly when she said: 'Those moments felt like a time immemorial, which started with the beginning of history and crossed all the ages.'

Targeting women's body and sexuality was a policy used in Israeli prison interrogations of Palestinian female detainees. Women complained about the refusal of the interrogator or the prison guard to provide them with sanitary pads during menstruation. Detainees who were sentenced and placed in prison rooms would rip some of the rags used as bed sheets or covers and use these; others in solitary confinement, in isolation cells or during interrogation would be left bleeding all over their only pants. Salwa expressed her feelings on this issue thus:

During interrogation I had my period; I asked for napkins, for cotton, anything, but they refused. I begged for toilet paper, and they refused. They kept saying: 'You stay the way you are because you are smelly and filthy and we want you to die, and then we will say you committed suicide …' My blood filled my underpants and pants and during these days I was in a lot of pain.

Salwa

The above discussion of Palestinian women political detainees' experiences in Israeli prisons, the terror, pain, physical, psychological and sexual torture, the racism, cultural, social and religious humiliation and so on, constitute only one part – albeit an unforgettable one – of their overall struggle and resistance. As Chapter 5 will demonstrate, women's struggle for their integrity, freedom, self-respect and humanity was continued if not heightened further during their terms in prison and after their release. For almost all women during our conversations, the end of the interrogation session and the beginning of the actual sentencing represents a new phase of prison life: one of energy, organization, education, resistance and empowerment; in the words of Ghada, 'The prison for me was a site of national struggle, education, empowerment and resistance'. The main difference in the two phases of struggle – the one before prison and that while imprisoned – is one of focus and priority. Before imprisonment, the women devoted all their energy, time, thoughts and activism towards the national cause: the liberation of the homeland. During imprisonment, while keeping the overall cause alive, women shifted focus and devoted more time, power, and strength towards and became increasingly resolved about their own empowerment through education, the discussion of social and gender issues, and the fight for their rights as women. It is these issues and the women's continuing struggle and resistance after prison to which we shall turn in Chapter 5.

5

Prison as a Site of Resistance

Chapter 4 discussed the experiences of Palestinian women political detainees in Israeli detention camps and prisons. It focused on the cruel treatment female political detainees received at the hands of Israeli prison officials (such as interrogators, guards and wardresses). It also demonstrated that the targeting of Palestinian women's bodies and sexualities constituted a primary goal for the Israeli prison authorities: inflicting utmost harm on women in order to force them to submit. This chapter, while focusing on women's own perception and experience of challenging the prison and its darkness, argues that the policies and tactics used in Israeli prisons are aimed at intimidating, threatening and forcing Palestinian women to submit have not succeeded. Palestinian women political detainees have strongly challenged the authorities, defied their orders and resisted their victimization with special strength. This chapter will also account for the ways in which women dealt with and redefined time and space as well as the female body. Finally, it will follow the women after their release and record their experiences of 'freedom'.

Women's resistance to torture in prison was no less innovative than the methods of torture used against them. Whether during individual discussions or during the focus group, our conversations revealed that resistance towards and the defiance of prison authorities were omnipresent acts. For most women political detainees, the prison was deemed to be *a site of resistance*: a walled living space, as some maintained. For Palestinian women, moving from life under occupation to prison was synonymous with moving from the 'large prison' to the small one. Since 1967, Palestinians have been living and continued to live in a basically interrupted and ruptured geography: they have been denied the right to movement and travel, and restricted by hundreds of military checkpoints, with Gazans isolated from West Bankers, living in villages and towns cut off from each other and surrounded by Jewish settlements and roads for Jews only; and the inhabitants of both the West Bank and Gaza have been prevented from meeting their families in the territory of 1948 Palestine. As one detainee said, 'Living at home under occupation and living in prison are the same, the only difference is the locality; whereas at home you live in 1967 occupied Palestine, in prison you are in 1948 Palestine [Israel], but in neither case you are allowed to travel and see your national territory.'

Women involved in the armed struggle were well aware of the possibility of detention or imprisonment, as our conversations revealed, and were also aware of the challenges and torture they might face there – or even the possibility of being killed during their mission. Most if not all of them also admitted that they were ready, at least mentally, to face their interrogators. This was seen as an inevitable consequence of the struggle against colonialism and occupation. Facing the interrogator, challenging prison authorities and defying their orders and so on was not an issue of whether it would happen or not, nor ultimately of women's perceptions of such possibilities, but rather was an issue of how women political detainees resisted and challenged the prison authorities.

As discussed in Chapter 1, prison resistance on the part of female (and male) detainees was partly individual and partly collective in nature, with the individual form corresponding to the first stage of incarceration as women were on their own, largely in isolation cells. Collective resistance occurs at the second stage, after charges had been laid and women were held in shared rooms. Corresponding to the nature and forms of struggle and resistance in prison is the political and actual commitment and readiness by which women had joined the armed struggle and ended up in detention camps. This was evident in the different experiences of the women interviewed.

There was a generational difference among the detainees in our conversations. For example, first generation political detainees (those detained in the late 1960s and early 1970s) exhibited a strong determination of resistance, which drew its strength from local, national and international experiences. Aisha, Rawda, Itaf and Sonia, for example, were closer in age to the Nakba and to the memory of it, memories that directly impacted on their growing up Palestinian. This generation was also exposed to organized training camps where they were introduced to international and regional revolutionary literature and to practical military training. In other words, these women were part of the revolutionary era of the time. This is not to say that the second generation political detainees, those who were incarcerated in the late 1980s, were not equally committed or sufficiently revolutionary in their thinking. As Ameena from this latter group stated: 'I was ready for interrogation, I was aware of their methods of torture through *adab al-sujoun* [prison literature], especially the works of Felicia Langer [the Jewish Lawyer and supporter of the Palestinian struggle] and Walid Fahoum [the Palestinian lawyer, author and activist], as well as the experiences of ex-detainees'. However, the younger generation in this group was less exposed to organized revolutionary training.

Most women in both groups were aware of sexual harassment in prison and many said that they prepared themselves 'mentally' for that possibility. Here is what Iman had to say:

> Let me tell you this: I was aware of their means of torture, especially sexual torture. At the age of 17, I read Lea Tsemel's book on torture of Palestinian political detainees in Israeli prisons.[1] I was also aware of the fact that they intentionally emphasized their use of sexual threats against us women, knowing we Arabs consider women's sexuality a taboo. One of the interrogators sat me on a chair, opened my legs and put his legs between mine. He used to hold my hand in a sexual way. I never submitted and every time showed him he could not scare me.
>
> Iman

Some second-generation women militants partook in the armed struggle as women independent of any organizational affiliation. Instead of using the international struggles as their role model, as in the case of first generation, second generation women militants found role models in the earlier 'veteran' generation for them to follow. Here is what Rawda said about Aisha who was already in prison when the former was detained:

> The first day, when I arrived at the detention camp in Ramla prison, I recall somebody knocked on our door. I opened the door … [a pause]. It was Aisha. She immediately said: 'Ahlan wa-Sahlan [welcome], I smell, on you, the scent of Tayybe and Deir Jrir!' [these are two neighbouring villages in Ramallah district: Rawda came from the former and Aisha from the latter]. For me, Aisha was a role model. I was young [15 years old] when Aisha was arrested. I remember how angry I was when they [the Israeli occupation forces] destroyed her [family] home. At the time I wished it was my house instead of hers. Ever since we were young, Aisha has been considered a role model for the whole village. I remember a blind man who used to go around the village every day speaking highly of Aisha. He would say: 'This is the very first girl to leave the village to the town for education.' In my mind Aisha represented a

role model as she signified the strong Palestinian woman. We followed her story while she was in prison, read about her in the local papers, and heard about the torture she underwent as well as the resistance she put up against the interrogators. I expected to see her totally broken from the torture she received. But when I arrived at the prison and saw her for the first time, I found this blond, beautiful-looking woman to be full of life. Along with Aisha, I also met Sonia: a funny and witty woman. These women made it easy for us, the new comers, to accept ourselves, survive the prison and resist as well.

Rawda

Rawda's experience was particularly telling not only at the political national level and the extent to which Palestine, in this case, the village of 'Deir Jrir' was ingrained in the conscious of the political detainees, but at the social level as well. Despite the traditional environment of the Palestinian village that tended to limit women's mobility, Aisha's incarceration, we learnt, was not condemned, but rather was condoned and discussed positively by younger women outside of the prison.

Whether belonging to the first generation of women fighters or the second generation, all the women political detainees in our conversations spoke of their strong resilience and resistance while in the Israeli prisons. They resisted as individuals while facing their interrogators; they also resisted collectively using different techniques, including the organizing and staging of hunger strikes and protesting work conditions and conducting work stoppages, among other methods.[2] On the question of work stoppage, Munia commented: 'on all Israeli independence days, we would stop working in the kitchen and go on demonstration protesting their independence and our colonialism.' Salwa and her comrades in prison refused to work in the factory. According to her: 'They wanted to force us to work in the factory for soldiers' clothes, but we refused. As a result they punished us, took away our books, pencils and notebooks. In turn, we held a strike for 15 days'. In the following sections, accounts of acts of individual and collective resistance on the part of Palestinian women political detainees will be discussed.

Individual Resistance in Israeli Prisons and Detention Camps

The distinction made in this chapter between individual and collective resistance aims at demonstrating the strength and resilience which each woman exhibited when confronting the violence of the prison guard, interrogator or warden; it also aims at enabling each woman to voice her own experience through her own words. Resistance is a learnt practice, which comes through others' experiences or existing prison literature (let alone through the very act of resisting itself). The forms of resistance to be discussed here include the political, social-gender, sexual and personal, but first an examination of some individual forms of resistance is in place here.

Refusing Orders

Iman's story of resistance was recounted in Chapter 4. Her story told us of how, when beaten by a female guard, she retaliated. Despite the long sentence she received for defending herself against the guard, Iman was adamant not to allow the prison authorities to abuse or humiliate her, resisting every harsh treatment she received at the hands of the guards. In an incident of confrontation with the female soldier who took her to prison, Iman had refused to listen to her orders when she demanded she stop making noise with her feet. She justified her resistance in this way: 'I have my dignity. I do not hate anybody, not even Jews, but I will not allow anybody, especially the colonial occupier, to humiliate me more than what they have already done and still are doing in our big prison of Naa`leen'.[3]

During her interrogation, Haleema 'A.' insisted on refusing to answer her interrogator's order to state her name. Here is how she put it: 'When he asked for my name, I refused to answer ... I told him: "You have my name in your files!"' He insisted on me saying my name, and I insisted on giving him the same answer. 'You know!' she looked at me and said, 'these things make you stronger and more self-confident.'

Ahlam's experience of resistance to her prison guards was already discussed in Chapter 4. Her refusal to apologize to the judge during her court hearing is another example. Before her appearance at the court, Ahlam's lawyer from the West Bank advised her to apologize to the judge so that the latter reduces her sentence as a minor. She adamantly refused telling the lawyer 'I will never apologize: these are military courts whereby the occupied is judged by their occupiers ... none of them was hurt.' Her response angered the lawyer who after sentencing her for a five-year prison term, told her parents: 'she deserves it, I told her to apologize, but she was rude, stubborn and refused to do so!' The lawyer left her case and instead another lawyer from Nazareth who was in the hearing volunteered on her behalf and asked the court to reduce her sentence on account of her age. Instead, Ahlam was handed a three-year prison term.

Ahlam used both verbal and physical means of resistance against her interrogators and oppressors. In Chapter 4, we heard of how she attacked the female soldier who was beating her friend Rawda. As for her use of verbal abuse against her abuser, it is important to note that during our conversation, Ahlam was very reluctant to repeat the 'bad names' she was frequently called by the interrogators. However, when she heard the interrogator using labels such as *sharmouta* against her, Ahlam was not silent. She would use the same language in return, saying words to the effect of: 'You and all of yours are *sharameet* [plural for *sharmouta*].' Ahlam's strong resistance was recognized by the prison authority. In one incident as she was leaving the court, one of her interrogators looked at her and said: 'You are terrible ... they taught you how to become rude and nasty.' Ahlam responded immediately: 'It is you and your atrocities who taught us how to become fierce resisters!'

In Chapter 4, we learned how Iman and Alian resisted the orders of their interrogators to remove their veils, insisting that they keep them on. Salwa, moreover, had fiercely resisted the orders of the prison authority to share the same room with Jewish women criminals, in her words, with 'drug dealers, whores and prostitutes.' She was consequently moved to a room housing other political detainees.

Refusing to Collaborate

Extracting a confession from the political detainee – and most often through the use of force – is deemed by the prison administration to be the highest priority during the interrogation period. Such confessions, which aim at incriminating the political prisoner and which often implicate other individuals they want to gather information on, are constructed by the prison administrators (mostly the interrogators) and are presented on paper in Hebrew to the detainee. In most cases, these written confessions are not given to the detainees for review beforehand. Instead, they are placed on the table in front of the interrogator as he 'explains' in Arabic what the confession says. Most if not the overwhelming majority of detainees refused to sign such papers; they considered signing confessions to be acts of treason and collaboration with the prison authorities and the occupying state. Almost all of the women in our conversations stated that they refused to sign such papers. Whereas some refused to sign without providing a reason to the authorities, others explained their refusal by saying that they could not read the language in which the confession was written. However, even the two detainees who were from Jerusalem and knew the Hebrew language refused to sign by using the language of the confession as a justification. In some cases, women were specifically asked to 'co-operate' with the prison authorities in order to secure their 'release'. As Rasmiyya said in an interview with Antonius: 'They used to urge me to join them and become an informer: "Join us and we'll release you, and you can go to the US and we won't demolish your home"' (quoted in Antonius 1980: 48).

Defying orders and challenging the interrogator even when the latter threatened them with sexual abuse and rape was a common tactic used by political detainees. Various political detainees, as shown in Chapter 4, knew about Israeli prison authorities' tactics of using women's bodies and sexuality as a tool to force them to submit. This knowledge was internalized and turned by some of the women into an internal power by employing the torturer's tool of torture – their bodies – into a site of resistance. Here is Haleema 'A.' on this point:

In one session of interrogation when the interrogator said 'I will fuck you now,' I was wearing pants and a shirt. I unbuttoned my shirt and told him: 'Do what you wish ...' Deep inside me I knew they were exploiting our traditional values and playing on the issue of sexuality. I basically wanted to give him a clear message that his threats did not frighten me and that I knew what his intentions were.

Haleema 'A.'

Ahlam voiced a similar experience:

They [the interrogators] threatened to sexually molest and rape me several times ... The occupiers understand the mentality of the Arab woman – they know how we feel and our points of weakness. When they find the detainee strong, they emphasize sexual harassment ... One day he [the interrogator] told me, we are going to do this and this [that is, threatening to rape her], he came closer to me with the intention of unbuttoning my shirt. I looked him in the eye and said: 'Don't bother, I will unbutton them!'

Ahlam

Our conversations with the women revealed various other means of resistance used by the detainees both individually and collectively. Such means include, for example, occupying bathrooms for long periods of time while the prison guard waited outside; refusing to divulge their names despite the additional torture they would receive at the hands of their interrogators and walking very slowly while ordered otherwise.

All the women during our conversations spoke proudly of their resistance in prison, the fact that the prison shaped their personality and strengthened their resilience and steadfastness. Those who did not resist the interrogator directly expressed their agency, pride in their deeds and their strength. For example, after spending 25 days in the Moscobiyya Detention Centre, Amne was moved to Al-Khalil prison: 'I never thought they would send me to that prison, because it was strictly for males.' She added: 'When I arrived there, they immediately told me: "Here we do not take it easy with prisoners ... you will not leave this prison until you reveal everything."' Sarcastically, Amne responded: 'God help you!' implying that she refused to divulge any information. On another occasion, Amne relayed: 'Throughout my interrogation, they [the prison authority] kept telling me: "Say you are sorry and regret what you did and you will be all right." My response was always: "If you think I made a mistake I apologize!"'

Itaf's experience in this respect is particularly interesting: 'My detention made me much stronger, more knowledgeable, and I gained more self-confidence and felt more independent there. I did not waste time in prison ... I made use of every hour I spent in prison.'

The Personal in Prison

Most of the women stated that maintaining self-confidence, strength, resilience and an unflinching will to resist was also an attribute of the reality of detention. Detention sharpens women's personality and political resolve; 'It,' as Aisha said, 'sharpens one's position and makes woman unwilling to negotiate her ideals and principles, let alone changing them.' This, however, does not preclude moments of human weakness and even breakdowns among women political detainees. After all, women political detainees are human beings who have feelings, emotions, fears and needs. A number of women in our conversations admitted to having gone through moments of harsh psychological distress in which they became depressed and spent hours alone and crying. Such moments occurred for the most part during the interrogation period and while they were confined to their isolation cells. Others explained such moments of distress as a result of learning about the passing away of a dear family member – especially a parent.

In Chapter 4, we learned about the strong relationship Ahlam had with her father. The latter passed away while Ahlam was still in prison. Despite the powerful personality and resilience she demonstrated in prison, her father's death was the only event which, as she related, had weakened her and caused her to cry. During our one-on-one conversation, Ahlam suddenly started crying. When asked her what was wrong, she responded with: 'because of the loss of my father.' After describing her reaction to his death, she added: 'He visited me just one week before he passed away and told me he felt his time was up! When he left I never cried.' When asked why this was so, she responded:

In prison you live a different reality. There you are forced to remain strong. At that moment I thought that, if I cried, I might lose my resilient and revolutionary character and that the female guards would take advantage of my weakness. During that day, one guard in a military uniform approached me, saying: 'How can you not cry or be sad at your father's death? Under such circumstances, we sit on the floor for over a week and cry.' I responded with, 'I do not cry ...,' but from the inside I was in pain and torn. Still, I had to be strong in front of them.

Ahlam

When she was alone, and especially when she was in bed, Ahlam would cry a great deal. Her father died young. Haleema 'A.', like most of the other women in this study, never cried in front of her jailers, even during the harshest moments of torture. However, as she stated, the death of her mother made her cry a great deal, but silently and not in public:

The moment when I felt most torn psychologically occurred nine months after my detention, when I learned about the passing away of my mother. I remember when I was in Ramla prison, I applied for permission to visit my family for the day, but the prison authority denied my request. The same day I was called to the office of the prison chief. I immediately felt that something was wrong with my mother. In her office there was a nurse – I am a very sensitive woman and emotionally fragile, although very strong against the occupiers, but weak from the inside. They told me: 'We are sorry, your mother passed away.' Despite the harshness of the moment, I held myself together and did not shed a single tear. When I got back to my room and was with my comrades I sat and started to cry. At the time, the most difficult moment for me was how to go home and not find my mother with whom I lived most of my life there. She was 62 years old.

Haleema 'A.'

Amne's experience was similar. She described the circumstance of her father's death and its impact on her as follows:

Five months before my release, the exchange deal of 1995 happened. Since I was the least sentenced among the 15 women in the room, I was convinced that I would be among the released. The day was a day of visitation and my family was waiting for me outside the prison, but my name never came up and I was not released. Between this time and the time I was released [six months later] my father died. I was devastated, telling myself that if I had been among the released, I would have at least seen my father before his death. It is interesting how I learnt about his death. The girls brought the newspaper. One of the younger detainees whom I had taught how to read was reading the name of my father. She was very confused. I read it too but told her: 'Do not worry, it is all right. God have mercy on him.' The rest of the detainees in the room could not take the news and a moment of total silence engulfed the room. In prison we stepped a lot on our feelings, we suppressed our feelings, out of fear of showing signs of weakness. The prison authority opened the door of our room so that condolences could be given. I never cried when I was with the women, but cried a lot when I was alone and in bed.

Amne

Crying silently out of public view or suppressing one's own feelings was also regarded as a form of resistance. These women did not want to show their Palestinian comrades in detention – and definitely not the prison officials – that they were weak. Despite their deep injuries, they wanted to stay strong in front of each other and not allow their emotions to break them.

Some of the women attributed part of their steadfastness in prison to the support they received from their family members. Additional personal and moral support for the detainees emerged after their prison terms, as none of the parents were aware of their daughters' involvement in the military struggle. But, their reaction to the news of their daughters' detention and the impact it had on them, while varied, was supportive at its core.

Resistance Despite Bringing Family to Prison

Israel's policy of collective punishment, inherited from the British colonial rule over Palestine, has been and continues to be used against occupied Palestinians. This policy includes home demolitions, the cancelling of family visits, the imprisonment and even torture of family members, as well as various other means all policies intended to put more pressure on female political detainees to confess, to inform or to collaborate (Daka 2011; Baker and Matar 2011; Ben-Ari and Barsella 2011; Abdo 2011a). Although most such policies failed to achieve the prison's aim, the impact of such tactics on female detainees was varied. For some, bringing a family member to the prison, especially a mother, while personally painful, actually proved to be a great morale boost and a further encouragement to remain steadfast and resistant, while others, especially at the beginning of their detention, expressed feelings of sadness and guilt at the presence of a family member in the prison, especially of a father.

Amne, for example was very proud of her husband's support, which enabled her to remain steadfast in prison. She relayed the following:

> before my arrest, I used to tell my husband: 'arrest is a likely for me' … partly kidding and partly serious … 'for how long can you wait for me?' He used to say: '10 years'. My arrest in other words did not impact my family negatively. When I was released my husband and my three children were waiting at home. My daughter heard that I was told: 'if I only apologize' … she told me: 'Mama we people do not apologize to the Israelis!'
>
> Amne

Ahlam was strongly supported by her brother, especially in the courtroom when she was handed a five-year term in prison despite being a minor. At that time, she says: 'My brother stood up and addressed the judge saying: "I address my talk to the Israeli people: as long as there is occupation, there will always be resistance.'"[4] Salwa, as discussed in Chapter 4, had a similarly positive experience in terms of support from her family, especially when they brought her mother to prison. Salwa was proud of that experience and revealed that the support of her mother made her much stronger in prison. We also learned about the support Aisha received from her mother and sister-in-law. Iman's experience was no different in this respect:

> The most difficult thing for me was when they arrested my mother and brother in an attempt to put pressure on me. My mother was interrogated. They asked her about 'problems' I had with my family. My mother responded: 'What my daughter did was not because of problems in her family.' They thought I was religious, a limited and closed person, a woman oppressed by my family and one who wanted to escape my family's treatment. My mother looked at them and said: 'My daughter lives a very peaceful and nice life, the life she wants to live. She believed in what she did and did not do it for any other reason.' My mother's words gave me a great boost and strengthened me further.
>
> Iman

While most women in our conversations spoke of the support they received from family members (mother, father, Brother ... etc.), Rawda's experience was slightly different. As we saw in Chapter 4, Rawda was quite hurt when her father was called in by the prison authorities: when they called him they lied to him about her behaviour, presenting her as a fallen woman, which angered her father and he wished her dead.

Collective Resistance Among Female Political Detainees

The transition from the interrogation period, during which time women for the most part were placed in isolation cells, to a 'more public' area of detention in which women shared the same space, represented a significant change in the experiences of women political prisoners. Here the norm became women living in shared rooms, while the isolation cell became an aberration used in special instances for punishment. Sharing the same space had undoubtedly facilitated women's resilience and unleashed their creativity and skills. Women were able to establish direct connection with each other, communicating collectively around shared concerns.

Until the late 1980s, women of different political affiliations were placed together, but after the First Intifada and as the number of female political detainees rose dramatically, political or party affiliation became the factor determining which room women were assigned to. Nonetheless, as most women admit, co-operation and a sense of unity among all Palestinian detainees regardless of political affiliation were characteristics of their experience in prison.

Women organized themselves as a collective, dividing themselves into different committees. Some were responsible for 'formal' education, while others were for organizing political discussions and for consciousness-raising sessions. They would also select or elect from among themselves someone to liaise between different political parties, while another would act as the spokesperson to represent them against the outside world. This latter person would represent their interests and needs and would transmit their complaints to the prison authority, to officials visiting the prison, to the Red Cross, to human rights organizations and so on. Here is how Ghada described the state of women political detainees in the late 1970s and early 1980s:

> We were united and had the same position against the prison administration. We had an executive committee which oversaw all our activities. We had several working committees; each was made up of two to four women. The executive committee was responsible for presenting our demands to the prison administration, representing us to the Red Cross and so ensuring that we remained united against the wishes and continual attempts on the part of the prison authority to break us or divide us. I remember when we were in the same prison with female Jewish criminals who used to fight among themselves and the prison guards used to tell them: 'You need to learn from these Arab women. You need to learn from them cleanliness and tidiness.' We would work on educating ourselves. We organized many consciousness-raising sessions. We had monthly programs which would stipulate what books we read and what topics we were to discuss. Both the Red Cross and our parents would supply us with books. The books sent by our parents were mostly political books. Our parents would replace their covers with the covers for cookbooks. We were busy all day: in the morning we would work and in the afternoon we would conduct our organizational and political sessions.
>
> Ghada

The refusal of women political detainees to allow the prison authorities to hang Israeli flags on their doors or windows during Jewish holidays was but one form of collective resistance practised by them. This incident was referred to by several women as a victory they won as a result of protests and demonstrations they waged in prison. Quite common among women's political detainees' collective struggles were strikes, including hunger strikes as well as work stoppages. Several women in our conversations mentioned an incident of work stoppage at the garment factory they worked in, a work stoppage that occurred because the prison authorities had ordered them to sew military uniforms. Salwa's account above is an example.

The type of collective action and forms of resistance taken up by women political detainees, it should be noted, depended on the location of the prison in Israel. The geography in which the prison is located defines the types of labour – of course forced labour – women political detainees were (and are) required to perform. For example, Nve-Tertza, the women's prison in the Arab city of Ramla (Israel), is located in an area with agricultural production and women incarcerated there (and especially those from the first generation) worked on the land or in the garment factory in the prison. But there is an irony about this prison and the forced labour performed there. As Aisha and Rasmiyya, two ex-political detainees, reported, the irony was that, despite the forced nature of labour in Ramla, women did not mind working there. Ramla, which neighbours Jaffa, holds an important place in the memory of Palestinians, especially in relation to memory of the Nakba. Ramla and Jaffa, the city of oranges, were cleansed of their indigenous Palestinians. Rasmiyya, as noted in Chapter 4, came from Jaffa, and since then her childhood dream had been to return there. It is that affection which made her defend labouring in prison. For unlike those who worked in the garment factory and had experienced several days of work stoppage, especially when forced to sew garments for the Israeli soldiers, working on the land has in fact connected women to their geographic or territorial identity – 1948 Palestine. As Palestinians under Israeli occupation of 1967 women like Aisha and Rasmiyya were (and still are) prevented from visiting their original places of birth. Being in prison inside the 1948 boundaries and seeing one's own place of birth was considered by these women to be a blessing.

Not all women political detainees went to the same prison, although Nve-Tertza prison (for both female criminal and political prisoners) was the major detention centre for women between the late 1960s and mid-1980s. After the late 1980s – and in order to accommodate the tens of thousands of new political detainees after the First Intifada, especially the youth – Telmond prison north of Tel-Aviv became the main prison. No agricultural land was available in or around Telmond prison nor was agricultural labour required. Female political prisoners at this prison used to work inside the prison, either in the kitchen or distributing food. Moreover, because of the concentration of youth at Telmond prison (primarily after the Second Intifada), veteran detainees there such as Amne and Haleema 'A.' spoke highly of the organizational work they did among the *Zahrat* (teenage females in political organizations).[5] 'At the time,' Haleema 'A.' said, 'I was almost the age of their mothers, still we all played together, danced and sang together. I never made them feel like children.'

The issue of hunger strikes, which recently reached a climax after the hunger strike held for about eight months by Samer Al-Issawi from Jerusalem, has galvanized strong national and international solidarity with Palestinian political detainees. Al-Issawi was close to death when as a result of local and international pressure he was released in December 2013 by the Israelis (Murphy 2013a). Hunger strikes as a method of protest by Palestinian political detainees have always been used by men and women. In general, and this is true for both women and men, hunger strikes were collectively organized, but the process of organization was varied. In some cases they would be started by one individual, after which others would join in out of solidarity. For example Ittaf Alian led a hunger strike on her own for over a month:

> I, for example, set a record in the number and duration of hunger strikes initiated in protest against the harassment and sufferings I went through for four and a half years. I set the longest record in the history of the Palestinian prisoners' movement with my 40-day hunger strike in objection to my administrative detention.'
>
> Alian (2011: 186)

After several days various other political prisoners joined Alian in her hunger strike.

Alian's situation was quite interesting. She was first released in 1997 under the so-called peace process, but several months later she was in administrative detention. She put on a hunger strike for 40 days, contesting her administrative detention, and was freed several months later. Abdel-Nasser Ferwana observes, that during the same year the Israelis ended the use of administrative detention with women. While the new policy did not apply to male Palestinian political detainees who could still be administratively detained, the new policy in terms of Palestinian females was short lived. A decade later, in 2007, Hana Shalabi was put in administrative detention for 25 months. She was released in the 2010 prisoner exchange that resulted in the release of Shalit, the captured Israeli soldier. But several months later, Hana was once again detained under the same law. In protesting against administrative detention, stripping her and humiliating her, Hana began a hunger strike that lasted for over 45 days. She garnered international solidarity for her and other male detainees, including Akram Rikhawi who, it was reported that 'on 22 July 2012 he ended his 102-day hunger strike upon reaching an agreement that he would be released on 25 January 2013, six months prior to his original release date'.[6] However, Rikhawi resumed his hunger strike on 24 January 2013 after learning Israel has reneged and refused to release him (Murphy 2013b).

In fact, with every passing day a new name is added to the list of political detainees and to the list of hunger strikers. On 23 April 2013 the hunger strike days recorded for administrative detainee Samer Al-Issawi, mentioned above, reached over 265 days. Issawi spent his last days in prison hospital with his body shackled to his bed. On 23 April, Al-Issawi's lawyer and sister signed a deal for his release in which he would be released 8 months later. Al-Issawi was released on 23 December 2013. Al-Issawi, like Hana Shalabi mentioned above, is among a large number of people who have been re-detained administratively after their release. National and international solidarity with these and other prisoners has been growing in the past decade or so. In Canada, as one example, a nation-wide movement made up of human rights activists, students and women's organizations has started several solidarity campaigns in support of the hunger strikers and against political detention in general. The international solidarity gained by the hunger strikers, along with local/national solidarity activities expressed in sit-ins and hunger strikes by over 1,600 political detainees and their family members forced the Israelis to reach an agreement whereby it gave in to some of the demands of the political detainees.

Education as a Collective Means of Resistance: 'The Prison as Academy'

For many women political detainees, the prison had significantly impacted their growth and development and acted as a major educational resource and consciousness-raising tool. Although most women political detainees in our group were highly educated – some with university education and others occupying teaching positions – a few among the younger generation, as for example with Ahlam, as will be clear shortly, were not as lucky and were arrested while still at school. The educational sessions as well as the social and political discussions held in prison, it is argued, were detrimental to these women, as they contributed to their development. On this, Rawda related:

> The prison represented an important stage in my life; it in fact has shaped my political and social consciousness. I am thankful to all the women detainees, especially Aisha whose impact on me was tremendous ... we started reading books, for example, Nawal Saa`dawi [an Egyptian renowned feminist]. In prison we discussed Saa`dawi's work and we celebrated International Women's Day. Such discussions have created a conceptual shift in my thinking. The women in prison were highly educated politically. For me feminist consciousness was further developed in prison. Since I joined political detention I made sure to teach all women who needed a math certificate for graduation from high school. I did that by teaching Lawahedh Jaa`bary and various others the subject of math.
>
> Rawda

The year 1979 marked an important transitional period for women political detainees. During this year most veteran (first generation) political detainees, who had already been detained for over ten years, were released in a major exchange deal between Israel and the PLO. Their departure created a vacuum in the prisons, especially in the areas of organization and leadership. Their departure also placed additional pressure on women who were imprisoned as political detainees in the late 1970s, such as for example Rawda, who explained the impact that this change had on her in this way:

I remember the dates when the various detainees were released in 1979. I remember at the time that we were new to the prison and the veterans had left and that the detainees needed leadership … When the veteran detainees left, and overnight, I felt I had grown up by many years. Their departure placed a big responsibility on my shoulders. I remember how we immediately started dividing responsibilities among the other detainees. We well knew that if there was no management, organization and delegation of responsibilities, then the prison authorities would exploit this [that is, this lack] and divide us. When I was arrested, I had already finished university. I was a math teacher and wanted to help the other women to complete their matriculate. I succeeded in teaching various women math and oversaw their successful application for the matriculation exams.

Rawda

The hard work to improve themselves in prison, through the various social and political discussions, political detainees would hold in Israeli prisons, was eloquently explained by Sonia:

The most difficult thing for me was the first two years after prison. We were among the first group of women detainees. Rawda was among us … We were building the homeland in prison and dreaming about how we would change the world around us. We had big dreams and worked hard on ourselves, to be informed of everything around us.

Sonia

Whereas Rawda was a teacher, Ahlam was a student who loved learning and education:

I always wanted to be educated, I consider prison to be an academy … it is a university for resistance, education and a training ground for the cadres of the revolution. The prison has shaped my personality. Since my release until this very moment, I have never stopped learning and contributing to the community.

Ahlam

Itaf was no less enthusiastic about the educational qualities political detainees received from other detainees: 'We spent our prison years reading, learning, and discussing Palestinian and world politics,' she said.

Amne also was highly positive in this regard, saying: 'My personality was actually shaped in prison, through the lessons, discussion sessions and the struggle we waged in prison.' And so too for Iman, who said that for her prison was a source of education. She had not been well educated during her youth, and this prison education resulted in her becoming a more informed and educated woman. It is no exaggeration to say that reading and writing were used as critical strategies of resistance in prison: these were weapons in the struggle itself. The educational or academic diversity of women political detainees made it possible for them to turn the prison into an educational institution and the prison rooms into class rooms. The Arabic, English and even Hebrew languages were taught as well as courses in maths, the sciences and history. This allowed the younger women who joined the armed resistance without completing high school to prepare for matriculation exams and to continue their education while in prison.

The strong relations, the bonding and the solidarity established between women political detainees enhanced their power and forced the prison authorities, on various occasions, to answer their demands. The very presence of pencils and paper used in their educational sessions were the achievement of women's collective resistance in prison. In addition to the educational sessions, women wrote poetry, prose and plays and performed in plays. Aisha made the same point several times, that 'detention released the best of women's skills and abilities.' It is in this context that Alian states:

> As women, our achievements inside prison were at times greater than those of our fellow male prisoners. For instance, when the occupation forces tried to classify the prisoners and divide them in preparation for a prisoner exchange deal, all the women made a firm decision to reject the deal, while the male prisoners adopted the position of 'accept and demand'. Remarkably, those who accepted the deal back then were not released and some of them are in prison up to this very day.
>
> Alian (2011: 186)

The sense of responsibility towards younger and newer detainees was heightened among first generation women political detainees. This was especially so after 1979 and the first exchange deal between the PLO and the Israeli authorities, which saw the release of the first batch of political detainees who had been imprisoned for one or more life sentences. Rawda's statement above, especially her insistence on the importance of organization among the detainees as a tool of defiance against the prison's authorities, is a testimony to the women's heightened responsibility and concern for not wasting time; rather, their effort was to make the best of their incarceration, supporting and empowering other women who were incarcerated.

The sense of solidarity and collective struggle emerged in Amne's experience as follows:

> I remember once we were five women in the same room and close to our room there was a room for Jewish women *jinaeyyat* [women with criminal charges, for example, drug dealers]. They were often fighting with each other, screaming and yelling. One day, one of them was smoking marijuana and the stench was filling our room. We were all coughing and choked from the smoke. We started stomping our feet against the door of our room until a prison guard came and asked what was going on. We demanded that we be allowed to leave the room. She [the prison guard] allowed us to get out of the room. We were rebellious in prison.
>
> Amne

The Changed and the Changer

Prison literature in general and the above discussion so far recognizes the radical changes women political detainees undergo in various spheres of life, including the political, organizational, general awareness, education and gender development. In this literature, however, there is much less information on or knowledge about the possibility of an opposite phenomenon, that is, the possibility for change among prison officials through the action of women political detainees, regardless of the extent or degree of such change. In a normal situation of political detention, it is often the case that the political detainees are subjugated to and the victims of oppression by prison guards and wardresses. Political detainees especially females, are seen as silent victims of oppression. Instead, our conversations suggest that to this norm there was also the exception: women political detainees exercised their agency and tried to influence prison wardresses and perhaps change their political position as well.

The spatial proximity between women detainees and their wardresses and guards on the one hand and the relationship between the two necessitated by the prison conditions, on the other, had created a special human or personal relationship between women. Various women political detainees spoke of the close relations that they had established with Israeli wardresses and female guards, whereby the latter became sympathetic to the detainees' cause, understanding their position and being responsive to some of their needs. Here is what Amne had to say:

> One day in Telmond [prison], we needed needles to sew something. We asked our prison wardress to get us needles from the male section [of the prison] and she was co-operative. She went to the men's ward and brought us needles and a bottle of shampoo. When we saw the shampoo, we said we did not ask for shampoo. She responded: 'I could not tell the male guards that I was bringing you needles; this is why I brought the shampoo too.'
>
> Amne

Amne explained this sympathetic action on the part of the wardress as normal human behaviour when they get to know the 'Other' better. Telmond prison included both political detainees as well as female Jewish criminals, and all were in the same section. According to Amne, Palestinian political detainees demonstrated more civility, intelligence and self-respect than the Jewish inmates, another reason for the close relationship with the wardress.

In other cases of what could be seen as influence of the women political detainees on prison guards and wardresses, the women I interviewed told me stories about political discussions and debates between the women and some of their prison wardresses. Topics discussed included the Palestinian right to live in freedom, Israeli colonialism and occupation, and the ordeals of the Palestinian people in general. Some were even proud of themselves, considering such events to be achievements they had made while in prison – changing the occupiers' point of view and making them feel the guilt of their deeds. Here is Salwa's story, in this regard:

> One day I asked her [the wardress] where she was from. She said 'Poland'. I then said, 'This is my homeland and you are here stealing my land.' We talked several times, then I noticed that she began to soften her speech and speak to me with some respect. I really think she learned something different than what they [Israelis] tell her. But some time later I learned that she was fired from her job because of me! When I left prison, I saw her in a demonstration in Jerusalem organized

by the Israeli Peace Now Movement. We talked and she looked at me and said: 'I understand you now, I understand what you were telling me in prison, and I sympathize with you. After leaving my job in prison I decided to join Peace Now in support of your people.'

Salwa

In our one-on-one conversation Aisha also mentioned the phenomenon of wardresses changing their position on Palestinian resistance. In her interview with Antonius (1980), she had elaborated on this issue, saying:

The prison wardress, Raya Epstein, was from Russia. At first she used to tell visiting journalists that we were black-hearted killers of children, that we were backward, underdeveloped, that we understood nothing. But after ten years of contact, of communication and discussions, she changed her opinion and began telling people that we were educated and aware, that we felt we were Palestinian nationalists.

Cited in Antonius (1980: 50)

Although the above stories were of an exceptional nature rather than the norm in Israeli political detention camps, Palestinian women considered such 'changes' as an important part of their agency and power they garnered as fighters and political prisoners.

In a limited temporal and spatial framework, such as the case of a prison or a training camp which holds both women and men, gender contradictions are often minimized as each considers the other as 'equal'. Camaraderie between men and women, Julie Peteet noted, was a consequence of facing the same dangers and trusting one another's military abilities. 'Women,' she writes, 'spoke of a euphoria, a new sense of who I am and my strength and of carrying the same load as men' (Peteet 1991: 150). She adds:

Women's heightened consciousness of their abilities unfolded through action, an action motivated by national consciousness and the conviction that women have a right to participate. Most important, the military experience awakened women to their potential equality to men. The belief in women's unsuitability, both physical and emotional, for training and combat was contested as they proved themselves as committed and able as men. Their strengths were made apparent to themselves and others.

Peteet (1991: 151)

Peteet's observation was made about women fighters in military training camps in Lebanon. Nonetheless, the description she provides is applicable to the case of political women in detention camps. Women spoke of camaraderie relations with other male political prisoners, they spoke of mutual respect and solidarity in resistance actions taken up in prison, and some positive aspects of these relationships continued after leaving the prison environment.

The exposure of women to intensive political discussions and analysis, their physical proximity to each other, and the presence of a variety of ideological positions held by people in the prisons had different effects on them, cementing for some their existing ideological convictions while in others leading them to change political affiliations and adopt different political (that is, party) paths – the turn was often either to the left or within the left. Thus, for example, Itaf's statement: 'In prison I was impressed with the ideology and thoughts of the leftist parties. I left and joined the DFLP. Various other women, especially within the left (for example, within the PFLP and the DFLP), also changed their affiliations.' Aisha, for example, switched from being a member of the PFLP to becoming one of the DFLP. Others changed their political affiliations after they left the prison, while still other women removed themselves from belonging to any political party altogether, becoming as they said 'independent'.

The Intimate and the Sexual in Prison

Although politics, struggle, resistance and liberation constituted the topics most discussed among women political detainees, they were not the only ones. Conversations with political ex-detainees suggest that not all experiences of struggle and resistance were harsh, mentally demanding, or required a particular strength, resilience and seriousness. There were moments which passed so quickly but left a great sense of defiance as well as relief in women's memories. These moments related to the intimate discussions about personal life, sexual desires, and gender relations in general, but also to the 'fun days' in which women also exhibited their power of defiance. Here is one such moment described by Amne:

> One day the Committee in Solidarity with Palestinian Political Detainees – a Jewish committee – came to visit us and brought us clothes. We were five women in the room. The clothes consisted of

red pants, yellow T-shirts and orange blouses! They were very cheap … probably one or two shekels each. We all wore the same clothes and for two days and two nights we slept in them and did everything in these clothes. The next day we went to breakfast all wearing the same tasteless and multi-coloured clothes and sat at the same table looking like little schoolgirls in uniform. After breakfast, we went out to the *fora* [recess or break]. We started marching like soldiers and chanting national songs. The woman who led the march was a bit wacky and had a loud voice. It was quite a scene … [outburst of laugh by all at the focus group]. Although we considered this fun, the prison guards did not feel the same way; they shouted at us and punished us by sending us back to the cell before the end of our *fora*.

Amne

Everybody in the focus group kept laughing at the story until Kholoud intervened, saying: 'So all of you were worth five shekels!' leading to further laughter. Amne continued:

As I told you we used to sleep with these clothes, lest the guards come and confiscate them. The next night one prison guard came to the room and started collecting all the clothes she found around. Some were washed and still wet, others dirty and still others were taken off because it was too hot to wear them all at once at the same time at night during sleeping time. The guards insisted that these clothes were given to us by the PLO and we insisted that it was the Jewish solidarity Group. The Jewish Committee by the way had to declare these clothes to the prison officials before giving them to us, so the prison knew the source of these clothes, still we managed to cause them troubles.

Amne

At that moment in the group conversation, while the atmosphere was relaxed and laughter was quite loud because of Amne's story, Sonia, with a big smile on her face, interjected:

When I was detained, I was a second year university student. I was not a traditional detainee [socially conservative] as were, for example, Aisha, Mariam, Rasmiyya, and others. I entered the detention with a lot of experience and activism and was never afraid. On my first day of detention, the prison wardress entered my room and found me lying down on my back with my head on the lap of another woman who had tweezers in her hand and was plucking my eyebrows. The wardress thought I was a criminal prisoner and not a political detainee. She left the room without any question.

Sonia

Sonia's words came as a shock to some younger women. As they explained later they did not expect to hear this from a university professor! Sonia continued:

I am by nature an open-minded woman. I speak directly to the issue. I am frank and have always had the ability to speak in great detail. Sometimes I even describe things in a graphic manner. Of course, some of the detainees at the time were not like this, but most others were very friendly, close and trusting. I will give you an example: In prison, we had secret meetings. Before any woman could join such meetings, we would put her through a test of trust … that never happened to me. I joined these secret meetings with not a single question asked of me.

Sonia

At that point, Rawda intervened to attest to the witty and very 'frank character of Sonia'. She described Sonia as 'a most open-minded woman, one who would share her very intimate experiences with the others without any hesitation.' Sonia resumed her story, saying: 'Before detention, I was in love with three different men at the same time … when we used to sit and discuss social issues in prison I used to ask the other detainees: "Who do you think I should be with when I leave prison?" They would unanimously vote for Anees.'

Strong personalities who combine resilience, revolutionary spirit, academia or high education are not an exceptional phenomenon in Palestinian resistance. Such personalities have always existed outside the small prison as will be discussed later in this chapter.

In prison, women discussed many intimate and personal issues including first love, relations with husbands, and relations with male comrades outside and inside detention. One woman, for example, spoke about how she helped her male lover to marry a different woman. Another told a story about how she went to her lover's house and proposed to him: 'I offered my hand in marriage,' something almost unheard of in an Arab traditional society. During the one-to-one interviews one woman announced that 'for the first time' she spoke about a 'very close' [meant a lesbian] relationship she had with another female comrade in prison. The relationship, she said, lasted until after prison, when 'the husband [of her friend] found out and threatened to divorce her if she met her female lover again.'

Given the rather socially conservative nature of Palestinian society, revealing such intimate personal stories indicated the degree of openness and sexual freedom some of the women possessed. In addition, public discussion of topics such as the sexual in an environment where the national has long been and continues to be prioritized over all other gender–social issues is itself a complex issue. A tension often emerged in the focus group, especially when issues of an intimate and sexual nature arose. 'Groups,' Lloyd-Evans has argued, can be 'participatory and empowering as participants find strength in numbers and feel in control of the research process; one also notice those within the group who are more dominant and have more powerful voices' (Lloyd-Evans 2006: 155). The risk in this is that those who feel they have a 'controversial' or 'opposing' view in relation to the rest of the group – in our case 'opposing' to those of veteran women, described as politically and nationally progressive, but socially conservative – can be silenced, especially given a sensitive subject like sexuality. This was our experience in the focus group discussion. During the conversation, Kholoud discussed a particular case in which a young woman detainee was 'caught masturbating' in her room by one other political detainee, and instead of talking to her about sexuality and human sexual needs, she was scolded and punished. Aisha, who had just joined the focus group, was very angry about Kholoud 'airing women's private stuff in public,' and accused her of being 'Westernized'. The tension which developed at that moment between some (but not all) of the veteran ex-detainees and the younger ones clearly demonstrated power relations in groups of women with different claims to authenticity and national stature.[7]

Remembrance and Forgetfulness in Prison

Settler colonialism in general and its prison institution more specifically are designed to break the will of the subject populations in order to make them conform to the colonial order. Political detention aims at breaking the will of political detainees, at fracturing their determination and forcing them to submit to the authority's wishes (Langer 1979; Bechara 2001; 2003; Harlow 1992; Abdo 2008). The use of different forms of torture is also designed to serve the same purpose. Such tactics are known to the detainees and in fact pose a major challenge to most of them. Considering that most political detainees are kept in isolation cells for long periods of time, unable to tell the time or distinguish between day and night, the concept of time and telling the time, along with the concept of space become major challenges for them. Surviving the period of their incarceration without breaking or submitting to the prison authority is considered a major achievement in the struggle of political detainees. In the process of survival, detainees develop specific skills and talents, one of which is how they deal with time.

In her *Stolen Lives: Twenty Years in a Desert Jail*, Malika Oufkir (2001) relates how Mariam, her sister, possessed a special sense of time. In attending to sunbeams which entered her small window, 'when asked about the time any time during the day she would answer: ten to three or four fifteen. She never errs on this' (Oufkir and Fitoussi 2001: 169). Similarly, in his *Tilka al-Atmah al-Bahira* (The Brilliant Darkness), francophone Moroccan novelist Tahar Ben Jalloun (2001) describes in great detail the acute sense of time (minute, hour, day and date) possessed by his protagonist, Karim, despite the fact that he spent his years in a dark cell in which there was no light or window (Ben Jalloun 2011: 106).

How Palestinian women used the time to educate themselves, how they organized their time around lectures, seminars, reading sessions and writing, and how they utilized time to its best, was very important to them. For some, time took a heavy toll, as it seemed too long and probably indefinite, while for others the time during one day was hardly enough to accomplish their planned activities. Although in most cases time was well utilized, there were moments in which time was spent watching what could be described as 'nothingness'. In Chapter 4 Munia's story about watching cockroaches in the cell consumed a lot of her time and some of the time of her friends she kept inviting to see the whereabouts of the cockroach, whose 'antennae' showed or 'moustache' grew. 'Come! The cockroach started walking,' Munia called her friends in the cell, adding: 'This cockroach inside does not hurt us. Hurt and injury comes to us from the outside!'

Whereas Munia and her prison mates watched the cockroach, other women also spent time watching and thinking of ways to get rid of the mice and rats they had in their cells. Other women complained about the lack of time in their possession to complete all they wanted to do. Here is Amne on this:

> Time! I did not have enough time to do what was needed to do in prison. To begin with, I was selected to hold the post of women's representative to the prison's authorities. I take their complaints to the prison officials, I represent them to the Red Cross and other foreign delegations which visit us. I also worked in the kitchen. Time for me passed very quickly. After six months in prison, I started counting how much more I had until I completed three years and what I needed to do in that time. Inside our prison cell we established a 'think-tank'. In our prison [Telmond] we had a lot of books donated to us by the Red Cross and our families. The 24 hours in a day were not enough. We were six in the cell. We had a library with books on Marx and Marxism, political books and literary books; we learnt embroidery. Each one teaches the other a skill. Our parents would bring the material and we would do the work and send most of it to our loved ones outside of prison.
>
> Amne

In prison, times and dates can have different meanings to different people; for some, remembering times and dates was crucial for their personal memory while for others it made no difference to them. During our focus group, a debate between Rawda and Sonia on remembering evolved, when Rawda observed: 'I remember all dates, including the dates of strikes, arrests and releases of every woman.' To this, as we saw in Chapter 4, Sonia was very surprised stating that she did not remember a thing, not even the date of her own court sentence: 'dates for me are meaningless.'

Life After Prison

When in prison, women struggled to become free and to leave it. They hoped for a better future, a receptive environment and an accepting community. Many women upon their release were celebrated by their family, the community and other women's organizations. During visitations by friends and comrades, some even were pleased in seeing newspaper clips which carried their photos and short articles about them while in prison. Aisha and Haleema 'A.' spoke at length about the *hafla* (party) put on for them by family and comrades. Here is Haleema 'A.'s' experience:

> The first day of release was celebrated like a wedding. At the door of the prison the family and comrades were there waiting, they were singing and dancing in the streets. For a month and a half and twelve hours a day our house was full of well-wishers. After my release [in 1990] I started doing volunteer work, until the coming of the PNA [Palestinian National Authority, in 1994]. I was a lawyer, I worked with Nadil-asir [a political detainee club – today the Ministry of Detainees] with the Mandela Institute and Ad-dameer [all are human rights organizations concerned mainly with prisoners]. I must say there was very little money there.
>
> Haleema 'A.'

Such celebrations, however, did not last long. After all, 'for female fighters, the struggle is almost always personal as much as it is national since national commitments will not erase her personal transgressions as far as family and society are concerned' (Al-Samman 2009: 334). Still, most women in our conversations had to go back, face new challenges and fight to gain or regain a position in their society.

Until the 1990s, the one and only active Palestinian association which celebrated the release of women detainees was Ina'ash al-Usra in Ramallah. This charitable society held several parties for released women and awarded them special gifts expressive of the importance of their struggle and their steadfastness. Names of released female political prisoners also appeared in local newspapers basically as announcements, with a little information on each.[8]

It should be noted that when these women were detained, they did not exactly move from a state of sovereignty, freedom and independence into the dungeon; their move was from a large open-air prison into a smaller walled and contained one. Still, for many, the outside world had changed and was different than when they were detained. Kholoud, for example, noted the change in the currency she found when she was released from prison: 'from *quroush* [pennies], to shekels, this was a big change for me.' Technological change within a period of about one decade was also impressive for some. Upon her release, Itaf for the first time saw a telephone: 'When it rang for the first time, I held it upside down and could not hear the caller. I also saw TV and running water for the first time in my village.' Ramallah was very different for Aisha and Itaf. They used to know Ramallah as a large town with plenty of green spaces; by the time of their release, it had become very populated, with many apartment buildings and few green spaces. Munia reflected on changes she found in Jerusalem, saying:

> When I left Jerusalem for prison, there was no Street #1. After my release, the first thing that shocked me in Jerusalem was to see this street. I knew I used to go to the Wall from that area. I asked my brother (who brought me home) to take me to the Jerusalem Wall; he said he couldn't because the road to the Wall had changed and we could not go from this road.
>
> Munia

When she saw the Wall for the first time, Munia explained in a face-to-face interview:

> I never cried when I left my father or my mother, but when I saw the Sibat [a historic alley] and the Aqsa [the Aqsa Mosque] and the Wall in front of my eyes I sobbed and cried hard ... I really missed this place.
>
> Munia

It is no surprise that the prisoner's return to 'freedom' was full of challenges and issues to be struggled over, the most important of which was finding employment. Women struggled to find jobs; they struggled to continue their education; they struggled to occupy a respectable space in their society; and they struggled to regain their status as freedom fighters and history makers. They were frustrated and disappointed in, for example, seeing their struggle before and during prison of little worth to the 'free society'. They were disappointed to find that the skills and knowledge they gained had little employable value and were further disappointed in cultural-traditional practices which had not changed in patriarchal character despite their struggle for gender equality, at least on the national level.

Back to the Social Struggle!

The prison is capable of erasing time and melting space and temporality within its walls and the walls of the interrogation rooms. When leaving the prison, both time and space re-emerge having a new function and a new role they had not possessed before. The way 'free' women deal with the new and open space, and the way they deal with and face the movement of change in the 'free' world were some of the important issues discussed in the conversations.

One common feeling expressed by most women was that despite the space that life outside the prison offers, it was still too small to accommodate the needs, dreams and desires of ex-political detainees. Words like 'estrangement' and 'alienation' were used by a number of women as expressions to their feelings after their release and when they were face-to-face with the world outside the 'small' prison. Women in prison increased their gender and even feminist consciousness and considered themselves more free and liberated than most other Palestinian women, yet when released they found life outside to have hardly changed in its traditional and patriarchal orientation. The disappointment after leaving prison and facing reality was well described by Sonia:

> The most difficult thing for me was the first two years after prison. We were among the first group of women detainees – Rawda was among us.[9] We were building the homeland in prison and dreaming to change the world around us. We had big dreams and worked hard to inform ourselves of everything around us. When I left the prison, I discovered that the world was not waiting for me and that life outside prison had not stopped when I was imprisoned. I discovered the world goes on and life continues with me or without me.
>
> Sonia

As the following experiences demonstrate, of the many important concerns raised by women regarding their disappointment with society, such as the failed 1994 Oslo Agreement, the corruption and gender discrimination, and the widening gap between the rich and the poor, two major issues seemed of particular concern: first, securing a place within society, getting married and establishing a family, and second, economic security, primarily finding employment. Here is Iman's experience after her release:

> When I left prison, I got married to an Ethiopian man of Christian background. I have a child who is eight now. My husband has the US green card and used to come and visit. After our marriage, he left for

the US to work, and when he came to take me and the child to join him, Israel knew he had married me, they denied him entry. I am currently working at the Ministry of Sports. I must admit, the prison made me more educated. I still have a very good relation with my brother and mother. I want to say that I donned the veil in prison as a form of defiance and expression of belief. None of my sisters don veils; I am the only one in my family. I never tell my sisters what to do nor do they interfere in my life. Also, after I left prison I started university, but after the first year, Israel imposed a curfew on us and made our movement almost impossible, so I could not complete my education.

Iman

The relative ease in which Iman faced life after prison was not shared by several others. For example, Amne encountered many objections from her family. They objected to her smoking and staying out late, and her brother, a sheikh, wanted her to veil. All her family members donned the veil except for her:

When I left prison, I broke all traditional norms. I decided to go and ask for his hand [the man she loved]. When I arrived at his house to ask for his hand, I was sitting with his mother, father and himself. I asked his parents for his hand. His mother told me: 'I do not want to marry my son. He is still young [Amne was 22 and the man she loved 29]. I could hardly deal with the fact that my nephew is imprisoned for life, I cannot deal with it any more.' In the meanwhile, his father said we needed to wait until he established himself. As for him, he was totally silent, as if he was deaf. I looked at him and said to myself: 'I am not here to ask for charity or for their pity. I have integrity and pride. I am a fighter and will not compromise. Anyway I am not a traditional woman and not made to stay home. This weak and submissive man is not for me.' I left his house and decided to forget him. I was convinced that strong and independent women need strong and independent men!

Amne

Amne married a 'decent' man, as she described him. 'He was an ex-political prisoner and spent much of his time in prison getting educated. He also wanted a strong woman and not a traditional one.' Amne moved with her husband to Beit-Lahem, Amne considered Beit Lahem to be more open than traditional Nablus.

The issue of marriage or establishing a family after detention was not an easy task for women ex-detainees. Even male ex-detainees were reluctant to marry ex-detainees. This reluctance is further exaggerated in a society where marriage has been and remained a family issue with heavy involvement of the parents, as we saw above in the case of Amne. Moreover, in a largely socially traditional society such as that of Palestine, the question of equality in the national struggle does not automatically translate into gender equality or equality at the social level. As argued above, gender equality might be true or might seem true within a closed space (e.g. in prison or in training camps), but not in society or in the struggle at large. Alian, herself an ex-political detainee married to an ex-political detainee, concurs with this bitter reality. According to her:

> Even given the compassion of the Palestinian nation towards prisoners, the reality proves otherwise. For example, marrying an ex-prisoner raises various controversies and is usually accompanied by fear, doubt and the wish to keep a distance; as the saying goes, 'Praise the evil from afar'. There are only few exceptions, mainly those who experienced detention themselves and therefore pay more respect for detained women. Among them is my husband and companion Walid Al Hodali.
>
> Alian (2011: 187)

Not all male ex-political detainees are open to or willing to marry women with similar experiences (ex-political detainees). Quite to the contrary, the norm among male ex-political prisoners is not to partner with female ex-political prisoners, and those who do are the exception. Of the over two dozen women ex-detainees I encountered in my research, only three female ex-political detainees were married to political ex-detainees either during or after their term of imprisonment. One of them was Alian herself who made the above statement. Alian spoke highly of the support she received from her husband and children during and after her incarceration.

It is true that women's struggle and resistance strengthens women's resilience and defiance and in some cases also improves their status within the family. But for some women, family dynamics after a daughter's incarceration can get sour and women can be most affected. The difficulties some ex-prisoners encounter after their release, whether manifested in family resentment of the whole idea of female incarceration or out of fear their daughters will not be able to find suitable partners and have their own families, place a great deal of pressure on them. It is worth noting that the family referred to by most women in the conversations does not refer to the nuclear family, but rather to the extended family, the *hamula*, which includes grandparents, uncles, aunts and cousins and sometimes even the neighbours. The whole *hamula* often interferes in the life of the individual, especially insofar as women are concerned – placing pressure on the nuclear family. Here is what Rawda had to say:

> My parents were under a lot of social pressure from the community and the extended family. They were shunned by them all. People were scared to talk with parents of detainees, especially to parents of us who were in the armed resistance.
>
> Rawda

Some women, for example Aisha, remained single and continued to command the respect of society at large, although she was not very successful in finding a job after her release. Other women were disappointed for yet other reasons. Sonia's experience, although unique, is quite telling. When she was released, Sonia was determined that the first thing she was going to do was look for Anees, the person she loved, and spend her life with him. However, when she found him, Sonia was put under a great deal of pressure, not due to social, but political (party) pressure, as she was forced by the political party of which she was a member to choose between her love and her membership in the party:

> Before detention I was very independent and determined. For me God was not the one in heaven but the *tanzeem* (organization). I was already organized with the DFLP. When I left prison the *tanzeem* I belonged to was in a very bad shape ... One day a comrade from the same *tanzeem* came and told me: 'The *tanzeem* tells you to leave Anees' – the man I loved – or 'The *tanzeem* will have to make its decision. We gave you a position in the leadership and you should be in a relationship with one of your comrades and not an outsider.' Anees did not belong to any *tanzeem* ... he was independent and a free man.
>
> I responded: 'Listen! I will not leave Anees and let the *tanzeem* do whatever it wishes' [*illi byitlaa' bi-eedo yitlaa' bi* ...]. After that incident, I resigned from the *tanzeem*.
>
> Sonia

Sonia's experience confirms a long-held feminist position on gender and nationalism, on gender and politics. In her 'The Relationship between the Social and the National', Islah Jad criticizes Palestinian intellectuals, especially those on the left, emphasizing the gap she finds between their talk and practice, and between their social-gender consciousness on the one hand and their political and national progressive positions on the other. Jad's position, shared by other Palestinian feminists, is that Palestinian progressive intellectuals are for the most part on the left and quite radical on the political front, yet conservative if not socially reactionary (Jad 1995: 169). 'Men,' Kholoud said during the focus group, 'allow everything for themselves and deny it to women.'

Itaf, Aisha and various other militants were not released to their home, family and community in Palestine; rather, these women were expelled, often deported to Jordan. Some of them, including Aisha and Itaf, came back to Palestine with the PLO after Oslo. While in exile, Itaf, almost alone, tried to build her family. Her experience of the social future of women ex-detainees is interesting, as she insisted on marrying a man whom she knew to be very sick and who had been told that he had not much time left to live. Itaf had a theory on who the men are who might marry a woman ex-detainee. Her theory was based on her own experience and the types of men who asked for her hand. She divided men willing to marry ex-political detainees into six types or categories:

After my release from prison, various men came to ask for my hand. I used to sit with these men, eager to know why they wanted to marry me. I found that different men had different reasons for marrying an ex-detainee: first, some wanted to brag about marrying a *munadela*, and second those who were after the money. Those days [the early 1980s], released political prisoners were given an allowance of 3,000 dinars as a gift [by their *tanzeem*]. They [PLO] were also quick at offering us jobs [this was in Jordan].[10] A third group consisted of ex-detainees, many of whom were released with various injuries, especially psychological ones. I was afraid to marry into this group. Fourth is the charitable category, those who thought by marrying an ex-detainee they would do her a service. Fifth, the older men – I was 27 when a 65-year-old man came to ask for my hand. I asked him, why me in particular? His answer was: 'I want to save you from people's talk.' Although I lived by myself in Amman, I had a lot of pressure from my sister's family to marry.

Itaf

The issue of marriage emphasized above is intended as a window on the general social and gender dynamics within Palestinian society insofar as women activists and militants are concerned. Seeking marriage by women upon their release was synonymous to achieving and thereby holding a socially respectable position in their society, signalling their true welcome back to the larger family. The actual challenge 'freed' women found upon their release lies in a complex set of social relations, relations expressed by Rawda who was engaged when she was detained as follows:

> When I left prison, I thought that I was not thinking much about marriage, but I was wrong. In fact, I did, but when in prison, he sent me a message which I did not like. At the time, we had enough problems in prison and I did not need more. I wrote him back saying: 'That's it. I am sentenced for eight years, consider our relation over.' I felt good about this. He was not satisfied with my answer and sent his family, and they wanted me back. When I left prison I was 35 years old, still, I refused to go back to him. My prison experience enhanced my feminist beliefs. I refused to marry in the same [traditional] way. I am a Christian and knew I could not find a Christian man to marry me, and the idea of marrying a Muslim man did not occur to me. I did not want to struggle for my personal or private issues, until one man who was in prison with us was released. He told me about his prison experience and we became close. But he was Muslim, which meant another struggle. It is at that point that I thought it is my right to marry someone with whom I can share my life and experiences – still, I was divided between him and my family.
>
> Rawda

Rawda's marriage experience speaks of issues which are social concerns to many: the absence of civil marriage, and the restrictions on Muslim–Christian marriages:

> The Christian communities around me started coming to our house to convince me not to marry him because he is Muslim, saying 'You are a role model and an example for other women. You made us very proud, but your marriage will make it difficult for our daughters to find good husbands.'
>
> Rawda

In addition to social pressures from extended family and the community, the Israeli state, through its prison institution also intervenes in women's personal choice. Rawda's decision to choose her life partner as an ex-political detainee and from a different religion, has paid politically and personally. During that time and before making up her mind about marriage, Rawda was called again by the prison authority for questioning, where the following discussion took place: 'We know you want to get married.' I responded that 'this was a personal matter for me.' They said: 'Why marry this man? He is a terrorist'. I left the Israeli intelligence office and decided I was going to get married.

This marriage was very costly for Rawda:

I was repudiated by everyone in my town, I waited very long for their approval. I have been married for quite some time, still, my cousins continue to shun me. They do not talk to me at all. Right up until today, when I visit my town [Tayybe], people continue to discuss the issue with me.

Rawda

For Rawda, this struggle was harder and even longer than the one she waged in prison:

I believe I am a fighter and it is my right to live with a partner of my choice. I am equal to my husband, we share everything at home. He was in prison for 17 years. He is really a role model as a male human being.

Rawda

Employment Among Women Ex-Detainees

Reintegration into the society and community was not a smooth process for many women ex-detainees. Various women complained about the lack of labour opportunities – in fact, of their actual exclusion from employment after their release. For example, Haleema 'A.' expressed her frustration thus:

Although the *tanzeem* [in this case, the PFLP], the society at large and my family were supportive, I faced discrimination on the employment front – no one would give me a job. I applied to jobs everywhere but was always rebuffed. Deep in my heart I knew that the reason was my political affiliation, which is different than that of the PA.

Haleema 'A.'

Like other feminists and women activists, Haleema 'A.' was convinced that the PA discriminates not only on the basis of gender, but also on the basis of political affiliation as well.

After leaving prison, I found a lot of support from my family, the PFLP and the community around me. The only problem I faced was finding a job. There was a lot of discrimination against political ex-detainees, and the reason is because of the different political leanings and organizations of these detainees.

Haleema 'A.'

Haleema 'A.'s' opinion is in sync with Palestinian feminist research, which claims that 'With heavily patriarchal structures, nationalist entitlements – such as posts in the authority – are primarily given to males who are part of the militarized hierarchy of the major political organization, Fateh' (Jad, Johnson and Giacaman 2000: 139). Haleema 'A.'s' story was particularly significant for the excuse used for not employing her as related to her by a PA official: In order to practise law, she needed a *huson solouk* (a record of 'good behaviour': a clean record). This bizarre claim, coming out of the mouth of the man responsible for the employment of ex-detainees, was highly resented by Haleema 'A.':

Because of my detention, I do not have *huson solouk*. For several years I was frustrated, then I went to Radi al-Jirae'i – the PA man in charge of the employment of ex-detainees in the PA – and told him, 'I cannot afford to pay rent, I have no money, I am a lawyer who practised for many years before prison, I do not have *huson solouk*, give me any job so that I can live.' But because of my political affiliation [which was not Fateh], they refused. There was a lot of vacancies for lawyers, they brought lawyers from Jordan, but refused to take me.

Haleema 'A.'

After many years of volunteer work Haleema 'A.', a practising lawyer before her detention, was able to find a job as a legal consultant at the Women's Centre for Legal Aid and Counselling (WCLAC). The claim that the type of 'political affiliation', namely Fateh, which is the largest *tanzeem*, or other *tanzeem*s such as the PFLP or the DFLP, influences ex-detainees chances of getting employment or more support was echoed in various conversations held with the women. The claim has been that members of Fateh were more successful in obtaining government and other jobs after their release (e.g. as with Salwa and Kholoud), while others, namely women belonging to other political parties, were less fortunate and faced major difficulties in finding employment.

Itaf was another unfortunate soul in terms of finding employment after her release in 1985. Reflecting on this issue, Itaf said: 'What I found most appalling is the reaction of the women's or feminist organizations, whose response was exactly the same as that of male institutions. All claimed I needed a certificate to be employed.' After some years Itaf took a job with one feminist organization which she considered to be exploitative and which failed to 'give her the credit she deserved.' When we met, for the first time, in 2008, Itaf was still in the same job and still complaining: she was very unhappy and not satisfied with her feminist employer:

> I did not have a *tanzeem* to support me. The most I was offered was a secretary job. Worse still has been the shabby treatment I received from the women's organizations. Three years ago a job vacancy for editorial manager was available. I had been doing this type of work [editing] for many years, but because I had no degree my name never showed up on the magazine I edit every month. I did not have a BA and therefore I never received proper compensation for the worth of my work and contribution.
>
> Itaf

Not unlike Haleema 'A.' and Itaf, Rawda also went through a very difficult time trying to find a job. Rawda was already a maths teacher before her incarceration. She stated that she applied to many schools and other educational institutions, but to no avail:

> I had the same experience. No one would give me a job. After a long search I found an advertisement in a local newspaper which said that a Muslim charitable organization in al-Bireh was looking for a principal for a school for the deaf and blind. This was my education and expertise. In fact, I was the only person qualified for this job in the area. I accepted the job despite its huge responsibility and minimal salary.
>
> Rawda

Despite Rawda's large responsibility in this job – that is, establishing an elementary school for the deaf and the blind – and despite the large drop in salary she took, from 360 dinars per month before detention to 70 dinars per month in this job, Rawda was proud of the offer. She was the first Christian woman ever to be employed in this Muslim charitable organization: 'For me as a Christian political detainee, the only party who employed me was this organization!'

Social hardships, discrimination in the labour force, and continual gender discrimination regardless of the grave sacrifices made by women political ex-detainees were the lot of most of them. '*Mujtama'a la yarham*' (a cruel society), several women complained. Was it worth the struggle? Was it worth all the sacrifices women committed for their national independence, against colonialism and occupation? To such questions, all women and despite the disappointment of some after their release, answered in the affirmative, saying words to the effect that they did not regret what they had done at all – words similar to those uttered by Leila Khaled as we saw in Chapter 4. There were though a couple of women who said that if they were to partake in the resistance movement again, they would do it differently. Both women said the situation in the 1960s–1980s was different. Haleema 'A.' for example elaborated:

> Today, the situation is very different … the objective conditions have changed dramatically. Then there was a strong revolutionary movement worldwide. I was a member of the PFLP and had a very strong will for resistance using any and all means for the sake of Palestine. I studied the history of Palestine and was very committed towards its liberation and the return of my people to their homes and lands.
>
> Haleema 'A.'

Earlier in this chapter we discussed some of the differences in women's attitudes towards the struggle. For some the political and the national and the cause have dominated their struggle, while others have combined the political with the social and the gender, and were also involved in raising feminist consciousness through reading and discussion sessions. With time, however, more women, especially of the older generation, also began to bring out issues other than the political or national or the cause as equally important issues on their agenda. For example, one could see some change in Aisha's attitudes: from a struggle where the political/national discourse was dominant and even overriding in her first autobiography

(Odeh 2004) and the interview to the third autobiography (Odeh 2012) where she discusses more intimate and personal issues, including love relations, family issues and gender concerns. Such a shift was also evident in the attitude of Leila Khaled and the difference between her autobiography (Khaled 1973) where the national dominated the discourse, to her later interviews. For example, in her interview with Katherine Viner, Khaled says: 'At the beginning, we were only interested in the revolution. We were not mature enough politically.' When asked whether she defines herself as woman first or Palestinian first, she responded: 'a woman and Palestinian at the same time' (Viner 2001). In the same interview Khaled said: 'I have learned that a woman can be a fighter, a freedom fighter, a political activist, and that she can fall in love, be loved … be married, have children, be a mother' (Viner 2001).[11]

Conclusion

The choice to discuss women's experiences of political detention as a result of their involvement in the anti-colonial struggle during the decades of the 1960s through to the 1980s served several objectives. As discussed in Chapter 1, it served as a reminder of the significance of the global anti-colonial struggle occurring during those three decades and the important place women occupied in the anti-colonial movements. This epoch, I have argued, revealed a relatively hidden chapter in the history of women's resistance in various parts of the world. (Re)presenting certain aspects of women's varied experiences as political detainees confirmed commonalities and similarities among women political detainees regardless of the nature of the state, whether colonial, settler colonial or so-called liberal democratic. Regardless of the actual nature of the state under discussion, for example, the United States, Israel or Great Britain, it was clear that states criminalized the anti-colonial struggle and as such also criminalized individual women political prisoners, considering them to be terrorists rather than freedom fighters. Still, criminalization of political activism was strongly resisted by the women in the struggle. Representing women's histories of anti-colonial struggle, by focusing on their daily experiences as political prisoners, has affirmed the high degree of resilience and resistance put up by such women against their prison authorities.

One particularly significant finding in the study of the incarceration of women involved in the armed anti-colonial struggle in general has been the extent to which the state, through the prison institution, tries to control women. State patriarchy, which in prisons targets women's bodies and sexuality in ways very different than it does men's, aims at controlling and disciplining them not only as women but more importantly as agents of change. Controlling women's activists is a means for controlling the rest of the society. In the process of enforcing such control the state targets women's bodies as a means for such control. Sexual harassment and humiliation in all forms, including attempted rape and rape, are used to deter women from participating in the struggle. Data available, whether from the case of women in Northern Ireland as discussed in Chapter 1 or

Palestinian women as discussed throughout this book suggest that women also use their bodies as a site for challenging and resisting prison authority.

It is commonly acknowledged that the act of imprisonment of political activists, of individuals involved in resisting state policies, is political in character. This political act, however, is never isolated from the wider context of the state and its hegemonic ideology. The history of the period under discussion (1960–1980) was also the history of national liberation movements in many Third World countries and a period of anti-colonial and anti-imperialist struggle in various Western countries, including the United States and Britain. Whereas at the time the international community through the United Nations has sanctioned national struggles for liberation, the United States on the contrary has resisted and even fought such movements, considering them terrorist. Considering liberation struggles as terrorist and violent while masking a much worse form of violence, namely, state violence was discussed in Chapter 2.

Chapter 2 discussed the old form of imperialism (colonial and settler colonial forms) and argued that new imperialism, despite its hegemonic ideological structure and the difference in language, wording and context it uses in the service of its interests are connected: new imperialism is the continuation of old imperialism; it has the same aims but different means of expression. Chapter 2 also exposed the rather shocking continuation of dehumanizing and vilifying of Palestinian women involved in the armed struggle, by both Orientalist and imperialist feminists alike. The only difference here was in the large body of literature found more recently, and the little interest and concern which these women received until the late 1980s. From Robin Morgan's initial writing on freedom fighter Leila Khaled, to Dworkin's and her likes among Israeli and US imperialist feminists, Palestinian women's freedom fighters have been depicted as terrorists, villains and as lacking any agency. It is regrettable that feminism, which is supposed to work for and defend any and all forms of oppression against women, instead of doing its job, allies itself with the state and with imperialism and stands against some women.

Contextualizing the Palestinian struggle nationally and international-ally has acquired a cultural dimension as well. During the decades under discussion, people fought for their rights and resisted colonialism through various means, including spoken word or poetry. This culture, known as resistance culture and more specifically resistance literature, has travelled through print and spoken media and was shared among people in struggle in different parts of the globe. The discussions with ex-political detainees revealed women's familiarity with international resistance literature, which they read and studied as part of their training for the struggle. In addition to the presence of international resistance literature, Palestinian women were heavily impacted by the rich body of regional (*Arabic*) literature and national (Palestinian) resistance literature. For women in the armed struggle, cultural resistance (poetry and prose) went hand in hand with their actual armed resistance.

Still, the particularly rich culture of resistance, including prison literature and resistance literature expressed mainly in poetry (e.g. by Mahmoud Darwish and Tawfiq Zayyad) and novels (e.g. by Ghassan Kanafani) have had a tremendous impact on all women in the national and anti-colonial struggle.

Our conversations with the women, as demonstrated in Chapter 4, have shown the fallacy of the Western (including Israeli) imperialist perspective and especially its racist Orientalist form directed towards Palestinian women involved in the armed struggle. These conversations demonstrated women's resilience and their strong will in challenging and defying Israeli colonialism, despite the violence and atrocities committed against them by the state and its prison institutions. Women's lived experiences before and during their incarceration, as discussed in Chapter 4, reveal a great deal of personal and political willpower and strength in order to be able to join the armed resistance regardless of the personal price they will pay. By detailing the terrible forms of physical, mental, psychological and sexual torture faced by women political detainees, Chapter 4 provided an additional proof to the argument that the actual violence is that of the state and its institutions, including that of the prison. Women involved in the armed struggle were convinced that their struggle is aimed at protecting and defending their families and their land: they were struggling for their freedom from oppression and colonialism. This position was uttered by various women in their encounters with the Israeli military courts.

The victimization, criminalization, torture, humiliation and constant intimidation practised against women political detainees were countered by a great deal of resistance by these women. Most importantly, Chapter 5 documented the creative individual and collective work women engaged in, as a mode of survival and resilience. One such act included the way in which they have turned the prison into a school, a university or an 'academy' (as one woman said), producing more educated women and preparing them for a better future when released. In addition to 'formal' education, they also held discussion groups and reading sessions in which they discussed a variety of issues, from world politics to issues of resistance and organization, to social-gender issues, through various readings, including by feminists such as Egyptian Nawal Saa'dawi. All this was intended to prepare them for a better future. Of equal importance in terms of the various forms of resistance invented by political ex-detainees as discussed in Chapter 5 has been women's response to the prison's authority use of their body and sexuality as a tool of torture. In response to the prison's tactics, women political detainees it was argued have also turned their bodies into a site of resistance, demonstrating to the occupier that they were aware of the former's tactics and that they were willing to challenge and defy them.

Finally, the dissatisfaction expressed by many women in the inability of the 'free' society outside prison to accommodate them was a rather disappointing reality for some of these women. As discussed in Chapter 5, one of the reasons for such disappointment was that these women left the 'small' prison only to find themselves in a much larger open one: a society still under occupation, colonialism and expanding Israeli settler colonial policies, with the further impoverishment this brought to Palestinians. As explained in Chapter 5, several of these women could not find a job when released. For others, the patriarchal structure of the Palestinian Authority (PA), which prioritized men in general and male ex-political prisoners over women, was seen as an important factor in their disillusionment as 'free' women. Finally, a small section of the women referred to the rupture of the Palestinian political life as a reason for their dissatisfaction. This rupture occurred while some of them were either in prison or expelled and prevented from returning to their homes until 1994 as part of the Oslo Accords. This situation has led to further fragmentation of the Palestinians, breaking up the PLO: recognizing Fateh and supporters of Oslo as legitimate forces, while forces opposed to Oslo (e.g. the PFLP and DFLP), where most women in the armed struggle at the time had belonged to, where delegitimized.

Afterword

I wrote this book during a very difficult phase in the history of the Arab world. Many, if not most Arab peoples are glued to their television screens watching the destruction and chaos throughout the Arab world: the devastation of Libya, the terrorist attacks in Iraq, the struggle between the Egyptian army and the Muslim Brotherhood, and most importantly, the atrocities inflicted upon the Syrian people and the destruction of religious sites and symbols of thousands of years of civilization. After completing this book, I was wondering with all of this turmoil engulfing most Arab countries how important this book, celebrating women's struggle and resistance, is especially as it deals with a historic period rather than the current one.

Despite my strong belief in this project, its value in reviving the revolutionary struggle of women in the Arab world and beyond, and its implications for the younger generation, I still questioned the value of this research at this moment in our/Arab history. The Arab world, I fully recognized has and continues to pay little to no attention to the armed struggle, let alone women's armed struggle. The latter by many seems to have been an issue of the past, with no relevance to the present, let alone to the future.

In November 2013, Al-Mayadeen devoted a whole week to celebrating Arab women who were involved in the anti-colonial armed struggle in their countries. A special event throughout this week was devoted to the Algerian freedom fighter, Jamila Bouhaired. The week of celebration also brought to light the meaning and value of the armed resistance for various peoples, through the invitation of women fighters from various parts of the world, including Cuban Aleida Guevara, Palestinian Leila Khaled and, Therese Halasa, among many others. The large crowd which, mostly from the youth, who attended the celebration was a pleasant surprise not only to Al-Mayadeen but to me as well. For me, this event served as a strong impetus for getting this book out to the public. The message in this celebration, similar to the message of this book, became very clear: women's revolutionary history, their history of struggle and resistance, no matter how much these women and their roles are silenced and removed from official history, it remains a constituent part of their people's liberation and independence.

Notes

Chapter 1: Forgotten History, Lost Voices and Silent Souls: Women Political Detainees

1. This paper was presented at a conference at the Centre for Research on Migration, Refugees and Belonging (CMRB), University of East London on Friday, 16 November 2008.

2. See Hillary Clinton's statement on the situation in Burma, at: www.change. org/petitions/u-s-secretary-of-state-demand-release-of-political-prisoners-and-an-end-to-hostilities-in-burma

3. Page references here refer to the formatted and revised online version of the article.

4. There were others subsequent to the first act in 1974. For more information on such acts, see: http://en.wikipedia.org/wiki/Prevention_of_Terrorism_Acts

5. Further details on these struggles are found in 'Female Political Prisoners in Northern Ireland/Strip-Searching', at: www.webster.edu/~woolflm/ireland. html

6. Incidentally, today (3 December 2013) Jamila Bouhaired's life is being celebrated in Lebanon, as 'the life worth living' and as 'an outstanding Arab woman who occupied a leading position in the Algerian armed revolution against French colonialism.'

7. In this book I adopt the term *fidai`* and not the spelling found in the Oxford dictionary.

8. For more than three weeks during the months of November and December 2013, the Al-Mayadeen television channel, which broadcasts from Lebanon, celebrated the life of Jamila Bouhaired with extensive programmes: interviews with comrades and acquaintances from various Arab countries, archival work on her struggle, movies made about her, discussions with various Arab women fighters, including Palestinian Leila Khaled and Therese Halasa, among many others, see: www.almayadeen.net

9. The drama *Dhakirat al-Jassad* was aired daily throughout Ramadan of 2010 by many Arab satellite TV stations. For an analysis and critique of this drama, see N. Abdo (2010), 'The Arabic Drama: A Critique -A-', Ramadan Series 2010, *Hadeeth An-Nas,* 8 October 2010, p. 14. Nazareth.

10. For more information on the case of Róisín McAliskey, see Coalition of Irish Republican Women, 2007, 'Stop the Extradition of Róisín McAliskey', 30 May, at: www.indymedia.ie/article/82825. More information on various

Irish women freedom fighters is also available on websites of the Coalition of Irish Republican Women at: http://eirinagealai.wix.com/cirw; and at: www.myspace.com/irishunity32

11. Mirvat Amin and Manal Ghanem gave birth while in prison, without adequate medical or health care, deprived of being accompanied by any relatives during delivery. For more on the physical and psychological torture of these women, see Iqbal Tamimi, 'Israeli authorities imprison Palestinian women even after their death', *uruknet.info*, 17 June 2008, at: www.uruknet.info/?p=44962

12. For more information on individual cases of sexual abuse in Israeli detention camps, see the June 2004 report by Addameer Prisoners Support and Human Rights Association (Palestine) and Sumoud Political Prisoner Solidarity Group (Canada) on the 'Status of Palestinian Political Prisoners in Israeli Prisons, Detention and Interrogation Centers', at: www.addameer.org/etemplate.php?id=243

13. As journalist Jonathan Cook writes: 'Dirani's accusations have been corroborated by affidavits from other soldiers who served in the prison. One interrogator, TN, says: "I know that it was customary to threaten to insert a stick. The intention was that the stick would be inserted if the subject did not talk."' For more information on the case of Mustafa Dirani, see Cook's (2003) 'Is "Facility 1391" Israel's version of Guantanamo Bay?', *The Daily Star*, 15 November 2003, at: www.dailystar.com.lb/News/Lebanon-News/2003/Nov-15/45092-is-facility-1391-israels-version-of-guantanamo-bay.ashx#axzz2zXrLkhL8

14. It is important to note here that the Palestinian Documentation centre (*Markaz Ad-Dirasat Al-Falastiniyya*, Beirut) which archived Palestinian events was destroyed by Israel in its 1982 invasion.

15. Abdel-Nasser Ferwana, is an ex-political prisoner and researcher expert in Palestinian political detainees. He publishes frequent reports on the state of Palestinian political prisoners. The information here was written on 18 August 2010.

16. Stark violations of human rights and the terrorization of the population under Hassan II did not make it easy for the Oufkir family. With the help of international lawyers and human rights organizations, the family asked to be sent into exile. They were again placed in prison for three more years until their exile verdict was issued. For more details on Malika Oufkir and her family life involving 20 years in prison, see Oufkir, Malika and Michèle Fitoussi. 2001. *Stolen Lives: Twenty Years in a Desert Jail*. New York: Miramax Books.

17. All quotations here are taken from the Arabic version of the book, published in 2000, keeping the author's spelling in the original Arabic form. In 2008, Fatna El-Beih's book was translated into English by Mustapha Kamal and Susan Slyomovics under the title *Talk of Darkness* (Austin, TX: University of Texas Press). In this translation, Fatna El-Beih's last name appeared as El-Bouih.

18. In her *Resistance Literature*, Barbara Harlow (1987) pays special attention to this fact, considering diaries and personal novels of political prisoners as a vital source of information on the topic of political detainees and political prisoners.

19. The end of colonialism in these countries did not, however, put an end to colonialism worldwide; Haiti for one continues to be under occupation. To this, we must add the military occupation of Iraq and Afghanistan and of course the seemingly endless occupation of Palestine.

20. The recent picture release on Facebook by a female Israeli prison guard posing in a picture with three blindfolded Palestinian political detainees brings to mind the recent history of Abu Ghraib prison, with the photo of a US soldier torturing Iraqi male political prisoners with her dog. See: 'Israeli officer poses for Facebook in front of Palestinian prisoners', *France 24 Observers*, 16 August 2010, at: http://observers.france24.com/content/20100816-female-officer-poses-facebook-front-palestinian-prisoners

Chapter 2: Anti-Colonial Resistance in Context

1. It is worth noting that the current author was present at the 1990 Moscow World Congress of Women as a member of the Canadian women's delegation. At this conference I had the chance to meet with the Palestinian delegations including Leila Khaled and the women members of the Israeli communist party including the lawyer defender of Palestinian political prisoners, Felicia Langer.

2. We all remember for example, the 'smart' weapons used in the US attack on Sudan in 1998 which in fact destroyed Al-Shifa pharmaceutical factory.

3. Richard Falk, Keynote address, Group 78 annual conference, 25–27 September 2009. Ottawa.

4. In most Western, especially American, literature and media, notions like the Middle East, the Muslim World and the Arab World are used interchangeably or are lumped together. In this homogenous construction of a region, to be an Arab means you are necessarily Muslim.

5. There is a plethora of literature documenting Israel's non- and even anti-democratic rule. Some of the literature focuses on Israel's settler-colonial rule, its constant confiscation of indigenous Palestinian land and its economic and political discrimination against its own Palestinian citizens (Morris 2001; Abdo 2011b; Davis 2003; Jamal 2007). Another vast set of literature describes Israeli racism against its Mizrahi Jewish citizens (for example, Adeeb 2003; Hever, Shenhav and Motzafi-Haller 2002; Khazzoom 2005).

6. Historically the USA has vetoed every UN decision criticising Israel. As I have argued elsewhere (Abdo 2012), over the last 60 years the USA has vetoed over 50 UNSC decisions related to Israel. What is ironic is that when, in October 2011, Russia and China vetoed a UN proposal which would have allowed the

West to intervene militarily against Syria, the Western world and especially the US administration was 'shocked'. Susan Rice, the US representative to the UN, had the following to say about the veto: 'I am disgusted by the reaction [i.e. the veto] of the Russians and Chinese', see Jamie A. FlorCruz, 'Why China didn't back U.N. plan for Syria', *CNN.com*, 10 February 2012, at: www.cnn.com/2012/02/09/world/asia/syria-china-florcruz. It appears that Rice is either unaware of the history of her country or is implying that the USA alone should make decisions affecting the world.

7. The public announcement of US Secretary of State Hillary Clinton in support of Saudi women's right to drive is little more than lip service following upon domestic pressure applied by various American feminists who urged her to make such a statement. See 'Secretary Clinton: Publicly Support Saudi Women's Right to Drive', a petition organized by a group of American feminists sent to various US officials including Clinton (www.change.org/petitions/secretary-clinton-publicly-support-saudi-women-s-right-to-drive). Her support is not for feminism, and definitely not for Saudi women and men's human rights, rights that are routinely violated by the Saudi government. In fact, the ironic alliance between democracy and fascism, as Chomsky points out, explains the deafening silence of the USA about Saudi Arabia's abuses of human rights and recent legal changes there which criminalize human rights activists. It also explains US complacency towards al-Qaeda, which is wreaking havoc in Syria. Later in this chapter, Chomsky's assertion on the ironic relationship between democracy and fascism will be explained further.

8. Named after Mark Sykes and François Georges-Picot, this infamous 1916 treaty represented a British and French plan to divide up the Middle East and place it under the control of both countries. It was through this agreement that Britain obtained control over Palestine, allowing for the establishment of the Jewish state, while France colonized Syria and Lebanon (see e.g. Sand 2012: 170–71).

9. For Arabs, the terms *shaheed* (for males) and *shaheeda* (for females) express a person's willingness to sacrifice him- or herself in defence of the nation, land or the collective honour. Yet Tzoreff, as in the case of most authors here, uses the terminology in a derogatory way such that the terms for martyr are interchangeable with terms such as 'suicide bomber', 'terrorist' or 'murderer'.

10. A critique of some of this literature has been provided elsewhere, see Abdo 2008.

11. This is true for the work of Schweitzer (2006), Tzoreff (2006), Reuter (2006), and Patkin (2004), but more so for the work of McGirk, Hamad and Klein (2007).

12. For a detailed discussion of the Israeli state policies towards Palestinian citizens, see my *Women in Israel: Race, Gender and Citizenship* (Abdo 2011b).

13. Ahmad Said was the head, director, and announcer of the Voice of the Arabs, a transnational radio programme broadcast from Egypt during the 1950s and the 1960s. The Egyptian radio was nationalized by the then leader Gamal Abdel-Nasser. It broadcast revolutionary songs, was committed to fighting Israel, to regaining stolen Palestine, and promoted pan-Arabism.

14. The story is also related in Antonius (1980: 43).

15. In a mammoth oral history project conducted among Palestinian women refugees from various geographical locations begun in the late 1990s by the Women's Section in the Ministry of Planning and International Affairs and later adopted by the Palestinian Women's Research and Documentation Centre, hundreds of tape recordings were made of women, documenting their experiences and their direct and indirect involvement in the armed struggle. Women's voices were transcribed in two volumes: *Women's Political Role in the Thirties* (Abdel-Hadi 2007) and *Women's Political Role in the Forties* (Abdel-Hadi 2008). It is worth noting that during my work as a gender consultant to the Ministry of Women's Affairs in 2005, I obtained several tapes that were not included in the above publications; these include recordings of Khazneh Al-Khatib, Zakiyya Hleileh, Jamile Sabah and Hagar Dhafir. All these women spoke of their carrying guns and other equipment to the guerrilla fighters. They also spoke about being trained to use arms and using them.

16. The term *thawra* (revolution) was the term primarily used to express Palestinian resistance throughout the first three decades of its existence, after its emergence in the 1960s. In fact, the same term was also used for the events of the 1936–39 revolution, which included a six-month general strike throughout Palestine. However, since the late 1980s, and especially after the 1993 Oslo Accords, the so-called 'peace process' came to replace the notion of revolution, rendering the latter an 'outdated' concept. This change in terminology was endorsed by Palestinian officials and enforced by them despite the dissatisfaction of the public in general. The Second Intifada and the 2012 armed resistance in Gaza against the Israeli aggression demonstrates this dissatisfaction.

17. For the full article, Dr Eyad Sarraj 'Why We Have Become Suicide Bombers: Understanding Palestinian Terror', see: www.missionislam.com/conissues/palestine.htm

18. The interview Benny Morris gave to *Haaretz* became very controversial; Ash argues that Morris became 'sick':

> his sickness is of the mental-political kind. He lives in a world populated not by fellow human beings, but by racist abstractions and stereotypes. There is an over-abundance of quasi-poetic images in the interview, as if the mind is haunted by the task of grasping what ails it: 'The Palestinian citizens of Israel are a time bomb,' not fellow citizens. Islam is 'a world in which human

lives don't have the same value as in the West.' Arabs are 'barbarians' at the gate of the Roman Empire. Palestinian society is 'a serial killer' that ought to be executed and 'a wild animal' that must be caged.

Ash (2004)

Chapter 3: Colonialism, Imperialism and the Culture of Resistance

1. The PLO is an umbrella organization historically composed of different political parties (organizations), the main ones being Fatah, the Popular Front for the Liberation of Palestine (PFLP), the Democratic Front for the Liberation of Palestine (DFLP) and the Communist Party. Of all these organizations, Fatah was considered to be the only non-leftist party. Many organizational changes occurred within the PLO, especially after 1993 and the Oslo Accords, at which time the DFLP was split into two parts: one allying itself with Fatah and which joined the leadership in the Occupied Territories, while the other part remained in exile and did not approve of the Oslo Accords.

2. The full story of French Moroccan Nadia Bradley and a group of *fidai`yyeen* was recently published by Abdel-Nasser Ferwana, manager of the statistics department, Palestinian Ministry of Detainees' Affairs, under the title 'The Moroccan freedom fighter who forced her way to Israel', see: www.palestinebehindbars.org (in Arabic).

3. Elsewhere I have discussed the different political movements among Palestinians in Israel, among the 1948 Palestinians as they prefer to be called (Abdo 2011b: 142).

4. Ahmad Fouad Najm is Egypt's most famous colloquial Arabic poet and lyricist. He has been a harsh critic of all Arab regimes, especially the Egyptian regime under Sadat and Mubarak. In 1962, he met the blind composer and singer Sheikh Imam, and their activism led the Imam–Najm duo to prison in 1968, serving three years. They were also frequent guests of Egypt's state prisons during 1972–79. The popularity of this duo peaked after the 1967 Arab defeat. In addition to the many songs Imam sung for the workers, peasants and poor and against the Egyptian regime, the duo also wrote and composed material celebrating and commemorating international revolutions. A couple of famous poems/songs: 'Guevara', written and sung after the death of Che, and 'ABC', written and sung after the liberation of Saigon, which was seen by Palestinian revolutionaries as a sign of hope in their struggle against Israeli colonialism (Al-Jadid 1995). It is worth noting that Najm and his daughter Nawwara have been very active in the January 2011 revolt as well as two years later in the June 30 2013 massive revolt against the rule of Muslim Brothers. Poet Ahmad Fouad Najm passed away on 4 December 2013.

5. The name *Harakat al-Qawmiyyeen al-Arab* is sometimes translated as the Arab Nationalist Movement (ANM).

6. According to David McDonald the lyrics mentioned here belong to a Nuh Ibrahim, described as a 'provocateur and broadcaster' for the 1936–39 Palestinian Revolt. McDonald adds that Nuh's work was broadcast over Arab radio stations and was also 'orally transmitted force for inspiration during the 1936–39 Revolt' (McDonald 2006: 13).

7. Writing at this historical juncture in the Arab Middle East which, since September 11, has experienced major changes and challenges, we must note that the meaning of the term 'suicide bombing' has also changed. The bombs placed by Iraqi and other Islamic extremists, including al-Qaeda and similar fanatic organizations, do not have the same meaning indicated in the analysis provided throughout this book. All forms of struggle Palestinians have adopted against Israeli colonial occupation have been anti-colonial forms and not terrorist acts.

8. For more information on this visit, see: www.opednews.com/articles/Jean-Ziegler--This-World-by-Siv-O-Neall-081125-155.html (accessed 16 April 2014).

9. According to its website, PalestineRemembered.com is a Palestinian NGO which is 'dedicated to retaining Palestinian refugees' memories before, during and after the Nakba', see: www.palestineremembered.com/MissionStatement.htm (accessed 16 April 2014).

10. Sivan, incidentally, is among the very few Israeli-Jewish film-makers who works with Palestinian film-makers and produces documentaries recording the history of Palestinians since 1948.

11. The Israelis, of course, deny any responsibility. This is all a guess on my part, based on an unreliable source: http://en.wikipedia.org/wiki/Kanafani (accessed 16 April 2014).

12. In its June 2012 fact sheet on Palestinian Prisoners, Miftah estimates the number of Palestinian political prisoners in Israel since 1967 at over 750,000.00. According to the same report, 'over the last 43 years, an estimated 10,000 Palestinian women have been arrested and/or detained under Israeli military orders, this number included' (Miftah 2012).

13. Elsewhere, I recount my own experience as a student in a private school in Israel. I recall the embarrassing and humiliating response of our grade 11 Arabic language teacher when one of my classmates composed a sentence critical of Israel (Abdo 2011b: 166).

14. This translation of mine is based on the lyrics of the poem, which were turned into a song by revolutionary singer Marcel Khalifeh. This song, like many others, is carved into the memories of most Palestinians. Mahmoud Darwish read this poem on August 2008 in Ramallah. The current author attended the event. This famous song has also become very popular, being recited by Palestinians in all of their geographical distributions.

15. This poem has appeared on several websites, including: http://sumofmind.com/2011/09/18/mahmoud-darwish-on-this-earth/ (accessed 16 April 2014).

Chapter 4: Political Detainees and the Israeli Prison System

1. It might be noted here that Ban Ki-moon's visit to Gaza came immediately after a visit he made to Lebanon, not to help the latter with much needed aid and support against Israeli's constant threats, but to demand that the government disarm the Lebanese resistance, especially Hezbollah. The aim of his visit to Gaza was not much different, as he went to ask the Palestinian Authority (the PA) to disarm the armed resistance.

2. The Moscobiyya is a detention centre in Jerusalem, to which almost all the women in our conversations were sent to first for interrogation. Some stayed there for days, others for weeks and yet others for months. After laying charges women were transferred to prisons in Israel.

3. It should be noted that various other scholars, including Dorit Naaman (2007) and Eyad Sarraj (2005), shed a more positive light on Palestinian (women and men) participation in the armed struggle during and after the Second Intifada, by contextualizing and historicizing such acts. A context, I may add, which was missing in the works of Johnson and Kuttab (2001).

4. Aisha was among 76 Palestinian political detainees released in exchange for one Israeli soldier captured by the Palestinians. Most of those released were deported.

5. Being poor, Ahlam could not afford a lawyer. In court, she was handed a five-year sentence, but a Palestinian lawyer and citizen of Israel who happened to be in the court decided to take her case pro bono and demanded a reduction of her sentence as she was a child. The judge reduced the sentence to two years of actual detention and three years with probation. She was released in 1979. Her lawyer advised her to disappear for three years, so that the charges would be annulled. She got married and moved from Nablus, her hometown, to Beit Lahem and stayed away from her daughter, whom she left with her family for four years.

6. In my conversation, two participants had the same first name, namely, 'Haleema'. to differentiate between them, I use the letters 'A.' and 'F.', which represent the first letter of the respective participants' family name.

7. Although only less than two weeks were left for the completion of her sentence, Haleema 'F'. was included in the 1985 exchange of prisoners.

8. It is worth noting that these words were taken from *Fal-Tasma'a kulled-Dunia* (Let the Whole World Hear), a poem by Tawfiq Zayyad, see Chapter 3.

9. I used the full name of Aida because her story was aired publicly. Aida Said has been living in exile (in Dubai, UAE) since her deportation after spending many years in Israeli prison. Her story was aired live on Al-Jazeera, 'Ziara Khassa' (A Special Visit) in February 2006.

10. The term 'child' used here and in other instances of detainees, while it refers to teenage women, I still kept the term for several reasons: first, because this is the term used by the women themselves; second, because

there is no term which is equivalent to teenager in Arabic (the term used, especially for females, namely *muraheqa*, has negative connotations and I do not want to use it); and third, to emphasize Israeli establishment's violation of International Humanitarian Laws by imprisoning children and torturing them. It is worth noting that, out of 570,000 Palestinian political activists and resisters arrested between 2000–2012, over 9,000 were children (both male and female) under the age of 18. For more information, see Abdel-Nasser Ferwana, '5100 Palestinians Currently Imprisoned By Israel', *Palestine News Network,* 5 May 2014 at: http://english.pnn.ps/index.php/prisoners/7487-ferwana-5100-palestinians-currently-imprisoned-by-israel

11. The Arabic terms used by the soldiers *beitak beitak* and *roukh min houn* – represent Ashkenized Arabic terms. Ashkenazi Jews, unlike Mizrahi Jews, cannot pronounce some Arabic letters, also, the terms *beitak beitak* are never used in Arabic this way. *Beitak* literally means 'your home', and is used for the male only!

12. Leena Nabulsi from Nablus was shot dead at close range on 15 March 1976 by Israeli soldiers while walking home from school; she was 15 years old. The famous Palestinian artist Suleiman Mansour painted a portrait of her wearing her school outfit, lying on the ground with blood coming out of her head. Leena became a symbol of the Palestinian struggle, especially during the First Intifada. Her portrait has entered almost every home in Palestine. Ahmed Qabour, a famous Lebanese singer and composer made a song in her tribute, which became very popular as well. Some of the lines, which were written by Hasan Daher and entitled *Fil-daffa* (in the West Bank), read:

> in the West Bank I have seven children
> the first suckles history
> the middle is named Guevara
> and the eldest is a revolutionary
> Leena was a child making her future
> Leena fell
> but her blood was still singing
> for Jerusalem, for Yafa [Jaffa]
> for Areeha [Jericho]
> Myself, my children and my wife are screaming
> my homeland will be set free.

13. As mentioned in Chapter 3, the first Land Day in 1976 was organized as a mass protest by Palestinian citizens of Israel who were (and still are) suffering from the constant settler-colonial policies of the state and its constant confiscation of Palestinian land by Israeli tanks, which roamed the cities and villages. Since then, the day of 30 March has become an annual protest and commemoration of the Land Day and the murdered citizens in all towns and villages populated by the Palestinians in Israel.

14. It is worth noting that Israel does not recognize political resisters as such, regardless of their citizenship status. Instead, it considers all political prisoners, including its own citizens as being a 'security risk' and treats them as 'terrorists' or suspected terrorists. In their introduction to *Threat: Palestinian Political Prisoners in Israel*, Abeer Baker and Anat Matar (2011) devote considerable attention to discussing Israel's legal policies and regulations around these issues.

15. Moscobiyya refers to a complex which was built by persons known in Arabic as *Al- Moscobiyya* (Russian missionaries from Moscow). Such buildings are found in cities having a majority population of Christians, such as Nazareth and Jerusalem. Historically, these complexes were built as cultural centres with libraries and for the holding of social events, and were used by Russian missionaries in Palestine. The British colonial government turned them into a police detention centre; Israel continued to use them this way.

16. According to B`Tselem's (the Israeli Information Center for Human Rights in the Occupied Territories) report of 1 January 2011, updated on 29 December 2013, 'Administrative detention was promulgated as part of the emergency laws introduced by the British colonial government in Palestine. This same law was reintroduced and passed as a law by Israel in 1975. It allows for the detention of Palestinians for up to six months without a charge or trial. Worse yet, the period can be repeatedly renewed, completely circumventing due process. Over the years, tens of thousands of Palestinians have been incarcerated under this law and tortured for many months.' For more information on administrative detention see the Israeli The Israeli Information Center for Human Rights in the Occupied Territories, at: www.btselem.org/administrative_detention

17. I use the term 'bout' here as a literal translation of the Arabic term *jura'a*, used by all women in the conversation. *Jura'a* in Arabic is a term used in the context of medical treatment, such as a *jura'a* of chemotherapy or a *jura'a* of pills or other necessary medication.

18. Munia was referring to her prison cell in the Moscobiyya, which was an old building with many arches. The mice, she said, were walking freely between these arches.

19. In my *Women in Israel* (2011b), I discuss the different categories or labels given to Palestinians, both citizens and others, that attempt to strip them of their Palestinian national identity.

20. Such attempts as many noted were resented by most Palestinian Christians who see themselves as an integral part of their Palestinian nation. It is interesting that even right-wing papers such as the Canadian National Post, carried an article to that effect. Titled: 'Campaign to enlist more Christian Arabs in Israeli army met with anger, little success in Palestinian community', speaks to this effect. See Karin Laub, *Associated Press*, 27 December 2013. http://

news.nationalpost.com/2013/12/27/campaign-to-enlist-more-christian-arabs-in-israeli-army-met-with-anger-little-success-in-palestinian-community/

21. During our focus group the note-taker who had worked as a social worker for 25 years among young women in Jerusalem presented us with her experience dealing with young women who became victims of '*isqat*' and the ramifications this act had on the woman and her family. It might be noted here that none of the women in our conversation had gone through such an experience. But, during the First Intifada, the issue of '*isqat*' was raised as a concern by the Palestinian feminist movement in the West Bank.

22. Various international media outlets, including *Al-Jazeera* and *The Guardian*, have reported this case. Incidentally, Dirani together with various other Lebanese abducted by Israeli military forces were incarcerated and tortured in a secret facility known as 'Facility 1391'. As Chris McGreal reports in *The Guardian*, Facility 1391 is not found on maps. The facility was located inside an army intelligence base in northern Israel. See Chris McGreal, 2003, 'Facility 1391: Israel's Secret Prison', *The Guardian*, 14 November, at: www.guardian.co.uk/world/2003/nov/14/israel2

23. *Uzraeel* is a term used in Arabic to denote the angel of death.

Chapter 5: Prison as a Site of Resistance

1. Lea Tsemel is a Jewish anti-Zionist human rights lawyer who has represented Palestinians accused of violence in Israel's prisons.

2. It is worth noting here that all political prisoners were forced to work in prison, some in the kitchen, some in agriculture and others in garment factories.

3. Naa'leen, like Bila'een, is a village in the West Bank that was targeted by the Israeli Apartheid Wall and separated off from the rest of the West Bank. Weekly demonstrations, most of which turned into confrontations with the Israeli soldiers, have resulted in the killing of several members of these villages.

4. Ahlam showed a great deal of respect and love for her brother whom she described as: 'He was not educated. He was sentenced for three years during the First Intifada and was unable to continue his education. After the Second Intifada, in 2003 he was sentenced for life in prison. My brother had then joined the Aqsa Brigades.

5. Whereas the term '*zahrat*' was used for teenage female political fighters, '*ashbal*' was the term used for teenage male fighters.

6. See, Addameer, at: www.addameer.org/etemplate.php?id=491 (accessed 16 April 2014).

7. On the methodological level, I must note that we were very lucky that such a tension occurred towards the end of the day. The hard feelings which

developed after Aisha's intervention have made several women bitter and had the effect of silencing them as well.

8. Archives gathered from the society of Ina'ash al-Usra feature names and in some cases pictures of most women detained since late 1960s and their whereabouts after release. The newspapers which recorded such information included *al-Shaa'b*, *al-Fajr* and *al-Itehad*. All three papers belonged to leftist Palestinian parties, the first two belonged to the PFLP and the DFLP subsequently, while the latter is the newspaper of the Israeli communist party. Both *al-Fajr* and *al-Shaa'b* have ceased to exist, while *al-Itehad* is still functioning.

9. Sonia here refers to 1979 after the first prisoners' exchanged in which 'first-generation' political detainees, such as Itaf and Aisha were released and in fact deported outside of Palestine.

10. Although the PLO was out of Jordan in 1979, they maintained their functions, especially their charitable organizations in operation there.

11. Changes in gender and feminist consciousness, among Palestinian women political activists and militants, is a research project on its own right. What is important to mention, and as Ameena suggested, objective changes, nationally and internationally have changed between the period under consideration in this book (late 1960–1980) and the twentieth century. In the late 1980s the third wave of feminism (socialist feminism) emerged, while in the 1990s feminism part of the academy globally and in Palestine as well. After the Oslo Accord, in 1996 the Ministry of Women's Affairs was established in Palestine along with various other independent women's centres – objective conditions leading to the further development of feminist consciousness among individuals.

Bibliography

Books and Articles

abbas, Nuzhat. 2003. 'Narrating the Nation of Palestine', an interview of Nahla Abdo in *Herizons*, 16 (4): 18–22.

Abboud, Samer. 2014. 'Reflections on the Syrian revolution', *Al-Jazeera,* 20 March 2014, at: www.aljazeera.com/indepth/opinion/profile/samer-abboud.html

Abdel-Hadi, Faiha. 2007. *Women's Political Role in the Thirties*. Ramallah: Palestinian Women's Research and Documentation Centre.

Abdel-Hadi, Faiha. 2008. *Women's Political Role in the Forties*. Ramallah: Palestinian Women's Research and Documentation Centre.

Abdo, Nahla. 1989. 'British colonialism and Capitalist Class Transformation in Palestine: 1920–47', Ph.D thesis Library Archives, University of Toronto.

Abdo, Nahla. 1993. 'Middle East Politics Through Feminist Lenses: Dialoguing the Terms of Solidarity', *Alternatives*, 18 (1): 29–41.

Abdo, Nahla. 1994. 'Nationalism and Feminism: Palestinian women and the *Intifada*—No Going Back?', in Valentine M. Moghadam (ed.), *Gender and National Identity: Women and Politics in Muslim Societies*. London: Zed Books, pp. 148–170.

Abdo, Nahla (ed.). 1996. *Sociological Thought: Beyond Eurocentric Theory*. Toronto: Canadian Scholars Press.

Abdo, Nahla. 2002. 'Eurocentrism, Orientalism, and Essentialism: September 11 and Beyond', in Susan Hawthorne and Bronwyn Winter (eds), *September 11, 2001: Feminist Perspectives*. North Melbourne: Spinifex, pp. 372–392.

Abdo, Nahla. 2008. 'Palestinian *Munadelat*: Between Western Representation and Lived Reality', in Ronit Lentin (ed.), *Thinking Palestine*. London: Zed Books, pp. 173–189.

Abdo, Nahla. 2010. 'The Arabic Drama: A Critique -A-', Ramadan Series 2010, *Hadeeth An-Nas,* 8 October 2010, p. 14. Nazareth.

Abdo, Nahla. 2011a. 'Palestinian Women Political Prisoners and the Israeli State', in Abeer Baker and Anat Matar (eds), *Threat: Palestinian Political Prisoners in Israel*. New York: Pluto, pp. 57–67.

Abdo, Nahla. 2011b. *Women in Israel: Gender, Race and Citizenship*. London: Zed Books.

Abdo, Nahla. 2012. 'Why Talk Intervention in Syria?: It's not about human rights or democracy', 8 June 2012 at: http://rabble.ca/news/2012/06/why-talk-intervention-syria-its-not-about-human-rights-or-democracy (accessed 16 April 2014).

Abdo, Nahla and Lentin, Ronit (eds). 2002. *Women and the Politics of Military Confrontation: Palestinian and Israeli Gendered Narratives of Dislocation.* Oxford: Berghahn.

Abdullah, Muhammad H. 2002. *Ibrahim Tuqan: His Life and Poems.* Kuwait City: Abdul-Aziz Saud Al-Babtain Institute.

Abu Iyad with Rouleau, Eric. 1981. *My Home, My Land: A Narrative of the Palestinian Struggle,* Trans. Linda Butler Koseoglu. New York: Times Books.

Abu-Lughod, Janet L. 1971. 'The Demographic Transformation of Palestine', in Ibrahim Abu-Lughod (ed.) *The Transformation of Palestine: Essays on the Origin and Development of the Arab–Israeli Conflict.* Evanston, IL: Northwestern University Press, 139–163.

Abu-Lughod, Lila. 2002. 'Do Muslim Women Really Need Saving? Anthropological Reflections on Cultural Relativism and Its Others', *American Anthropologist,* 104 (3): 783–790.

Abu-Lughod, Lila. 2006. 'The Muslim woman: The power of images and the danger of pity', *Eurozine,* 1 September 2006, at: www.eurozine.com/articles/2006-09-01-abulughod-en.html (accessed 16 April 2014).

Abunimah, Ali. 2006. 'Hamas Election Victory: A Vote for Clarity', *The Electronic Intifada,* 26 January 2006, at: http://electronicintifada.net/content/hamas-election-victory-vote-clarity/5847 (accessed 16 April 2014).

Abunimah, Ali. 2014. 'Palestinian Christians "not really Arabs," says senior Israeli lawmaker', *The Electronic Intifada,* 13 January 2014, at: http://electronicintifada.net/blogs/ali-abunimah/palestinian-christians-not-really-arabs-says-senior-israeli-lawmaker (accessed 16 April 2014).

Adeeb, Uri. 2003. 'Mizrahi Jews in Israel: Presence and Future Possibilities', *Journal of Arab Unity Studies,* 16 (2): 17–62 (in Arabic).

Agah, Azadeh, Parsi, Shadi and Mehr, Sousan. 2007. *We Lived to Tell: Political Prison Memoirs of Iranian Women.* Toronto: McGilligan.

Agamben, Giorgio. 2005. *State of Exception.* Chicago, IL: University of Chicago Press.

Ahmad, Aijaz. 2009. 'US policy will lead to thousands of new recruits for al-Qaeda', *The Real News,* 12 May 2009, at: http://therealnews.com/t2/index.php?option=com_content&task=view&id=31&Itemid=74&jumival=3706 (accessed 16 April 2014).

Al-Ali, Nadje Sadig. 2007. *Iraqi Women: Untold Stories from 1948 to the Present.* London: Zed Books.

Al-Hassan, Omar. 2013. 'Crimes against Humanity: The Plight Of Palestinian Prisoners in Israeli Jails', *Global Research,* 6 April, at: www.globalresearch.ca/crimes-against-humanity-the-plight-of-palestinian-prisoners-in-israeli-jails/5330075 (accessed 16 April 2014).

Al-Hout Noueihed, Bayan. 2012. 'Nameless Women Made Palestinian History', *Al-Akhbar,* 8 March, at: http://english.al-akhbar.com/node/4968 (accessed 16 April 2014).

Ali, Abdullah Suleiman. 2014. 'ISIS Losing Ground in Syria to Jabhat al-Nusra', *As-Safir Newspaper*, at: www.assafir.com/Channel/63/%D8%B3%D9%88%D 8%B1%D9%8A%D8%A7/TopMenu#%21/ArticleWindow.aspx?ChannelID= 63&ArticleID=337413 (Arabic). Reprinted in English in *Al-Monitor*, at: www. al-monitor.com/pulse/security/2014/02/isis-losing-ground-deir-al-zour-jabhat. html (accessed 16 April 2014).

Ali, Tariq. 2008. 'Afghanistan: Mirage of the Good War', *New Left Review*, 50, March–April 2008, at: www.newleftreview.org/II/50/tariq-ali-afghanistan-mirage-of-the-good-war (accessed 16 April 2014).

Al-Hardan, Anaheed. 2008. 'Understanding the Present Through the Past: Between British and Israeli Discourses on Palestine', in Ronit Lentin (ed.), *Thinking Palestine*. London: Zed Books, pp. 236–253.

Alian, Ittaf. 2011. 'Female Prisoners and the Struggle: A Personal Testimony', in Abeer Baker and Anat Matar (eds), *Threat: Palestinian Political Prisoners in Israel*. New York: Pluto, pp. 183–187.

Al-Jabiri, Muhammad A. 1991. *Aa`beroun fi Kalam Aa'ber: Maqalat Mukhtara*. (those who pass between fleeting words: selected articles). Morocco: Dar Tubqal.

Al-Jadid Staff Writers. 1995. 'The Legacy of the Late Sheikh Imam, Creator of Modern Arabic Political Song'. *Al-Jadid Magazine*, November 1995, Vol. 1. No. 1. Beirut, at: http://almashriq.hiof.no/egypt/700/780/sheikh-imam/aljadid-sheikh. html (accessed 16 April 2014).

Al-Jazeera. 2006. 'Ziara Khassa' (A Special Visit), 24 February 2006.

Al-Jazeera. 2014. 'Senior al-Qaeda commander killed in Syria', at: www. aljazeera.com/news/middleeast/2014/02/senior-al-qaeda-commander-killed-syria-2014223172557381478.html (accessed 16 April 2014).

Alloula, Malek. 1987. *The Colonial Harem*. Manchester: Manchester University Press.

Alpert, Emily. 2012. 'French president says Algeria suffered under "brutal" colonialism', *Los Angeles Times*, 20 December 2012, at: http://articles. latimes.com/2012/dec/20/world/la-fg-wn-france-algeria-francois-hollande-colonialism-20121220 (accessed 16 April 2014).

Al-Mayadeen. 2013. 'Al-Mayadeen Honours the Algerian Fighter Jamila Bouhaired', November 2013, at: www.almayadeen.net/ar/news/lebanon-w340FcmTM0274KJ1AR,mig (accessed 16 April 2014).

Al-Nawwab, Mudhaffar. 2008. *Adab* (Arab Poetry), at: http://adab.com/modules.php ?name=Sh3er&doWhat=shqas&qid=64136&r=&rc=29 (accessed 16 April 2014).

Al-Saadi, Qahira. 2002. 'Qahira Sa'eed Ali al-Sa'adi', at: www.protection-palestine. org/IMG/pdf/QAHIRA_SAADI.pdf

Al-Samman, Hanadi. 2009. 'Transforming Nationhood from within the Minefield: Arab Female Guerrilla Fighters and the Politics of Peace Poetics', *Women's Studies International Forum*, 32 (5): 331–339.

Antonius, Soraya. 1980. 'Prisoners for Palestine: A List of Women Political Prisoners', *Journal of Palestine Studies*, 9 (3): 29–80.

Antoon, Sinan. 2007. 'An Iraqi Rhapsody: Poet & Novelist Sinan Antoon on the U.S. Destruction of the Iraqi State, His Latest Novel and the Sad Statement that Iraq Was Better Under Saddam Hussein'. *Democracy Now!*, 6 July. New York.

Ash, Gabriel. 2004. 'Diagnosing Benny Morris: The mind of a European settler', *The Electronic Intifada*, 27 January 2004, at: http://electronicintifada.net/content/diagnosing-benny-morris-mind-european-settler/4967 (accessed 16 April 2014).

Ashrawi, Hanan. 2001. 'Palestine: The world should intervene to end the Israeli apartheid'. *World Conference Against Racism, Racial Discrimination, Xenophobia, and Related Intolerances* – NGO Forum. 28 August, Durban: South Africa, at: www.i-p-o.org/palestine-ashrawi.htm (accessed 16 April 2014).

Ayyoub, Samir. 2010. 'Mahmoud Darwish: The Unforgettable'. *Palestine Remembered*, 10 August, in Arabic, at: www.palestineremembered.com/Gaza/al-Faluja/Story18433.html (accessed 16 April 2014).

Bahour, Sam. 2006. 'New Paradigm After The Victory Of Hamas', *Countercurrent.org*, 30 January, at: www.countercurrents.org/pa-bahour300106.htm (accessed 16 April 2014).

Baker, Abeer and Anat Matar (eds). 2011. *Threat: Palestinian Political Prisoners in Israel*. New York: Pluto.

Baker, Abeer and Anat Matar. 2011. 'The Arrest and Persecution of Elected Political leaders: Interview with Sheikh Muhammad Abu Tir', in Abeer Baker and Anat Matar (eds), *Threat: Palestinian Political Prisoners in Israel*. New York: Pluto, pp. 83–89.

Ball, Anna. 2012. *Palestinian Literature and Film in Postcolonial Feminist Perspective*. New York: Routledge.

Barsamian, David. 2003. 'Introduction', in David Barsamian and Edward Said (eds), *Culture and Resistance: Conversations with Edward W. Said*. Cambridge: South End Press, pp. xi–1.

Barrett, David. 2014. 'Terror chief warns of threat from Syria jihadists', *The Telegraph*, 23 January, at: www.telegraph.co.uk/news/uknews/terrorism-in-the-uk/10593185/Terror-chief-warns-of-threat-from-Syria-jihadists.html (accessed 16 April 2014).

Bechara, Soha. 2003. *Resistance: My Life for Lebanon*. Trans. Gabriel Levine. Brooklyn, NY: Soft Scull Press.

Ben-Ari, Sigi and Anat Barsella. 2011. 'Family Visits to Palestinian Prisoners Held Inside Israel', in Abeer Baker and Anat Matar (eds), *Threat: Palestinian Political Prisoners in Israel*. New York: Pluto, pp. 201–211.

Ben Jalloun, Tahar. 2001. *Tilka al-Atmah al-Bahira* (Cette aveuglant absence de lumière or, the brilliant darkness), Beirut: Al-Saqi (in Arabic).

Beyler, Clara. 2002. 'Messengers of Death: Female Suicide Bombers', in Hebrew, at: www.keren-inbar.co.il/INB/cache/pic_22500.pdf (accessed 16 April 2014).

Bhavnani, K. and Davis, A. 2000. 'Women in Prison: Researching Race in Three National Contexts', in France Winddance Twine and Jonathan Warren (eds), *Racing Research, Researching Race: Methodological Dilemmas in Critical Race Studies*. New York: New York University Press, pp. 227–235

Bishara, George. 2007. 'The persistence of memory'. Institute for Middle East Understanding, 13 May, at: http://imeu.net/news/article005276.shtml (accessed 16 April 2014).

Bishara, Suha. 2001. *Muqawamah* (Resistance). London: Al-Saqi (in Arabic).

Bishara, Suha. 2010 *Ahlam bi-Zinzana min Karaz* (Dreams of a Cell of Cherries). London: Al-Saqi.

Bloom, Mia. 2005. *Dying to Kill: The Allure of Suicide Terror*. New York: Columbia University Press.

Bloom, Mia. 2007. 'Female suicide bombers: a global trend', *Daedalus Journal of the American Academy of Arts and Sciences*, Winter, 136 (1): 94–102.

Bloom, Mia. 2009. 'Chasing Butterflies and Rainbows: A Critique of Kruglanski et al.'s "Fully Committed: Suicide Bombers' Motivation and the Quest for Personal Significance."', *Political Psychology*, 30 (3): 387–395.

B'Tselem. 2005. 'Detainees and prisoners: Statistics on Palestinian minors in IDF Detention 2001–2007', B'Tselem, The Israeli Information Center for Human Rights in the Occupied Territories, at: www.btselem.org/english/Statistics/ Minors_in_IDF_Detention.asp (accessed 16 April 2014).

B'Tselem. 2011. 'No Minor Matter: Violation of the Rights of Palestinian Minors Arrested by Israel on Suspicion of Stone-Throwing, July 2011', at: www.btselem. org/publications/summaries/2011-no-minor-matter

B'Tselem. 2013. 'Administrative Detention', first published 1 January 2011; updated 29 December 2013, at: www.btselem.org/administrative_detention (accessed 16 April 2014).

Cabral, Amilcar. 2009. 'Tell No Lies, Claim No Easy Victories', *Newritings*, 11 February, at: http://newritings.wordpress.com/2009/02/11/cabral-tell-no-lies-claim-no-easy-victories/ (accessed 16 April 2014).

Carlson, Paul R. 2003. *Media Bias and the Middle East*. Bloomington, IN: Xlibris Corporation.

Chesler, Phyllis. 2003. *The New Anti-Semitism: The Current Crisis and What We Must Do*. San Francisco, CA: Jossey Bass.

Chesler, Phyllis. 2009. 'A Jerusalem Conference to Combat Global Anti-Semitism: The Greatest Battle of the 21st Century'. *Pajamas Media*, 15 December 2009, at: www.phyllis-chesler.com/672/jerusalem-conference-anti-semitism (accessed 16 April 2014).http://pajamasmedia.com/phyllischesler/2009/12/15/a-jerusalem-conference-to-combat-global-anti-semitism

Chomsky, Noam. 1999. *Profit over People: Neoliberalism and Global Order*. New York: Seven Stories Press.

Chossudovsky, Michel. 2013. 'Hillary Clinton: "We Created Al Qaeda": The Protagonists of the "Global War on Terrorism" are the Terrorists'. *Global Research*, 1 June 2013, at: www.globalresearch.ca/hillary-clinton-we-created-al-qaeda/5337222 (accessed 16 April 2014).

Cohen, Roger. 2010. 'U.S. Illusions in Lebanon'. *The New York Times*, 13 December 2010, at: www.nytimes.com/2010/12/14/opinion/14iht-edcohen14.html (accessed 16 April 2014).

Cook, Jonathan. 2003. 'Is "Facility 1391" Israel's version of Guantanamo Bay?' *The Daily Star*, 15 November 2003, at: www.dailystar.com.lb/News/Lebanon-News/2003/Nov-15/45092-is-facility-1391-israels-version-of-guantanamo-bay.ashx#axzz2zXrLkhL8 (accessed 16 April 2014).

Cook, Jonathan. 2014, 'Saving Nazareth: What the struggle by Israeli Arabs for equality reveals about the State of Israel today', a public talk organized by National Council on Canada–Arab Relations (NCCAR), Ottawa, 10 March 2014.

Corcoran, Mary. 2006. *Out of Order: The Political Imprisonment of Women in Northern Ireland, 1972–1998*. Cullompton, Devon: Willan Publishing.

Daka, Walid. 2011. 'Consciousness Molded or the Re-identification of Torture', in Abeer Baker and Anat Matar (eds), *Threat: Palestinian Political Prisoners in Israel*. New York: Pluto, pp. 234–254.

Darwish, Mahmoud. 1980. 'Diwan Mahmoud Darwish'. 7th edn. Beirut: Dar at-Talia'a.

Darwish, Mahmoud. 1995. *Memory for Forgetfulness: August, Beirut, 1982*. Trans. Ibrahim Muhawi. Berkeley, CA: University of California Press.

Darwish, Mahmoud. 2004a. *Al-Aa`mal al-Jadida* (The New Works), in Arabic. London: Riad El-Rayyes.

Darwish, Mahmoud. 2004b. 'Edward Said: A Contrapuntal Reading', *Al-Ahram Weekly* 'Culture' 710, 30 September–6 October, at: http://weekly.ahram.org.eg/2004/710/cu4.htm (accessed 16 April 2014).

Darwish, Mahmoud. 2007. 'An Evening with Mahmoud Darwish', 7 July. Haifa: Israel.

Darwish, Mahmoud. 2011. *In the Presence of Absence*. Trans. Sinan Antoon. Brooklyn, NY: Archipelago.

Daugherty, D. M. 2002, 'The Women Hunger Strikers of Armagh Prison', at: http://hungerstrikecommittee.webs.com/womenhungerstrikers.htm (accessed 16 April 2014).

Davis, Angela Y. 1971. 'History is a Weapon: Political Prisoners, Prisons, and Black Liberation', at: www.historyisaweapon.com/defcon1/davispoprprblli.html (accessed 16 April 2014).

Davis, Uri. 2003. *Apartheid Israel: Possibilities for the Struggle Within*. London: Zed Books.

DeGenaro, Bill. 2011. 'The Rose and The Dictionary', Beirutbillblogspot, 18 May, at: http://beirutbill.blogspot.com/2011/05/rose-and-dictionary-by-mahmoud-darwish.html (accessed 16 April 2014).

Dworkin, Andrea. 1990. 'Whose Country Is It Anyway?', *Ms. magazine*, vol. I, no. 2, September/October.

Dworkin, Andrea. 2002. 'The Women Suicide Bombers'. *Femenista*, 5 (1): 19–28.

El-Beih, Fatna. 2000. *Hadeeth Al-A'tmah* (Talk of Darkness), Al-Fanak: Morocco (in Arabic).

El Fassed, Arjan. 2004. 'Naji al-Ali: The timeless conscience of Palestine'. *The Electronic Intifada*, 22 July, at: http://electronicintifada.net/content/naji-al-ali-timeless-conscience-palestine/5166 (accessed 16 April 2014).

Engler, Yves. 2014, 'How the Tories Propagate Jewish Imperialism', *Huffington Post*, 8 January, at: www.huffingtonpost.ca/yves-engler/jewish-imperialism_b_4558897.html (accessed 16 April 2014).

Fahoum, Walid. 1980. *Toyour Nve-Tertza* (The Birds of Neve-Tertza Prison). Al-Hakim: Nazareth.

Falk, Richard. 2009a. Keynote address, Group of 78 Annual Conference, 25–27 September. Ottawa.

Falk, Richard. 2009b. 'Report of the Special Rapporteur on the situation of human rights in the Palestinian territories occupied since 1967'. 11 February. New York: UN General Assembly.

Fanon, Frantz. 1965. *A Dying Colonialism*. Trans. Haakon Chevalier. New York: Grove Press.

Fanon, Franz. 1970. *Black Skin, White Masks*. Trans. Charles Lam Markmann. London: Paladin.

Ferwana, Abdel-Nasser. 2010. *August Report*. www.statscrop.com/www/palestinebehindbars.org (accessed 16 April 2014).

Ferwana, Abdel-Nasser. 2013. '204 Palestinian Political Prisoners Martyred in Israeli Prisons', in Arabic, at: www.palestinebehindbars.org/ferwana2apr2013.htm (accessed 16 April 2014).

Findley, Paul, 1995. *Deliberate Deceptions: Facing the Facts About The U.S.–Israeli Relationship*. Toronto: Laurence Hill Books.

Flapan, Simha. 1987. *The Birth of Israel: Myths and Realities*. New York: Pantheon.

Galleymore, Susan. 2009. *Long Time Passing: Mothers Speak About War & Terror*. London: Pluto Press.

Giacaman Rita and Penny Johnson. 1994. 'Searching for Strategies: The Palestinian Women's Movement in the New Era'. *Middle East Research and Information Project* (MERIP) 263 (42): 22–25.

Goldberg, David T. 2002. *The Racial State*. Oxford: Blackwell.

Goodman, Amy. 2008. 'Mahmoud Darwish, Poet Laureate of the Palestinians, 1941–2008'. *Democracy Now!*, 8 August, at: www.democracynow.org/2008/8/11/mahmoud_darwish_poet_laureate_of_the (accessed 16 April 2014).

Hajjar, George (ed.). 1973. *My People Shall Live: The Autobiography of a Revolutionary Leila Khaled*. London: Hodder & Stoughton Ltd, at: www.onepalestine.org/resources/articles/My_People_Shall_Live.html (accessed 16 April 2014).

Hammami, Rema. 1995. 'Feminist Scholarship and the Literature on Palestinian Women', *Gender and Society Working Papers Series No. 1*, (Women's Studies Program, Birzeit University).

Hammami, Rema and Rieker, Martina. 1988, 'Feminist Orientalism and Orientalist Marxism' *New Left Review*, I (170) July–August.

Hardy, Jeremy. 2007. 'A decade of injustice: Roisin McAliskey is facing a renewed extradition threat, but Stormont remains silent'. *The Guardian*, 22 August. at: www.guardian.co.uk/commentisfree/2007/aug/22/comment.northernireland (accessed 16 April 2014).

Harlow, Barbara. 1986a. 'Palestine and Modern Arab Poetry', *Race and Class*, January 1986, Vol. 27 (3): 102–103.

Harlow, Barbara. 1986b. 'Return to Haifa: "Opening the Borders" in Palestinian Literature', *Social Text*, 13–14: 3–23.

Harlow, Barbara. 1987. *Resistance Literature*. London: Methuen.

Harlow, Barbara. 1992. *Barred: Women, Writing and Political Detention*. Hanover, NH: Wesleyan University Press.

Harlow, Barbara. 1994. 'Writers and Assassinations', in Sidney J. Lemelle and Robin D. G. Kelley (eds), *Imagining Home: Class, Culture and Nationalism in the African Diaspora*, London: Verso, pp. 167–184.

Harlow, Barbara. 1996. *After Lives: Legacies of Revolutionary Writers*. New York: Verso.

Hayward, Susan. 2006. *Cinema Studies: The Key Concepts*. Abingdon: Routledge.

Hever, H., Y. Shenhav, and P. Motzafi-Haller (eds). 2002. *Mizrahim in Israel: A Critical Observation into Israel's Ethnicity*. Tel Aviv: Van Leer Jerusalem Institute and HaKibbutz HaMeuchad (in Hebrew).

Heikal, M. H. 2011. 'Four Middle East scenarios'. *Al-Ahram*, 29 September–5 October, No. 1066, at http://weekly.ahram.org.eg/2011/1066/eg1.htm (accessed 16 April 2014).

Hitti, Philip K. 2002. *History of the Arabs*. 10th edn. Basingstoke: Palgrave Macmillan.

Irving, Sarah. 2012. *Leila Khaled: Icon of the Palestinian Liberation*. London: Pluto.

Issacharoff, Avi. 2006. 'The Palestinian and Israeli Media on Female Suicide Terrorists', in Yoram Schweitzer (ed.), *Female Suicide Bombers: Dying for Equality?* Tel-Aviv: Jaffee Center for Strategic Studies, pp. 43–51.

Jad, Islah. 1990. 'From Salons to the Popular Committees: Palestinian Women 1919–1989', in Jamal R. Nassar and Roger Heacock (eds), *Intifada: Palestine at the Crossroads*. New York: Praeger, pp. 125–142.

Jad, Islah. 1995. '*Fil-ilaqa baynal-Ijtimai' wal-watani: muhawala li-fahm azmat alAhzab al-siyasiyyah al-Haliyyah*' (The Relationship between the social and the national: An attempt at understanding the crisis of existing political parties), in Azmi Bishara (ed.), *Azmat al-Hizb al-Siyasi al-Falastini* (Pluralism and democracy: The crisis of the Palestinian political party). Ramallah: Muwatin (Palestinian Institute for the Study of Democracy), in Arabic. pp. 163–172.

Jad, Islah, Johnson, Penny and Giacaman, Rita. 2000. 'Transit Citizens: Gender and Citizenship under the Palestinian Authority', in Suad Joseph (ed.), *Gender and Citizenship in the Middle East*. Syracuse, NY: Syracuse University Press, pp. 137–157.

Jajeh, Jennifer. 2013. 'Leila Khaled, the 1970s Palestinian revolutionary, is still passionate', *The National*, 16 February, at: www.thenational.ae/arts-culture/leila-khaled-the-1970s-palestinian-revolutionary-is-still-passionate#page2 (accessed 16 April 2014).

Jamal, Amal. 2007. 'Strategies of Minority Struggle for Equality in Ethnic States: Arab Politics in Israel'. *Citizenship Studies*, 11 (3): 263–282.

Jayawardena, Kumari. 1986. *Feminism and Nationalism in the Third World*. London: Zed Books.

Jayyusi, Salma Khadra and Tingley, Christopher. 1977. *Trends and Movements in Modern Arabic Poetry*, Boston, MA: Brill, pp. 285–287.

Jeffery, Simon. 2006. 'Hamas celebrates election victory', *Guardian* Tuesday 26 January, at: www.theguardian.com/world/2006/jan/26/israel1 (accessed 16 April 2014).

Jenkin, Tim. 1987. *Stolen Years*. London: Kliptown.

Johnson, Penny and Kuttab, Eileen. 2001. 'Where Have All the Women (and Men) Gone? Reflections on Gender and the Second Palestinian Intifada', *Feminist Review*, 69: 21–43.

Jones, Chris. 1997. '"Bombs" An Incomplete Look At Big Brother', 13 August, Special to the *Chicago Tribune*, at: http://articles.chicagotribune.com/1997-08-13/features/9708130348_1_prison-cell-bombs-alejandrina-torres (accessed 16 April 2014).

Juris, Jeffrey S. 2008a. 'Introduction: The Cultural Logic of Networking', in *Networking Futures: The Movements against Corporate Globalization*. Durham, NC and London: Duke University Press, pp. 1–26.

Juris, Jeffrey S. 2008b. 'Performing Politics: Image, Embodiment, and Affective Solidarity During Anti-Corporate Globalization Protests'. *Ethnography*, 9 (1): 61–97.

Kanafani, Ghassan. 1977a. 'Adab al-Muqawama fi Falasteen al-Muhtalla: 1948–1966' (Palestinian Resistance Literature in Occupied Palestine), in *Al-Athar al-Kamela* (The Full Effects), vol. 4, Beirut: Dar at-Talia'a, (in Arabic), (first edn), pp. 1–80.

Kanafani, Ghassan. 1977b. 'Al-Adab al-Falastinin al-Muqawem tahtal-Ihtilal: 1936–1968' (Palestinian Resistance Literature under Occupation 1936–68), in *Al-Athar al-Kamela* (The Full Effects), vol. 4, Beirut: Dar at-Talia'a, (in Arabic), (first edn), pp. 29–206.

Kanafani, Ghassan. 1980a, *Rijāl fish-Shams* (Men in the Sun), in *Al-Athar al-Kamela: al-Riwayat* (The Full Effects: The Novels), vol. 2, Beirut: Ghassan Kanafani Cultural Institute, Dar at-Talia'a (2nd edn): 37–152 (in Arabic).

Kanafani, Ghassan. 1980b. 'A'aed ila-Haifa' (Returning to Haifa), in *Al-Athar al-Kamela: al-Riwayat* (The Full Effects: The Novels) vol. 2, Beirut: Ghassan Kanafani Cultural Institute, Dar at-Talia'a (2nd edn): 341–414 (in Arabic).

Kanafani, Ghassan. 1980c, 'Umm Saa'd', in *Al-Athar al-Kamela: al-Dirasat al-Adabiyya* (The Full Effects: Literature Studies), vol. 2,. Beirut: Ghassan Kanafani Cultural Institute, Dar at-Talia'a, (2nd edn): 241–336 (in Arabic).

Kanafani, Ghassan. 1987. *Ard al-Burtuqal al-Hazeen* (The Land of Sad Oranges). Beirut: Dar ad-dirasat al-Arabiyya.

Kanazi, Remi. 2006. 'US Media Bias: Covering Israel/Palestine', 26 March, www.countercurrents.org/pa-kanazi230306.htm (accessed 16 April 2014).

Kassem, Fatma. 2011. *Palestinian Women: Narrative Histories and Gendered Memory.* London: Zed Books.

Khalidi, Rashid. 1997. *Palestinian Identity: The Construction of Modern National Consciousness.* New York: Columbia University Press.

Khalidi, Walid. 1992. *All That Remains: The Palestinian Villages Occupied and Depopulated by Israel in 1948.* Washington, DC: Institute for Palestine Studies.

Khazzoom, A. 2005. 'Did the Israeli State Engineer Segregation? On the Placement of Jewish Immigrants in Development Towns in the 1950s', *Social Forces*, 84 (1): 115–127.

Kimmerling, Baruch. 2003. *Politicide: Ariel Sharon's War against the Palestinians.* London: Verso.

Kogan, Rick. 1990. 'Cruel Punishment: A Rough, Raw Look At 3 Women In Prison', *Chicago Tribune*, 26 June, at: http://articles.chicagotribune.com/1990-06-26/features/9002220070_1_political-prisoners-alejandrina-torres-prison-system (accessed 16 April 2014).

Langer, Felicia. 1975. *With My Own Eyes: Israel and the Occupied Territories, 1967–1973.* London: Ithaca Press.

Langer, Felicia. 1979. *These Are My Brothers: Israel & the Occupied Territories, Part II.* London: Ithaca Press.

Lappin, Yaakov. 2012. '2 Balad members arrested at Nazareth protest', *Jerusalem Post*, 20 February, p. 2.

Lazreg, Marnia. 1988. 'Feminism and Difference: The Perils of Writing as a Woman on Women in Algeria'. *Feminist Studies*, 14 (1): 81–107.

Lentin, Ronit. 2000. *Israel and the Daughters of the Shoah: Reoccupying the Territory of Silence.* Oxford: Berghahn Books.

Lentin, Ronit, 2008. Presented at a conference at the Centre for Research on Migration, Refugees and Belonging (CMRB), University of East London, Friday, 16 November 2008.

Lentin, Ronit. 2010. *Co-memory and Melancholia: Israelis Memoralising the Palestinian Nakba.* Manchester: Manchester University Press.

Levy, Joshua. 2004. *The Agony of the Promised Land.* Bloomington, IN: iUniverse.

Lloyd-Evans, Sally. 2006. 'Focus Groups', in Vandana Desi and Robert B. Potter (eds), *Doing Development Research.* London: Sage publications, pp. 152–162.

Mahmoud, Riham. 2010. 'Establishing the Institute of Mahmoud Darwish in Shefa-Amr'. *Al Matraqa*, in Arabic, at: www.almatraqa.com/oldsite/showstry.php?toicid=5062 (accessed 16 April 2014).

McDonald, D. 2006. 'Palestine: Resisting the Occupation and Reviving Jerusalem's Social and Cultural Identity through the Arts', *Jerusalem Quarterly*, 25 (1): 5–19.

Makhoul, Ameer. 2012. 'What Palestinian political prisoners are fighting for'. *The Electronic Intifada*, 20 March 2012, at: http://electronicintifada.net/content/what-palestinian-political-prisoners-are-fighting/11076 (accessed 16 April 2014).

Mamdani, Mahmood. 2002. 'Good Muslim, Bad Muslim: A Political Perspective on Culture and Terrorism', *American Anthropologist*, September, 2002, 104 (3): 766–775.

Masalha, Nur (ed.). 2005. *Catastrophe Remembered: Palestine, Israel and the Internal Refugees: Essays in Memory of Edward W. Said*. London: Zed Books.

Masalha, Nur. 2012. *The Palestine Nakba: Decolonising History, Narrating the Subaltern, Reclaiming Memory*. London: Zed Books.

Masarwi, Riad. 2009. 'Tawfik Zayyad: Voice of his People', *This Week in Palestine*, No. 129, 25 January, at: http://thisweekinpalestine.com/details.php?id=2672&ed=165&edid=165 (16 April 2014).

Massad, Joseph. 2003. 'Liberating Songs: Palestine Put to Music', *Journal of Palestine Studies*, 32 (3): 21–38.

McGirk, Tim, Jamil Hamad, and Aaron J. Klein. 2007. 'Moms and Martyrs'. *Time*, 169 (20): 48–50.

McGreal, Chris. 2003. 'Facility 1391: Israel's Secret Prison', *The Guardian*, 14 November, at: www.guardian.co.uk/world/2003/nov/14/israel2 (accessed 16 April 2014).

Miftah (Palestinian Initiative for the Promotion of Global Dialogue and Democracy). 2012. 'Palestinian Prisoners: A Fact Sheet'. www.miftah.org/Doc/Factsheets/Miftah/English/Prisoners.pdf (accessed 16 April 2014).

Mirrless, Tanner. 2006. 'American Soft Power, or, American Cultural Imperialism?', in Colin Mooers (ed.), *The New Imperialists: Ideologies of Empire*. Oxford: Oneworld, pp. 199–228.

Mohanty, Chandra Talpate. 2002. '"Under Western Eyes" Revisited: Feminist Solidarity through Anticapitalist Struggles', *Signs: Journal of Women in Culture and Society*, 28 (2): 500–34.

Mojab, Shahrzad and Nahla Abdo (eds). 2004. *Violence in the Name of Honour: Theoretical and Political Challenges*. Istanbul: Bilgi University Press.

Mooers, Colin (ed.). 2006a. *The New Imperialists: Ideologies of Empire*. Oxford: Oneworld.

Mooers, Colin. 2006b. 'Nostalgia for Empire: Revising Imperial History for American Power', in Colin Mooers (ed.), *The New Imperialists: Ideologies of Empire*. Oxford: Oneworld, pp. 111–136.

Morgan, Robin (ed.). 1984. *Sisterhood is Global: The International Women's Movement Anthology*. Harmondsworth: Penguin.

Morgan, Robin. 1989. *The Demon Lover: On the Sexuality of Terrorism*. London: Methuen.

Morris, Benny. 1988. *The Birth of the Palestinian Refugee Problem, 1947–1949*. Cambridge: Cambridge University Press.

Morris, Benny. 2001. *Righteous Victims: A History of the Zionist–Arab Conflict, 1881–2001*. New York: Vintage.

Murphy, Maureen Clare. 2013a. 'Hunger striker Samer Issawi welcomed home in Jerusalem', *The Electronic Intifada*, 23 December 2013, at: http://electronicintifada.net/blogs/maureen-clare-murphy/hunger-striker-samer-issawi-welcomed-home-jerusalem (accessed 16 April 2014).

Murphy, Maureen Clare. 2013b. 'Akram Rikhawi renews hunger strike after Israel reneges on agreement to release him, *The Electronic Intifada*, 30 January 2013, at: http://electronicintifada.net/blogs/maureen-clare-murphy/akram-rikhawi-renews-hunger-strike-after-israel-reneges-agreement-release (accessed 16 April 2014).

Mostaghanmi, A. 1993. *Dhakirat al-Jassad* (Memory in the flesh). Dar al-Adab: Beirut (in Arabic).

Naaman, Dorit. 2007. 'Brides of Palestine/Angels of Death: Media, Gender, and Performance in the Case of the Palestinian Female Suicide Bombers', *Signs: Journal of Women in Culture and Society*, 32 (4): 933–955.

Nashif, Esmail. 2008. *Palestinian Political Prisoners: Identity and Community*. New York: Routledge.

Neruda, Pablo. 2007. *I Explain A Few Things: Selected Poems*. Ian Stravans (ed.). New York: Farrar, Straus and Giroux.

Nusair, Isis. 2008. 'Gendered, racialized and sexualized torture at Abu Ghraib', in Robin L. Riley, Chandra Talpade Mohanty and Minnie Bruce Pratt (eds), *Feminism and War: confronting US imperialism*. London: Zed Books, pp. 179–193.

Odeh, Aisha. 2004. *Ahlam bil-hurriyyah* (Dreams of Liberation). Ramallah: Muwatin (Palestinian Institute for Studies in Democracy), in Arabic.

Odeh, Aisha. 2007. *Youm Mukhtalef* (A Different Day). Dar al-Shurouk, Amman: Jordan (in Arabic).

Odeh, Aisha. 2012. *Thamanan Lil-Shams* (For the Sake of the Sun), Ramallah: Muwatin: Palestinian Institute for the Study of Democracy (in Arabic).

O'Neall, Siv. 2008. 'Jean Ziegler: "This World Order is not just murderous, it is absurd"', *OpEdNews Op Eds* 25 November 2008, at: www.opednews.com/articles/Jean-Ziegler--This-World-by-Siv-O-Neall-081125-155.html (accessed 16 April 2014).

Oufkir, Malika and Michèle Fitoussi. 2001. *Stolen Lives: Twenty Years in a Desert Jail*. New York: Miramax Books.

Pappe, Ilan. 1988. *Britain and the Arab–Israeli Conflict, 1948–1951*. London: St. Martin's Press.

Pappe, Ilan. 2001. 'The Tantura Case in Israel: The Katz Research and Trial', *Journal of Palestine Studies*, 30 (3): 19–39.

Pappe, Ilan. 2006. *The Ethnic Cleansing of Palestine*. Oxford: Oneworld.

Pappe, Ilan. 2004. *A History of Modern Palestine: One Land, Two Peoples*. Cambridge: Cambridge University Press.

Pappe, Ilan. 2008. 'The *Mukhabarat* State of Israel: A State of Oppression is not a State of Exception', in Ronit Lentin (ed.), *Thinking Palestine*. London: Zed Books, pp. 148–170.

Patkin, Terri Toles. 2004. 'Explosive Baggage: Female Palestinian Suicide Bombers and the Rhetoric of Emotion'. *Women and Language*, George Mason University. *HighBeam Research*, 5 May 2014, (27) 2: 79–99.

Peteet, J. M. 1991. *Gender in Crisis: Women and the Palestinian Resistance Movement*. New York: Columbia University Press.

Punamaki, Raija-Leena. 1988. 'Experiences of Torture, Means of Coping, and Level of Symptoms among Palestinian Political Prisoners'. *Journal of Palestine Studies*, 17 (4): 81–96.

Qatamish, Ribhi. 2003. 'Torture of Palestinian Political Prisoners in Israeli Prisons', trans by Nimer Sha'ban. Jerusalem: Addameer Prisoners Support and Human Rights Association, at: http://israelpalestinenewscompiler.files.wordpress.com/2009/04/torture.pdf (accessed 16 April 2014).

Qumsiyeh, Mazin B. 2010. *Popular Resistance in Palestine: A History of Hope and Empowerment*. London: Pluto.

Razack, Sherene. 2008. *Casting Out: The Eviction of Muslims from Western Law and Politics*. Toronto: University of Toronto Press.

Reuter, Christopher. 2006. *My Life Is a Weapon: A Modern History of Suicide Bombing*. Princeton, NJ: Princeton University Press.

Rosenberg, Susan. 2006. 'Female Political Prisoners and Anti-Imperialist Struggles', *Journal of Prisoners on Prisons*, Reprint of Vol. 2 (2) from Spring, 1990.

Sa`di, Ahmad H. and Abu-Lughod, Lila (eds). 2007. *Nakba: Palestine, 1948, and the Claims of Memory*. New York: Columbia University Press.

Said, Edward W. 1979. *Orientalism*. New York: Vintage.

Said, Edward W. 1980. *The Question of Palestine*. London: Routledge & Kegan Paul.

Said, Edward W. 1981. *Covering Islam: How the Media and the Experts Determine How We See the Rest of the World*. New York: Pantheon.

Said, Edward W. 1994a. *Culture and Imperialism*. Toronto: Random House.

Said, Edward W. 1994b. *Representations of the Intellectual*. New York: Vintage.

Sand, Shlomo. 2012. *The Invention of the Land of Israel: From Holy Land to Homeland*. London: Verso.

Sarraj Eyad. 2005. 'Why We Have Become Suicide Bombers: Understanding Palestinian Terror', at: www.missionislam.com/conissues/palestine.htm (accessed 16 April 2014).

Sayigh, Rosemary. 1979. *Palestinians: From Peasants to Revolutionaries*. London: Zed Books.

Sayigh, Rosemary. 1998. 'Palestinian Camp Women as Tellers of History', *Journal of Palestine Studies*, 27 (2): 42–58.

Sayigh, Rosemary. 2005. *Voices: Palestinian Women Narrate Displacement*, at: http://almashriq.hiof.no/palestine/300/301/voices/index2.html (accessed 16 April 2014).

Schweitzer, Yoram (ed.). 2006. 'Female Suicide Bombers: Dying for Equality?' Tel Aviv University: Jaffee Center for Strategic Studies (JCSS), Memorandum No. 84.

Schweitzer, Yoram. 2006. 'Palestinian Female Suicide Bombers: Reality vs. Myth', in Yoram Schweitzer (ed.), *Female Suicide Bombers: Dying for Equality?* Tel Aviv: Jaffee Center for Strategic Studies, 25–41.

Sfard, Michael. 2011. 'Devil's Island: The Transfer of Palestinian Detainees into Prisons within Israel', in Abeer Baker and Anat Matar (eds), *Threat: Palestinian Political Prisoners in Israel*. New York: Pluto, pp. 188–200.

Shammas, Anton. 2009. 'Accolade', in Mahmoud Darwish. *A River Dies of Thirst: Journals*. Trans. Catherine Cobham. Brooklyn, NY: Archipelago Books.

Shannon, Elizabeth. 1989. *I Am of Ireland: Women of the North Speak Out*. Boston: Little, Brown.

Shepherd, Naomi. 2000. *Ploughing Sand: British Rule in Palestine, 1917–1948*. New Brunswick, NJ: Rutgers University Press.

Shlaim, Avi. 1988. *Collusion Across the Jordan: King Abdullah, the Zionist Movement and the Partition of Palestine*. Oxford: Clarendon Press.

Shlaim, Avi. 2004. 'The "New History" of 1948 and the Palestinian Nakba', a lecture delivered on 18 March 2004 at the Palestinian Initiative for the Promotion of Global Dialogue and Democracy (MIFTAH), at: www.miftah.org/PrinterF.cfm?DocId=3336 (accessed 16 April 2014).

Shwar, Al-Khair, 2007. 'My name is Jamila Bou-Hired. I live with you but remain silent', (in Arabic) *Al-Sharq Al-Awsat*, 7 November 2007, at: www.aawsat.com/details.asp?article=444539&issueno=10571 (accessed 16 April 2014).

Slyomovics, Susan. 2005. 'Morocco's Justice and Reconciliation Commission'. *Middle East Report and Information Project (MERIP)*, 229, at: www.merip.org/mero/mero040405 (accessed 16 April 2014).

Smith, Dorothy E. 2005. *Institutional Ethnography: A Sociology for People*. AltaMira Press: Oxford.

Suliman, Mohammed. 2011. 'Edward Said on claims to the land and the occupation of Palestine', *The Electronic Intifada*, 27 August 2011, at: http://electronicintifada.net/blogs/mohammed-suliman/edward-said-claims-land-and-occupation-palestine (accessed 16 April 2014).

Sunday Times. 1977. 'Israel tortures Arab prisoners', a special investigation by INSIGHT, *The Sunday Times*, 19 June, available at: http://unispal.un.org/UNISPAL.NSF/0/FE3D603D74F5729B85256FE0006CC519 (accessed 16 April 2014).

Tawil-Souri, H. 2011. 'Where is the Political in Cultural Studies in Palestine?' *International Journal of Cultural Studies*, 14 (5): 467–482.

Tibi, Bassam. 1997. *Arab Nationalism: Between Islam and the Nation-State*. New York: St. Martin's Press.

Tsemel, Lea. 1982. 'Political Prisoners in Israel: An Overview'. Jerusalem, 16 November (a report obtained directly from author).

Tsemel, Lea and Walid Fahoum. 1980. 'Nafha is a Political Prison', 13 May (a report obtained directly from author).

Torres, Andrés. 1998. in Andrés Torres and José E. Velázquez (eds), *The Puerto Rican Movement: Voices from the Diaspora*. Philadelphia, PA: Temple University Press, p. 147.

Turok, Ben (ed.). 1980. *Revolutionary Thought in the 20th Century*. London: Zed Books.

Tzoreff, Mira. 2006. 'The Palestinian *Shahida*: National Patriotism, Islamic Feminism, or Social Crisis', in Yoram Schweitzer (ed.), *Female Suicide Bombers: Dying for Equality?* Tel-Aviv: Jaffee Center for Strategic Studies, 13–24.

Victor, Barbara. 2003. *Army of Roses: Inside the World of Palestinian Women Suicide Bombers*. New York, NY: Barnes & Noble.

Viner, Katharine. 2001. 'I made the ring from a bullet and the pin of a hand grenade', *Guardian*, 26 January 2001, at: www.theguardian.com/world/2001/jan/26/Israel (accessed 16 April 2014).

Wedde, I. and Tuqan, Fawwaz. 1973. *Mahmoud Darwish: Selected Poems*. Manchester: Carcanet Press.

Wihbe, Zahi. 2013. 'Interview with Anni H. Kanafani' in *Baitel-Qaseed*. *Al-Mayadeen*, 1 January.

Wood, Ellen Meiksins. 2006. 'Democracy as Ideology of Empire', in Colin Mooers (ed.) *The New Imperialists: Ideologies of Empire*. Oxford: Oneworld Publications, pp. 9–23.

Zakarin, Jordan. 2012. 'Who is Sam Bacile? Mystery of Anti-Islam Filmmaker's Link to Libya Embassy Riots Deepens', 12 September 2012, at: www.hollywoodreporter.com/news/sam-bacile-fake-name-libyan-embassy-attack-369849 (accessed 16 April 2014).

Zayyad, Tawfiq. 1994a. *Sujana'a al-Hurriyya wa-Qasaed Mamnou'a Ukhra* (The prisoners of freedom and other forbidden poems). Akka: Abu Rahmoun (in Arabic).

Zayyad, Tawfiq. 1994b. *Ashuddo Ala Ayadeekom* (I press on your hands: a collection of poems). Akka: Abu Rahmoun (in Arabic).

Zayyad, Tawfiq. 1994c. *Seera Thatiyya* (An autobiography). Akka: Abu Rahmoun (in Arabic).

Zayyad, Tawfiq. 1994d. *Ana Min Hathil-Madeena* (I Am From This City), Akka: Abu Rahmoun, (in Arabic).

Zine, Jasmin. 2004, 'Creating a Critical-Faith-Centred Space for anti-Racist Feminism: Relections of a Muslim Scholar-Activist', *The Journal of feminist Studies in Religion*, 20 (2): 167–188.

Zochrot. 2012. 'Who We Are', at: http://zochrot.org/en (accessed 16 April 2014).
Zureik, Elia T. 1979. *The Palestinians in Israel: A Study in Internal Colonialism*. London: Routledge & Kegan Paul.

Films and Documentaries

abid, Kasim (dir.). 2000. *Naji Al-Ali: An Artist With Vision*. Brooklyn, NY: Icarus Films, http://icarusfilms.com/new2000/naji.html (accessed 16 April 2014).
Bakri, Mohammad (dir.). 2002. *Jenin, Jenin*.
Chahine, Youssef (dir.). 1958. *Jamila the Algerian*.
Chomsky, Noam. 2011. 'The U.S. and Its Allies Will Do Anything to Prevent Democracy in the Arab World'. Interview by Amy Goodman. *Democracy Now!*, 12 May, at: www.youtube.com/watch?v=eDolf-TugxY (accessed 16 April 2014).
Dirbas, Sahera (dir.). 2009. *A Handful of Earth*.
Dworkin, John. 2012. *Peace, Propaganda and the Promised Land*, documentary, at: www.youtube.com/watch?v=cAN5GjJKAac (accessed 16 April 2014).
Hawal, Kassem (dir.). 1982. *Return to Haifa*.
Makboul, Lina (dir.). 2006. *Leila Khaled: Hijacker*, at: www.youtube.com/watch?v=iWg6-oQTSvw (accessed 16 April 2014).
Pontecorvo, Gillo (dir.). 1966. *The Battle of Algiers*.
Press TV. 2014. 'US playing double game on Syria', an interview with Kevin Barrett by *Press TV*, 3 February 2014, at: www.presstv.com/detail/2014/02/03/349017/us-playing-double-game-on-syria/
Sheikh Imam, n.d. 'Saqatat Saigon' (Saigon Fell), at: www.youtube.com/watch?v=8g8ooaUL6Lg
Sivan, Eyal (dir.). 1990. *Izkor: Slaves of Memory*.
Sivan, Eyal (dir.). 2009. *Jaffa: The Orange's Clockwork*.
Tarachansky, Lia (dir.). 2013. 'Seven Deadly Myths', at: http://leichik.webs.com (accessed 16 April 2014).

Index

Compiled by Indexing Specialists (UK) Ltd

1929 uprising 94, 95
1948 Palestinians 85, 90

A`qlain, Fatema abi 99
'A State of Siege' (Darwish) 110–11, 117
Abdel-Nasser, Gamal 93–4, 134, 137
Abu Ghraib prison 1, 28
Abu-Hanna, Hanna 110
Abu-Lughod, Janet 45
Abu-Lughod, Lila 58, 81
adab al-muqawama see resistance
    literature
adab al-sujoun see prison literature
administrative detention 31–3, 146,
    181–2
Afghanistan 57
African American detainees 22
African women detainees 23
agency
    Arab/Muslim women 56–7
    victimization and 71–7
    women political detainees 15–16,
        33–7
agricultural seasons 79–80
Ahlam, case 130, 132, 150, 153, 171–2,
    173, 175, 177–8, 184
Aisha, case 125, 128–30, 132, 136,
    142–5, 155, 169–70
Akhras, Ayat 62
Al-Bishtawi, Hamda 99
Al-Hout Noueihed, Bayan 95
Al-Issawi, Samer 181, 182
Al-Khalil prison 174
Al-Led prison 67, 180–1
Al-Mayadeen 212
Al-Nawwab, Mudhaffar 92

al-Qaeda 127
al-Saadi, Qahira 163–4
Al-Zir, A`ta 95, 96
A'lawites 54
Algeria 24, 26, 43, 98
Ali-Ali, Naji 104
Alian, Ittaf 10, 137, 145, 159, 181–2, 185,
    199
Ameena, case 131, 132–4, 137–8, 168–9
Amne, case 152, 155, 158–9, 176, 177,
    187, 189–90, 194, 198
ANM (Arab Nationalist Movement) 93
anonymity of interviewees 9
anti-colonial resistance *see* armed
    struggle
anti-Semitism 66
Antonius, Soraya 90, 188
Antoon, Sinan 116
Arab culture, denigration of 160–1
Arab-Jewish interrogators 153–4
Arab Nationalist Movement (ANM) 93
'Arab Spring' 4, 50, 52, 55
Arab women
    agency of 56–7
    Orientalist feminism 56–8
    silencing of 23, 26
Arabic proverbs 155–6
'Arabs'/'Christians' term use 157
Armagh Prison 23, 25, 27, 30
armed struggle 1, 3, 48, 105, 108, 109,
    212
    Algeria 24
    historical context 70–1
    honour 66, 75–6
    imperialism 47
    Irish women 23

armed struggle *continued*
  language and 11, 64
  Orientalism and 6
  reasons for joining 132–40
  religion/culture 61
  silencing of women 72
  see also freedom fighters
arrest of freedom fighters 141–5
aseera/asra see political detainees/
    prisoners
Ashrawi, Hanan 66
assassinations 105, 109

Badr, Liana 87
Bakri, Mohammad 102
Ball, Anna 87
Ban Ki-moon 124
beating of prisoners 150, 157, 161
'Behind Bars' (Zayyad) 120
Ben Jalloun, Tahar 148–9, 193
Bishara, George 102
Bishara, Suha 17, 38
blindfolding of detainees 38
Bloom, Mia 59, 60
body searches 139
borders 116–17
Borghalter, Edith 90
Bouhaired, Jamila 23, 24, 26
Bouteflika, Abdelaziz 98
British colonialism 44, 70–1, 94–5
B'Tselem organization 32

Cabral, Amilcar 101
Canada 66
capitalism 49, 51–2
cartoons 104
celebrations for released prisoners 195
charitable organizations 205–6
checkpoints, military 116–17, 126
Chesler, Phyllis 63–4
children
  as detainees 32–3
  detainees' separation from 158

the Nakba 80
sexual torture 28
Christian–Muslim marriages 202
Christian political detainees 157
'Christians'/'Arabs' term use 157
clean record (*huson solouk*) 204
clothing 189–90, 198
collaboration, refusal of 172–4
collective punishment 177
collective resistance 168, 178–86
colonialism 3, 4, 21–2, 26, 40, 42–83
  British 44, 70–1, 94–5
  French 24, 44, 98
  Israeli 101, 102, 105, 117, 118
  see also imperialism; settler-colonial
    state
Communist Party of Israel (CPI) 90
confessions 172–3
consciousness-raising 183–6
Corcoran, Mary 30, 39
CPI (Communist Party of Israel) 90
criminalization of freedom fighters
    18–19, 29–31, 72
crying 175–6
Cuban revolution 43
'cultural genocide' 78–9
culturalism 21–2, 59
culture
  Arab/Muslim women 57
  armed struggle 61
  familiarity with 8
  the Nakba 77
  racism 21
  resistance culture 5, 20, 59–70, 95
curfews 138

Darwish, Mahmoud 73, 85–6, 110–19,
    132
Davis, Angela 17, 22, 24
defamation of prisoners 161
Deir Yassin massacre (1948) 80, 136
democracy
  Arab world 53

Israel as 65
'new imperialism' 51–2, 54
Democratic Front for the Liberation of
    Palestine (DFLP) 127, 132, 189
depression 174–5
detainees *see* political detainees/
    prisoners
detention orders 31
DFLP *see* Democratic Front for the
    Liberation of Palestine
diaries 86
Dirani, Mustafa 28, 162
Dirbas, Sahera 103
'dirty protest', Armagh Prison 27, 30
distress of prisoners 174–6
documentaries 102, 103–4
Doyle, Mary 25
Dworkin, Andrea 45–6, 59–60

education
    political prisoners 34, 179, 183–6
    suicide bombers 61–3
El-Beih, Fatna 36–8
election, 2006 128
emotional distress of prisoners 174–6
employment, ex-prisoners 203–7
empowerment 166, 174
'exchange deals' 25
exile 25–6, 77, 116, 129
extended family (*hamula*) 200

factory work 180
Fahoum, Walid 147
Falk, Richard 51, 55
family relationships/support 128–32,
    158, 159, 175–8, 199–200
Fanon, Frantz 24, 39, 72–4, 102
Farrell, Mairéad 25
Fatah 127, 132, 205
female resistance literature 87–9
feminism 1–2, 21, 30–1, 41, 45, 72,
    128
    gender consciousness and 7

imperialist feminism 4–5, 56, 59–70
Orientalist feminism 4–5, 47, 56–8,
    59
feminist organizations 205
fidai see freedom fighters
films 102, 103–4
Findley, Paul 162
First Intifada (1987–1992) 87, 127
flag-hanging 180
Flapan, Simha 78
folk songs 85, 92–3, 95–6
food shortages 69
forced labour 180–1
Forche, Carolyne 116
freedom fighters (*munadelat*) 1–2, 7,
    11–12, 73–4, 90, 107, 124–5
    arrest of 141–5
    criminalization 18–19, 29–31, 72
    family relationships 128–32
    honour 76
    life before detention 126–32
    political affiliations 132, 179, 189,
        204–5
    political consciousness 128
    reasons for joining armed struggle
        132–40
    resistance culture 5
    silencing of 23
    terminology 48
    terrorism and 50
    see also political
        detainees/prisoners
French colonialism 24, 44, 98
funeral processions 95–6

Galleymore, Susan 63
Garedat, Hanadi 62
Gaza 55, 76, 124, 127, 138
gender
    equality 199
    feminist consciousness 7
    the Nakba 79
    treatment of detainees 14–41

genocide 78–9
Ghada, case 134–5, 139–40, 154, 163, 179
Goldberg, David Theo 14
Goldstone, Richard 55
'good cop'/'bad cop' interrogators 153
guards, prison 186–8

Halasa, Therese 25
Haleema 'A', case 141–2, 151–2, 153, 157, 162–3, 171, 173, 175–6, 195, 203–4, 206
Haleema 'F', case 131, 132, 138–9, 148, 153, 156
Hamas 76, 127–8, 132
hamula (extended family) 200
A Handful of Earth (Dirbas) 103
Handhala caricature 104
Hannah, Huda 99
Harlow, Barbara 5, 39, 86, 88, 97, 104, 105
Hassan, King 35
Hassan II, King 36
Hawal, Kassem 103–4
hearing, sense of 38–9
Hebrew language 82
Heikal, Hassanein 55
'Here We Shall Remain' (Zayyad) 119–20
hijacking of planes 133–4
Hijazi, Fouad 95
history
    Academy versus Activism 5–6
    memory and 98–100
    the Nakba 77–83
    Palestinian resistance 70–1, 74–5
    terrorism 63
    US imperialism 52
Hitti, Philip 93
Hollande, François 98
honour 60, 66, 75–6
hunger strikes 181–2
huson solouk (clean record) 204

'I Explain A Few Things' (Neruda) 91–2
'I Press on Your Hands' (Zayyad) 120–1
'Identity Card' (Darwish) 115
IDF see Israel Defense Forces
Idris, Wafaa 61–2
Imam, Sheikh 92–3
Iman, case 146–7, 169, 171, 178, 185, 197–8
IMF (International Monetary Fund) 40
imperialism
    armed struggle against 47
    ideology of 53–4
    new era of 39–43, 49, 50–6, 65–6, 71
    Orientalism 4–5
    resistance movements 3, 42, 70
    see also colonialism
imperialist feminism 4–5, 56, 59–70
Ina'ash al-Usra 8, 195
informers 173
'institutional ethnography' 2
International Monetary Fund (IMF) 40
internationalism 89–94
interrogation of detainees 146, 147–9, 158, 168
    agency/resistance 34, 36–7
    Arab-Jewish interrogators 153–4
    confessions 172–3
Intifada
    First 87, 127
    Second 57–8, 66, 76–7
Iraq 43, 57
Irish women 23
    see also Northern Ireland
Irving, Sarah 46–7
ISA (Israel Security Agency) 32
Islam, 'new imperialism' 54–5
isolation cells 147–9
isqat (prisoner defamation) 161
Israel Defense Forces (IDF) 32, 64–5

Israel Security Agency (ISA) 32
Israeli colonialism 101, 102, 105, 117,
    118
Israeli–Palestinian conflict 4, 63, 82
Israeli–Palestinian 'peace negotiations'
    1
Israeli state 14, 17, 44, 50–6, 65, 66,
    101, 102, 105, 117, 118
Itaf, case 135–6, 174, 195–6, 201, 205
Izkor: Slaves of Memory (Sivan) 102

Jad, Islah 201
Jaffa: The Orange's Clockwork (Sivan)
    103
Jamjoum, Muhammad 95
Jayawardena, Kumari 6
Jenin, Jenin (Bakri) 102
Jerusalem 196
'Jerusalem' (Al-Nawwab) 92
Jewish holidays 180
Jewish women prisoners 161, 179
Jews, 'hatred' of 66–7
'just wars' 50, 51, 55

Kanafani, Ghassan 85, 103, 105–9
Kassem, Fatma 81, 83
kees (torture method) 151–2
Keinan, Amos 118
Khaled, Leila 31, 47–8, 58, 133–4, 207
Kholoud, case 195, 201
Kuwait 106

Land Day 122, 139
language
    armed struggle 11, 64
    the Nakba 82
    resistance literature 39
Lazreg, Marnia 4
legal system, Israeli state 14
Lentin, Ronit 82
'Let the Whole World Hear' (Zayyad)
    121
literature on resistance 39, 66, 83

McDonald, David 96
Maki (Communist Party of Israel) 90
male political detainees 19, 28
marriage 198–203
martyrdom 73–4, 96
    see also suicide bombing
Masalha, Nur 78–9, 81
massacre at Deir Yassin (1948) 80, 136
'Mawtini' (Tuqan) 96–7
memoirs 88
memory
    and history 98–100
    the Nakba 77–83, 118
    'Memory for Forgetfulness' (Darwish)
        114–15
Men in the Sun (Kanafani) 106
menstruation 165
Middle East
    democracy and 65
    imperialism 55
    USA and 44, 51, 52, 53
military checkpoints 116–17, 126
moa'taqala/moa'taqaloon see political
    detainees/prisoners
Mooers, Colin 40, 49
Morgan, Robin 46–7
Moroccan prisons 149
Moroccan women detainees 34–7
Morris, Benny 78, 80
Moscobiyya Detention Centre 146
Mostaghanmi, Ahlam 26
movement restrictions, Palestinians
    158, 167–8
Muhammad V, King 34, 35–6
munadelat see freedom fighters
Munia, case 140, 149, 161, 196
Muslim–Christian marriages 202
Muslim women, Orientalist feminism
    56–8
'My Homeland' (Tuqan) 96–7

Naaman, Dorit 62–3
Nablus 87

Nakba Law (2011) 79, 101
the Nakba (Palestinian exodus, 1948)
    72, 75, 77–83, 97, 99, 101, 107
    Darwish's experiences 112
    Israeli state and 102
    'memoricide' 78
    resistance culture 103
Nasser, Gamal Abdel 93–4, 134, 137
national anthems 97
national anti-colonial resistance 39–41
nationalism, the Nakba 80–1
natural gas, access to 52
Nazareth 101, 119
Neruda, Pablo 91–2
'new imperialism' 39–43, 49, 50–6,
    65–6, 71
night raids 141–3
Nijm, Ahmad Fouad 92
Northern Ireland 18, 23, 25, 30, 40
novels 106–9
Nugent, Mairéad 25
Nve-Tertza prison 67, 180–1

'O Those Who Pass through Fleeting
    Words' (Darwish) 118
Odeh, Aisha 9, 39, 67–9, 88, 89, 90,
    164–5, 206–7
Odeh, Rasmiyya 10, 68–9, 77, 164
oil reserves, access to 52
olive tree symbolism 80
O'Neall, Siv 98
oral history 81, 88, 97, 99, 103
organizational work by political
    prisoners 181
Orientalism 4–6, 31, 46
Orientalist feminism 47, 56–8, 59
Oslo Accords 32, 132
Othering process 29–30, 45
Oufkir, Malika 23, 34–6, 193

PA see Palestinian Authority
Palestine
    1929 uprising 94, 95

regional/international struggles and
    89–94
Palestine Liberation Organization
    (PLO) 71, 127, 132
PalestineRemembered.com 99
Palestinian Authority (PA) 25–6, 111,
    204
Palestinian National Authority (PNA)
    97
Pappe, Ilan 78, 80
parties for released prisoners 195
Patkin, Terri Toles 60–1
patriarchy 86–7, 204
Peres, Shimon 101–2
permits to travel 159
personal life, prisoners' discussions
    189–92
Peteet, Julie 7, 188–9
PFLP see Popular Front for the
    Liberation of Palestine
physical torture 150–4, 161–2
plane hijacking 133–4
PLO see Palestine Liberation
    Organization
PNA (Palestinian National Authority)
    97
poetry 73, 87–8, 91–2, 109–23
political affiliations of prisoners 132,
    179, 189, 204–5
political consciousness of freedom
    fighters 128
political detainees/prisoners 1, 3, 6,
    14–41, 124–66
    administrative detention 31–3, 146,
        181–2
    Ahlam 130, 132, 150, 153, 171–2, 173,
        175, 177–8, 184
    Aisha 125, 128–30, 132, 136, 142–5,
        155, 169–70
    Alian, Ittaf 10, 137, 145, 159, 181–2,
        185, 199
    Ameena 131, 132–4, 137–8, 168–9

Amne 152, 155, 158–9, 176, 177, 187,
    189–90, 194, 198
author's experience 8, 12
beatings 150, 157, 161
clothing 189–90, 198
collaboration refusal 172–4
collective resistance 168, 178–86
committee work 179
consciousness-raising 183–6
criminalization of 18–19, 29–31
crying 175–6
death of parents 175–6
defamation of 161
denigration of Arab culture 160–1
education 179, 183–6
emotional distress 174–6
employment after prison 203–7
family relationships/support 158,
    159, 175–8, 199–200
focus group discussions 13
forced labour 180–1
Ghada 134–5, 139–40, 154, 163, 179
guards, relationships with 186–8
Haleema 'A' 141–2, 151–2, 153, 157,
    162–3, 171, 173, 175–6, 195,
    203–4, 206
Haleema 'F' 131, 132, 138–9, 148,
    153, 156
hunger strikes 181–2
Iman 146–7, 169, 171, 178, 185,
    197–8
individual resistance 170–8
influence on wardresses/guards
    186–8
interrogation 34, 36–7, 146, 147–9,
    153–4, 158, 168, 172–3
invisibility of 15–16
Itaf 135–6, 174, 195–6, 201, 205
Kholoud 195, 201
life after prison 194–207
life before detention 126–32
marriage 198–203
Munia 140, 149, 161, 196

organizational work 181
personal life, discussions about
    189–92
political affiliations 132, 179, 189,
    204–5
political education 179, 183–6
psychological torture 154–66
rape threats/rape of 163–5
Rawda 126, 131, 132, 139, 152, 155,
    169–70, 183–4, 194, 200, 202–3,
    205–6
refusing orders 171–2
release from prison 194–207
resistance inside prison 167–207
role models 169–70
Said, Aida 135, 137, 155
Salwa 148, 154–5, 165, 187–8
separation from children 158
sexual assaults on 161–6
sexual slurs used against 160–1
sexuality 189–92
Sonia 125–6, 132, 184, 190–1, 194,
    197, 200
terminology 9, 16–20
time, sense/use of 36–7, 193–4
torture of 149–66
transit to prison 145–6
wardress/guard relationships 186–8
work duties/strikes 170, 180–1
political parties 90, 127, 132, 179, 189,
    204–5
'politicide' 78
Popular Front for the Liberation of
    Palestine (PFLP) 127, 132, 133,
    189
'post-colonialism' 40
pregnant women
    the Nakba 80
    psychological torture 27
prison cells 147–9
prison literature (*adab al-sujoun*) 5, 88,
    100, 109–10, 121, 186
prison resistance 167–207

prison wardresses/guards 186–8
prisoner releases 183–4, 185
prisoners *see* political detainees/
    prisoners
prisoners of conscience 18–19
Prisoners of Freedom and Other
    Forbidden Poems (Zayyad) 121
prisons, terminology 17
prose poems 114–15
proverbs, Arabic 155–6
psychological torture 21, 27, 154–66
Puerto Rican women detainees 22–3
Punamaki, Raija-Leena 151

racialization/racism
    anti-colonial resistance 46–7
    culturalist literature 22
    definition 14–15
    imperialism 50
    Israeli state 14
    settler-colonial state 21
    silencing of detainees 20–2
    Zionism as 48
raids by Israeli soldiers 141–5
Ramallah 117, 129, 196
Ramla 180
rape 28, 29, 80, 163–5, 173
Rawda, case 126, 131, 132, 139, 152, 155,
    169–70, 183–4, 194
    employment discrimination 205–6
    extended family 200
    marriage 202–3
Razack, Sherene 71–2
'Red Tuesday' 96
refugeeism 116
refusing orders, political prisoners
    171–2
remembering (Zochrot) 82–3, 101
research methods 2, 7–13
resistance
    active resistance 34
    agency and 33–7
    anti-colonial 39–83

criminalization of detainees 30–1
history of 16, 20, 70, 94–8
literature on 39
suicide bombing 59–70
terminology 20
see also freedom fighters; political
    detainees/prisoners
resistance literature (*adab*
    al-muqawama) 5, 84–123
    Arab resistance literature 93–4
    female resistance literature 87–9
    function of 100
    genre of resistance 103–4
    historical context 94–8
    impact of 122–3
    internationalism 91
    novels 106–9
    poetry 73, 87–8, 91–2, 109–23
    prison literature 5, 88, 100, 109–10,
        121, 186
Resistance Literature (Harlow) 86, 88,
    105
Return to Haifa (Hawal) 103–4
Returning to Haifa (Kanafani) 107–9
revisionist historians 78
revolutionary literature 89
Rice, Condoleezza 55
Rikhawi, Akram 182
role models 169–70
Rosenberg, Susan 16, 22

Sa'di, Ahmad 81
Said, Aida, case 135, 137, 155
Said, Edward 4, 40, 43, 45, 48–9, 56,
    65, 116
Salwa, case 148, 154–5, 165, 187–8
sanitary protection 165
Sarkozy, Nicolas 98
Sarraj, Eyad 74–5
Sayigh, Rosemary 81, 83
school curriculum 111
Schweitzer, Yoram 61
searches by Israeli soldiers 27, 139

Second Intifada (2001) 57–8, 66, 76–7
self-sacrifice 73–4, 96
    see also suicide bombing
senses, human 38–9
settler-colonial state
    freedom fighters and 74
    Israel as 14, 17, 44, 55–6
    'new imperialism' 43
    racism/racialization 21–2
    Zionist project 70
sexual assaults/torture 28, 29, 80,
    161–6, 169, 173
sexuality 21–2, 46, 57, 76, 80, 189–92
sexualized language 10–11, 160–1
Sfard, Michael 159
shabeh (torture method) 151–2, 164
shaheeds/shaheedas see freedom
    fighters
Shalabi, Hana 182
Shamir, Yitzhak 118
Shaw Report 94
Shi'a Islam 54
Shin Bet 32
Shlaim, Avi 78
silencing of women 15, 20–6, 33–4, 41,
    42, 58, 72
Sivan, Eyal 102, 103
skills of political detainees 37–9
Smith, Dorothy 2
solitary confinement 38, 147–9, 163
songs 85, 92–3, 95–6
Sonia, case 125–6, 132, 184, 190–1,
    194, 197, 200
spoken word genre 88
the state 3, 17, 37
    see also colonialism; Israeli state;
    settler-colonial state
*Stolen Lives: Twenty Years in a Desert
    Jail* (Oufkir) 193
suicide bombing 59–70, 72, 74, 126
Syria 53

Tarachansky, Lia 82

Tawil-Souri, H. 104
Telmond prison 181, 187
terrorism/terrorists
    characteristics 60–1
    feminist debate 58
    freedom fighters and 50, 74
    history 63
    political detainees as terrorists 17,
        18, 29, 37
    sexuality 46
    terminology 33, 48
    US interests 53
    violence and 48, 72
'The Impossible' (Zayyad) 119–20
'The Rose and the Dictionary'
    (Darwish) 113–14
'They Stopped Me at the Borders'
    (Darwish) 116–17
time, prisoners' sense/use of 36–7,
    193–4
'To My Mother' (Darwish) 112–13
'toponymicide' 78
torture 3, 6, 29, 37, 124, 149–66
    kees 151–2
    physical torture 150–4, 161–2
    psychological torture 154–66
    sexual torture 28, 161–6, 169, 173
    shabeh 151–2, 164
transit to prison 145–6
travel permits 159
Tuqan, Fadwa 87–8
Tuqan, Ibrahim 96–7
Tzoreff, Mira 61–2

Umm Saa'd (Kanafani) 106–7
UN resolutions 162
United States of America (USA)
    anti-colonial resistance 22–3, 42–3
    'Arab Spring' 4
    Iraq/Afghanistan wars 57–8
    Islam and 54
    Israeli–Palestinian peace
        negotiations 1

'just war' concept 51
'new imperialism' 49, 52, 71
political detainees/prisoners 16–17,
    20, 28
support for Israel 44, 52–3, 55
university students 90–1

veil-wearing 198
victimization 21–2, 71–7
Viner, Katherine 207
violence and terrorism 48, 72

Wahhabism 54
'war on terror' 71–2

Washington, Mary Helen 20
'We Have on This Earth What Makes
    Life Worth Living' (Darwish)
    118–19
Western colonialism see colonialism
'whore' name-calling 160
women freedom fighters see freedom
    fighters
women's organizations 205
work duties/strikes 170, 180–1

Zayyad, Tawfiq 73, 119–22, 134
Zionist project 44, 45–6, 48, 70, 78
Zochrot (remembering) 82–3, 101

www.ingramcontent.com/pod-product-compliance
Lightning Source LLC
Chambersburg PA
CBHW032124020426

42334CB00016B/1061